Dorothy Parker

Dorothy Parker, 1932. Photo courtesy of UPI/ Bettmann Archive.

Dorothy Parker

A BIO-BIBLIOGRAPHY

Randall Calhoun

Bio-Bibliographies in American Literature, Number 4

GREENWOOD PRESS
Westport, Connecticut • London

Library of Congress Cataloging-in-Publication Data

Calhoun, Randall.
   Dorothy Parker : a bio-bibliography / Randall Calhoun.
     p. cm.—(Bio-bibliographies in American literature, ISSN
0742-695X; no. 4)
   Includes bibliographical references and index.
   ISBN 0-313-26507-0 (alk. paper)
   1. Parker, Dorothy, 1893-1967—Biography. 2. Parker, Dorothy,
1893-1967—Bibliography. 3. Authors, American—20th century—
Biography. I. Title. II. Series.
PS3531.A5855Z6 1993
818'.5209—dc20
  [B]   92-30882

British Library Cataloguing in Publication Data is available.

Library of Congress Catalog Card Number: 92-30882
ISBN: 0-313-26507-0
ISSN: 0742-695X

First published in 1993

Greenwood Press, 88 Post Road West, Westport, CT 06881
An imprint of Greenwood Publishing Group, Inc.

Printed in the United States of America

∞™

The paper used in this book complies with the
Permanent Paper Standard issued by the National
Information Standards Organization (Z39.48-1984).

10 9 8 7 6 5 4 3 2 1

I wish to express my gratitude and appreciation to Mr. Charles E. Carter, the former Corporate Counsel of the NAACP, Parker's literary executor. Mr. Carter invited me to the ceremonies interring Parker's ashes in the memorial garden named after her at the NAACP National Headquarters in Baltimore. Mr. Carter's generous trust in authorizing me to collect, edit, and ultimately to publish complete editions of Parker's work has not, I hope, been misplaced. Because this book is the first step in that process, I sincerely dedicate it to him.

Contents

Preface

An often cited story about Dorothy Parker will serve to illustrate the difficulty in writing about her life. After a younger woman had either stepped aside or had held the door for her and said "Age before beauty," Dorothy Parker, in her guise of Mrs. Parker, whisked into the Algonquin Hotel while she quipped "And pearls before swine."

Joseph Bryan, III, and Wyatt Cooper, two writers who had known Parker as a friend through time, maintain that the younger woman was Clare Boothe Luce. William C. Rogers, a classmate of Parker's second husband Alan Campbell, tells the same kernel story, but maintains that the target of the quip was Gypsy Rose Lee, and that he was present when the incident happened at the Long Island estate of Herbert Bayard Swope. And Robert Benchley's widow told the same story to Babette Rosmond for Rosmond's biography Robert Benchley. The core of the story is the same, but Mrs. Benchley made "some little chorus girl" the target of Parker's quip, and Mrs. Benchley maintained that she had been present when it happened. Whereas Bryan, Cooper, and Rogers make Parker's target almost equal to Mrs. Parker, Mrs. Benchley makes her a defenseless soul-- an unknown chorus girl trying to match wits with "America's wittiest woman."

Parker was not unknown to repeat her best lines--either orally or in print--so the facts may well be that the incident took place and it occurred, probably, more than once. But more interesting is whom the teller makes the target of the quip. The three men make Parker rise to an occasion; Mrs. Benchley makes Parker a catty, heartless bitch. Parker evoked such different feelings from everyone who met her that any biographer must have, always, a double vision. Any story related about Parker is as interesting for what it tells about the teller as it is informative about Dorothy Parker.

In his Introduction to the expanded and revised The Portable Dorothy Parker (1973), Brendan Gill wrote that "the essential facts" of Parker's life were "quickly told." In the more than a dozen years since that time, two major biographies have appeared: Leslie Frewin's The Late Mrs. Dorothy Parker (1986) and Marion Meade's Dorothy Parker: What Fresh Hell is This? (1988). With these two documented lives of her available, one can now find one's own favorite Dorothy Parker story and enjoy the rest. But a problem remains that Parker is still known primarily as the author of a few frequently anthologized poems like "One Perfect Rose" and "Resume" and stories like "Big Blonde," "Here We Are," and "Horsie." Anyone familiar with Parker's work is likely to know it only through Viking's The Portable Dorothy Parker, a book largely unchanged since its first appearance during World War II. When I began the research for this book, I had assumed--incorrectly as I found out--that The Portable Dorothy Parker comprised both the best of and the most of her work. I was, quite simply, wrong.

The biographical sketch in Chapter 1 contains some familiar and some new information, and provides, I hope, at the very least, good questions that others interested in Parker might help to answer. Whenever possible, I have cited Parker's own words or words from those intimate enough with her to call her "Dottie." If I reach any conclusion it is that the more information one collects about Parker's life, the less one knows, and the less sound any generalization about her life becomes. Chapter 2, the primary bibliography, is as complete as I could make it, given the limitation of time. The annotated secondary sources in Chapter 3 are as extensive as seemed practical and worthwhile. To have included every reference that mentions Parker or her work would be inimical to the purpose of this bio-bibliography series, which is to develop comprehensive research guides.

Details of the classification and organization of the primary and secondary bibliographies are explained in headnotes within the pertinent sections. Items in the primary bibliography are prefixed by alphanumerical codes determining their places in a classified outline, and these codes appear in brackets at other places in the book when references are made to them. Items in the secondary bibliography are enumerated in one sequence, and these bracketed numbers similarly are used for cross-referencing purposes. Numbers in parentheses are page references within the works mentioned. The Classified Primary Index and the General Index refer to page numbers in this book.

In the Appendix, I have included three biographical sketches of Parker. Richard Lauterbach's "The Legend of Dorothy Parker" offers a valuable assessment of her from a 1944 perspective. The notes are mine, not Lauterbach's. Wyatt Cooper's "Whatever You Think Dorothy Parker Was Like, She Wasn't" is a longer piece, dating from 1968, which offers both analysis of the woman and interesting anecdotes that would otherwise have been lost. Joseph Bryan's sketch, "Bittersweet", was first published in 1985. It is an appreciative but non-sentimental description of Parker.

Dorothy Parker

1. A Biographical Sketch

Dorothy Parker's parents, Jacob Henry Rothschild and Annie Eliza Maston, were married in 1880, and within four years had three children, Harold, Bertram, and Helen. When these children were eleven, ten, and nine respectively, the fourth and final child, Dorothy, was born, two months prematurely on 22 August 1893. J. Henry Rothschild was no relation to the famous banking family, but he was a prominent and wealthy garment manufacturer. On 20 July 1898, Annie Marston Rothschild died. In January of 1900, J. Henry Rothschild was married again to Eleanor Frances Lewis, who lived only until April of 1903. On 27 December 1913, J. Henry Rothschild died.[1]

In the above account of Parker's first 19 years, her biographers generally concur, but none agrees precisely about matters of her education. It isn't exactly known when Dorothy Rothschild first attended school, but sometime around 1900 and until 1907, she attended the Blessed Sacrament Academy administered by the Sisters of Charity Convent.[2] After this, Parker was boarded at a combination high school and finishing school, Miss Dana's, in Morristown, New Jersey. Exactly how long she was there is unknown. Parker's best biographer, Marion Meade [186], maintains she was there only one year, 1907-1908, after which her education ended "abruptly and inexplicably" (27). And if Meade is correct in writing that Eleanor Lewis died in 1903, then Leslie Frewin [179] cannot be correct when he writes that the "solid evidence" makes it known that Parker's "father and stepmother, who both accompanied her to the interview [to attend Miss Dana's school], were invited to enter their daughter at the start of a new term" (13).[3]

Whatever year she may have left, Parker was enrolled in the Art Student's League in Manhattan by 1912. It was there she may truly have begun writing.[4] By late 1913 or early 1914, Parker had taken her first job as a caption writer for Vogue.[5]

Parker's few extant comments about her formative years were all said much later in her life. About her education at a Catholic School, Parker told Marion Capron [D.19] in the 1956 Paris Review interview that

> Convents do the same things progressive schools do, only they don't know it. They don't teach you how to read; you have to find out for yourself. At my convent we <u>did</u> have a textbook, one that devoted a page and a half to Adelaide Ann Proctor; but we couldn't read Dickens; he was vulgar, you know. . . . But as for helping me in the outside world, the convent taught me only that if you spit on a pencil eraser it will erase ink. (76)

She also told Capron about her home life: "All those writers who write about their childhood! Gentle God, if I wrote about mine, you wouldn't sit in the same room with me!" (76). But near the end of her life, Parker did talk in considerable detail to Wyatt

Cooper [88], with whom she sat through a series of interviews that were to lead to either a biography or autobiography. About her childhood, Cooper wrote

> She could (and did) stand one's hair on end with a chronicle of the adversities of a waif with the unfortunate name of Dorothy, a chronic victim whose misadventures were enough to make a piker out of de Sade's Justine. (57)

Parker, according to Cooper's account, lived among ignorant nuns, hostile children, two unsympathetic older brothers and a sister, a wretched stepmother, and malicious servants. About her father, Parker told Cooper

> On Sundays he'd take us on an outing. Some outing. We'd go to the cemetery to visit my mother's grave. All of us, including the second wife. That was his idea of a treat. Whenever he'd hear a crunch of gravel that meant an audience was approaching, out would come the biggest handkerchief you ever saw, and in a lachrymose voice that had remarkable carrying power, he'd start wailing, 'We're all here, Eliza! I'm here. Dottie's here. Mrs. Rothschild is here.' (57)

Parker's life changed notably when her father died in 1913: "After my father died there wasn't any money. I had to work" (Capron 72). Parker began by playing piano for a dance studio and by writing:

> I lived in a boarding house at 103rd and Broadway, paying eight dollars a week for my room and two meals, breakfast and dinner. Thorne Smith [the author of Topper] was there, and another man. We used to sit around in the evening and talk. There was no money, but Jesus we had fun. (Capron 72)

Parker sold her first poem to Frank Crowinshield, the managing editor of Vanity Fair, for 12 dollars. Crowinshield secured her a job writing captions for advertisements at Vogue. When she arrived at the lavishly decorated offices of Vogue, Parker, still Dorothy Rothschild, took one look and said "Well, it looks just like the entrance to a house of ill-fame."[6] When looking through issues of the magazine from 1914 until 1917, one can discern the Parker touch: the often-cited "Brevity is the Soul of Lingerie" appeared in an underwear advertisement on 1 October 1916 (101). In January 1917, Parker wrote in an advertisement for girdles that "Women need not be suppressed in order to be Stayed" (63). And according to Caroline Seebohm [158] in her life of Conde Nast, The Man Who Was Vogue, some captions "never proceeded further than the proof stage: 'There was a little girl and she had a little curl right in the middle of her forehead. When she was good, she was very good, and when she was bad, she wore this divine night dress of rose-colored mousseline de soie, trimmed with frothy Valenciennes lace'" (60). Parker also wrote one poem for Vogue, "The Lady in Back," [F.10] a not very good poem about that ubiquitous character who tells the plot or the punchline of the entertainment on stage.[7]

In June 1917, Dorothy Rothschild became Mrs. Edwin Pond Parker, II. She was 23; he was 26. Edwin Parker had taken her to meet his family; she recalled nearly fifty years later that Edwin's grandfather, a former United States Senate chaplain, called the family together for prayer and asked "Oh Lord, grant to the unbeliever in our midst, the light to see the error of her ways . . . ." (Cooper 113) They had been married "for about five minutes" when Edwin Parker joined the 33rd Ambulance Corps and went to Summit, New Jersey. He was already alcoholic, and as an ambulance driver who was wounded in World War I, he had access to morphine to which he became addicted.[8] Being assigned to occupation duty in the Rhineland, he remained in Europe until August 1919. The marriage survived the war, but it did not last. The two separated on more than one occasion, and in 1924 Mr. Parker left New York to return to Hartford, Connecticut. Mrs. Parker did not go with him. They were divorced in 1928. To Wyatt Cooper, Dorothy Parker recalled that after Edwin had returned from Europe in 1919, "it was one sanatorium after another." (113) She retained the name of Parker for the remainder of her life, and again to Cooper recalled that "there once was a Mr. Parker" (61).

As painful as her husband's absence must have been, their separation did help the development of that social and, increasingly, literary phenomenon "Mrs. Parker." As Dorothy Rothschild, she had published "Any Porch," [F.9.a] a metrically regular series of conversational cliches among wealthy women who are indulged by their husbands, and who have servants whose major jobs are to frustrate their mistresses and to rear their children.[9] Full of the colloquial language and the cliched thinking that allows it, "Any Porch" shows what a careful listener Parker must have been. She told Marion Capron in 1956 that "I haven't got a visual mind; I hear things." (80) "Any Porch" looks forward to the characters which Parker would create in her fiction and it also contained the seeds of the subject for her six personal essays in Vogue [F.10].

These six personal essays are set in the fashionable world and the tribulations of those who inhabit that world are always the topic. The essays demonstrate the Parker prose style and her characteristically wry humor. In "Love Fashion, Love Her Dog," for example, Parker suggests what may be done with an out-of-fashion dog:

When a woman has a wardrobe stocked with bulldogs, and the style suddenly changes to Scottish terriers, what is she going to do about it? She can't have them made over unfortunately. She might lay them aside, for the proverbial seven years, until they become fashionable again. She might even bestow them, with her antiquated clothes, on some deservedly poor family. She might send them to the country to rest their jangled nerves after their social season.[10]

Society weddings are her target in "Here Comes the Groom." The groom is important in a wedding only because "it takes two to make a wedding." After the ceremony and the singing of "The Voice that Breathed O'er Eden," the groom must face the "climax of the atrocities. He must stand beside his bride, a target for congratulations" (36). Women too are subjects of ridicule in "Here Comes the Groom," as they are in "When You Come to the End of a Perfect Day." The theme of the essay--there is nothing a woman will not do in order to be beautiful--is made cleverly funny by the gallons of lotions and excruciating exercises, all leading to a "fitting finale":

ten wicked little instruments of cruelly glittering steel, to slip on one's fingers and make them taper gracefully. Each little instrument is provided with a screw. You fit the implement on your innocent unsuspecting finger, then screw it tightly. When the pressure is as tight as you can endure

without screaming, you give the screw a few more twists and leave it that
way all night.[11]

The essay concludes that the "world is full of women who endure this routine every
night," but "dauntless creatures like that can't have the vote."

In her 1954 informal history of Vogue, Edna Woolman Chase [60] described
Parker as a "small, dark-haired pixie treacle-sweet but vinegar witted."[12] Her essays and
antics had caught the attention of Frank Crowinshield who was the managing editor of
Vanity Fair.   In his 1944 reminiscence "Crowinshield in the Cub's Den," [42]
Crowinshield remembered that Parker had "the quickest tongue imaginable, and I need
not say the keenest sense of mockery". For example, in mocking the formality required
by the editors of Vogue, Parker would enquire of Crowinshield "To whom should one
address oneself for towels?" Crowinshield described Parker this way:

> her figure was slight, her eyes, with their tranquil and intensely thoughtful
> expression, a curious mixture of hazel and green. She wore her brownish-
> auburn hair in a bang, and with, very often, a bun at the back. She was
> reticent, self-effacing, and preternaturally shy. . . . She wore horn-rimmed
> eyeglasses, which she removed quickly if anyone spoke to her suddenly.
> She had, too--perhaps as a result of nervousness--a habit of blinking and
> fluttering her eyelids. . . . She walked, whatever her shoes might be, with
> short, quick steps. Her suits, in the winter at any rate, were tailor-made.
> Her hats were large and turned up at the brim. Green, as a colour, seemed
> to appeal to her greatly, whether in a dress, hat, or scarf.[13]

Crowinshield had Parker transferred from Vogue to Vanity Fair as a copy editor. In
1918, P. G. Wodehouse, drama editor and critic at Vanity Fair, took an extended leave,
and Crowinshield appointed Parker drama critic. In 1919, Robert Benchley and Robert
Sherwood were hired at Vanity Fair as managing and dramatic editors, respectively. The
antics of these three were not well-received by Conde Nast, but their abilities kept them
employed, Frank Crowinshield acting as the mediator between Nast and the "cubs." The
best account of the time these three spent together at Vanity Fair was written by Parker
herself in her poem "Our Office: A Hate Song." [F.9.a][14]

"Our Office" does indeed supply, as its subtitle declares, "An Intimate Glimpse
of Vanity Fair--En Famille." Parker begins by stating "I hate the office; / It cuts in on
my social life." There is a barb directed against the "cover hounds" who "never fail to
find exceptional talents / In any feminine artist under twenty-five." The editors "don't
mean to stay in it-- / Some day they will be Free Lances / And write the Great
Thoughts that Surge within them." Nast, whom Parker calls the Great White Chief, went
"to Paris on the slightest provocation," and had "some bizarre ideas / About his
employees' getting to work / At nine o'clock in the morning." Then with comic
inevitability, the boss

> has never been known to see you
> When you arrive at 8:45;
> But try to come in at a quarter past ten
> And he will always go up in the elevator with you.

The poem closes as it opens: "I hate the office;/ It cuts in on my social life." Any particular barbs in "Our Office" are certainly offset by the broader humor that inherently exists between employers and employees, but in spite of the not too kind picture of Nast, Parker continued working for Vanity Fair, writing her monthly drama reviews and having eight more personal essays published.

Parker was also beginning to develop a reputation as a character. An incident that happened during her husband's absence in France was recounted by Edna Chase:

> Albert Lee, who held the position of private assistant and counselor to Conde Nast, took the war very much to heart. An enormous map hung on one wall of his office and daily he followed the progress of the Allied forces, meticulously setting and resetting his lines of colored pins as the armies fluctuated back and forth across no man's land. Mrs. Parker found this procedure interesting. It fired her imagination; she yearned to help. Accordingly, on more than one cold and snowy morning, she arrived betimes, hurried to Mr. Lee's office, and lovingly rearranged his embattled armies. On the first few occasions the poor man checked frantically with the papers, thinking he had misread the dispatches. Gradually he came to suspect that German spies were tailing him. He was filled with apprehension and pride. Mrs. Parker was happy too. (136)

In 1956, Parker told Marion Capron the same story:

> Every day [Mr. Lee] would get the news and move the flags around. I was married, my husband was overseas, and since I didn't have anything better to do, I'd get up half an hour early and go down and change his flags. Later on, Lee would come in, look at his map, become very serious about spies--shout, and spend his morning moving his little pins back into position. (73-74)

People who fought the war from a skyscraper in New York received special contempt from Parker. Under her pen name of Helen Wells [F.9.c], Parker wrote two essays about the Mr. Lee's of the world. In "Fun--For the Boys on Leave," Parker criticizes the women whose "sacrifices" consist of giving soldiers limousine rides and lectures about French girls. In their noble efforts, the women will end the war because soldiers will eagerly wish "to get to the front--with as little delay as possible."[15] In January of 1919, Parker wrote "They Won the War." Again, the Mr. Lee's of the world are the object of her disgust:

> It's come to the point where I am starting to conceal the fact that my husband went to the front--it makes him seem like such a slacker.[16]

By January of 1920, Parker was beginning her sixth year of employment with the Conde Nast publishing empire. She could snipe at her boss as she did in "Our Office." She, Sherwood, and Benchley had received a memorandum expressedly stating that their salaries were not to be discussed, so the three of them made placards with their salaries listed and wore them around the office. That, too, could be tolerated--with Crowinshield calming Nast down. But in January of 1920, Parker wrote herself out of a job with

Vanity Fair. In a monthly drama review called "The Oriental Drama" [F.9.b], Parker
wrote that there was a "great deal" in George Scarborough and David Belasco's Chinese
drama The Son Daughter:

> And indeed, there is a great deal in it--mandarin coats and black wigs and
> red screens and pidgin English do much to divert attention from the play
> itself. (39)

The play itself was an expensively produced imitation of Samuel Shipman's East is West
and Parker apologized for her earlier and frank opinion of that play:

> If Mr. Samuel Shipman is in the house, I should be glad to have him
> observe me get down and crawl abjectly along the ground for anything I
> may have said about his brain child East is West. Last season, in the
> exuberance of youth, I used to think that no play along the same lines
> could possibly be worse; that was before the dying year brought The Son-
> Daughter. (94)

By comparison with what had come before, Parker's remarks about Billie Burke's
performance in William Somerset Maugham's Caesar's Wife seem tame:

> Miss Burke, in her role of the young wife, looks charmingly youthful. She
> is at her best in her more serious moments; in her desire to convey the
> girlishness of the character, she plays her lighter scenes rather as if she
> were giving an impersonation of Eva Tanguay. (94)

Tanguay was a burlesque house entertainer of the time; Burke was Florenz Ziegfeld's
wife. As major advertisers in Vanity Fair, Charles Dillingham, David Belasco, and
Ziegfeld complained to Nast; Billie Burke wrote directly to her pal Crowinshield.
Dorothy Parker was fired from Vanity Fair.
    The incident was reported in the New York Times that "over a pleasantly
decorated tea table at the Plaza, Mr. Crowinshield broke the news to Mrs. Parker that her
days as drama critic at Vanity Fair were over."[17] In his column "The Conning Tower,"
Franklin Pierce Adams told the gossip this way: "R. Benchley tells me that he hath
resigned his position with 'Vanity Fair' because they had discharged Mistress Dorothy
Parker; which I am sorry for."[18] Robert Sherwood was also fired because he had asked
for a raise from his weekly $25. Crowinshield reported that in 1944, but what he did
not report was that, according to Sherwood's biographer John Mason Brown [75], the
"music teacher of Conde Nast's daughter was coming in to take over his work." After he
was fired, Sherwood returned to Harvard's Hasty Pudding Club, where he and S. D. Sears
revised a play Barnum Was Right which had been interrupted because of the war.[19] In
the old Metropolitan Opera building, Benchley and Parker rented an "office so tiny that
an inch smaller and it would have been adultery" (Capron 74). They planned to write a
play, but Sherwood became the New York Life movie critic and Benchley became its
drama editor.
        The story that Parker retained the office she and Benchley had rented and had
MEN lettered on the door made the rounds and became--and has remained--part of the
mythology about Mrs. Parker.[20] In the second part of his biographical sketch of Robert

Benchley, "Funny Man," Joseph Bryan III wrote that the whole Vanity Fair incident was a "case in Saki's phrase, of 'cows buzzing around a gadfly.'"[21] Benchley had resigned in sympathy over Parker's being fired. Parker told Capron "It was the greatest act of friendship I'd ever known." (74) More than 40 years later, while she was teaching at Southern California, Parker told Lois Battle [D.22] that clobbering three plays had cost her job and since "that time, I've been free-lancing."[22]

It wasn't exactly true that Parker had been free-lancing. She took a job as drama critic for Ainslee's in May of 1920. Being fired from Vanity Fair could not have come at a more opportune time, at least from an historical perspective, for the development of the persona of "Mrs. Parker." Part of that persona is that of victim, and who could be better as victimizer than the biggest, most glamorous, most fashionable magazine of the day? And who could be a better victim than tiny, harmless, elfin Mrs. Parker?

"In Broadway Playhouses" was the name of Parker's monthly column for Ainslee's [F.1]. In this column, Parker continued to develop the sophisticated voice outraged at the paucity of entertainment on Broadway. Parker was able to strike with full vengeance at the Ziegfeld Follies. In September 1920, she called the 1920 Follies a national institution, "the only dangerous rival of baseball and profiteering as an all-American sport." (156)[23] She wrote that the new Follies needed a few good songs, "just to give the audience something to remember the evening by." (157) The "eccentric" dancing was the "most striking action of the evening, especially Jack Donahue's": "He proved to be, as you might say, the Harding of the occasion." Another show on Broadway, "The Scandals of 1920," was sure to become another national institution as well: "William Jennings Bryan, rent profiteering, the Mexican situation, and prohibition are satirized with much the same subtlety that characterizes the work of the Hippodrome troupe of trick elephants." (158) There was a nice innovation in the 1920s Scandals:

> A pretty touch is the introduction of four showgirls, wearing, instead of tights, coats of fresh and glistening paint, some of which they smear off with their hands, to show the audience that there is no deception. And yet, there are those who say that the American stage has not advanced artistically. (158)

Parker continued in this same vein for the remainder of her stay as Ainslee's drama critic. For example, she wrote that Nora Bayes both produced and starred in Her Family Tree, "an exceptionally beautiful production, with virtually no expense spared with regard to costumes and lighting. Where the economy was practiced was in the lines and songs." About James Barrie's play Mary Rose, Parker wrote

> I know that people say that they cannot figure out what Mary Rose is meant to mean. I know they say the cast is mediocre and the setting shoddy and Ruth Chatterton not the person to play the title role. They may be perfectly right; I'm sure I am in no position to say.[24]

A revue at the Century Theatre, The Midnight Rounders of 1921 contained sheet shadows, indifferent songs, and uninspired costumes. Parker wrote that "you cannot fully appreciate the Wisdom of Franklin's 'Early to Bed' until you see The Midnight Rounders."[25]

Parker was not yet so famous as she would become by 1926 and 1927, but these

Ainslee's essays have too long been over-looked as part of her contribution to American humor. They are no more serious dramatic criticism than her later and more famous Constant Reader essays [F.7.d] are serious book reviews. The few examples cited above could be multiplied indefinitely, but one more deserves some attention. In August of 1922, Parker reviewed Go Easy, Mable, a play

> billed on the program as 'The Musical Comedy Different.' During the first few moments of the piece, it seemed as a couple of letters had been omitted and that 'The Musical Comedy Indifferent' was what had been intended. It soon developed however that this idea was all wrong. Despite the presence of the buoyant Ethel Levey, and the curious misplacement in the cast of Estelle Winwood, it was quite plain that the slogan for Go Easy, Mable should have been 'The Musical Comedy Terrible.'[26]

One of Parker's classic lines is about Channing Pollock's The House Beautiful which Parker dismissed in The New Yorker while substituting as theatre critic for Robert Benchley [F.7.d] as "I may utter only that The House Beautiful is the play lousy." (21 March 1931: 36)

Nine years separate the two lines, and nothing was more influential in helping Parker to establish her reputation as Mrs. Parker than her involvement in the famed Algonquin Round Table. In his life and times portrait of Neysa McMein, Anything Goes, Brian Gallagher [182] defines the boundaries of the world of the Round Table: "the area between the East and Hudson Rivers and between Greenwich Village and 96th Street."[27] In a small world of 12 daily newspapers, the activities of the group could be chronicled as F. P. A. did in The World in his "Conning Tower" and his "Diary of Our Own Samuel Pepys." As Gallagher writes, the group had "the genius for projecting a sense of 'in-ness' to their readers: they made their own, often inconsequential, actions seem something of a sophisticated norm" (85). The Algonquin Hotel on 44th Street was simply a convenient physical locus for lunch and dinners among group members.

There is no way to date precisely the group's beginning or end. Frank Case, the Algonquin's manager and eventual owner, in his 1938 book Tales of a Wayside Inn [30] wrote that the group's beginning was in "1918 when Woollcott came home from the war and it continued without a break for more than ten years." But for Case, the Round Table had become only a "mellow and pleasant" memory by 1938: "The real Round Table flourished during the days when none of the boys or girls had yet done anything in particular; they were the hopefuls of the future."[28] The group may well have begun in the early summer of 1919 when Alexander Woollcott, the drama critic for the Times, was asked to lunch by Murdock Pemberton, Woollcott's childhood friend and, by 1919, a press agent. Pemberton and John Peter Toohey, another press agent, were trying to get Woollcott to mention an unknown client--named Eugene O'Neill--in his column in the Times. Toohey did not get a plug for his client, but he and Pemberton were treated to World War I stories which Woollcott always began with "When I was in the theatre of war . . . ." Woollcott had been stationed in Paris where he, F. P. A., and Harold Ross first met and wrote for Stars and Stripes, the Army's official newspaper. In September of 1919, Woollcott collected and published his tales and sketches of A. E. F. Battlefields under the title The Command Is Forward, by Sergeant Alexander Woollcott.[29]

Toohey and Pemberton planned their revenge: an elaborate lunch to welcome the "hero" home. Invited to the affair at the Algonquin were press agents, editors, and music and drama critics from New York's papers and fashionable magazines like Vanity Fair and Harper's Bazaar. Beginning another of his theatre of war stories, Woollcott was interrupted with "Seat 13, Row Q, no doubt" or "If you were ever in the theatre of war Aleck, it was in the last row-seat nearest the exit." According to Margaret Case Harriman [55], Bill Murry, music critic for the Brooklyn Daily Eagle, said the first (6); the second, according to James R. Gaines [123] was said by Harper Bazaar editor Arthur Samuels (28).

The Round Table members waxed and waned daily, but the Inner Circle became known as "The Board." They called their lunches the Board Meeting, until Frank Case gave the group its own waiter, Luigi; then lunch became "The Luigi Board," mocking the enormously popular fascination with the Ouija Board.[30] The oldest member F. P. A. (1881-1960) was the group's biographer and recorder in "The Conning Tower" and "The Diary of Our Own Samuel Pepys." Woollcott (1887-1943) was, according to Wolcott Gibb in 1938, the group's spiritual focus. In addition to Parker, the other members of the Board included Robert Benchley (1889-1945), Robert Sherwood (1896-1955), George S. Kaufman (1889-1961), Heywood Broun (1899-1939), Harold Ross (1892-1951), Donald Ogden Stewart (1894-1980), and Marc Connelly (1890-1980).[31]

Perhaps the high point of the group's public flaunting of themselves as individuals and as a group to which membership would be a rare privilege came in 1922 with the two Round Table revues No Sirree! and The 49'ers. The whole point of the two revues was to have fun, as was the whole point of the lunches at the Algonquin. The lunch conversation and the antics of the group have become the material for the legend of the Algonquin Round Table. Because the group incited envy among non-members, the Round Table regulars became known as Log Rollers. In order to avoid this charge, the group became especially vicious and critical towards each other and of each other's work, hence the name the Vicious Circle. But the criticism directed towards the individual or his or her work was never taken offensively. In fact, members could joke about their reputations as log-rollers and back scratchers. Robert Drennan [89] cites Woollcott on such an occasion: about "F. P. A.'s harsh review of a Heywood Broun novel [The Boy Grew Older, 1922], Woollcott remarked 'You can see Frank's scratches on Heywood's back yet.'"[32]

By 1934, Parker's work was actively sought after by any magazine of the day, and in February of that year, Vanity Fair published her essay "A Valentine for Mr. Woollcott." [F.9.b] In this public, affectionate, letter of friendship, Parker wrote about the peculiar quandary members found themselves in, when they wanted to praise another member's work:

> You might set fire to widows, deflower orphans, or filch the flag from soldier's graves and still be invited to all the literary teas; but if you admired in print, the traits and achievements of any member of your acquaintance, your jig was up. . . . The fear of becoming a log-roller was put into me during my formative years, and there was a good long stretch during which, in my endeavors to keep clean of the ugly charge, I said only the vilest of my nearest and dearest. (27)

The glossy side of the Round Table can make it "the greatest forum of presiding wits since the Mermaid Tavern."[33] For a sentimental and sympathetic view of the group, one needs to read Margaret Case Harriman's 1956 book The Vicious Circle [65]. However,

Gaines' book Wit's End has the long subtitle The Days and Nights of the Algonquin Round Table. He supplies abundant evidence to support his assertions that the dark side of the Round Table was a "Bronx Zoo of contemporary neurotics" whose "fragrant manners" masked their unhappiness, even to the point of self-loathing with Woollcott and Parker (29). And as Brendan Gill [A.13] warned in his introduction to the revised and enlarged The Portable Dorothy Parker in 1973, one must constantly remember that the little world that gave Parker and others their reputations was really "only a province, and like all provinces, it considered itself much bigger and more important than it was." (xv) Ernest Hemingway found the teapot tempests disgusting,[34] and other writers who were living in New York were not members: Eugene O'Neill, Edna St. Vincent Millay, Sinclair Lewis, and Steven Vincent Benet.

In addition to meeting in the Rose Room, group members often met in Neysa McMein's studio. In his portrait of the painter Neysa McMein, Woollcott [4], not surprisingly, romanticized the studio itself, its owner, and the "widely variegated" population:

> Over at the piano Jascha Heifetz and Arthur Samuels may be trying to find what four hands can do in the syncopation of a composition never thus desecrated before. Squatted uncomfortably around an ottoman, Franklin P. Adams, Marc Connelly and Dorothy Parker will be playing cold hands to see who will buy the dinner that evening. At the bookshelf Robert C. Benchley and Edna Ferber are amusing themselves vastly by thoughtfully autographing [McMein's] set of Mark Twain for her. In the corner, some jet-bedecked dowager from a statelier milieu is taking it all in, immensely diverted. Chaplin or Chaliapin, Alice Duer Miller or Wild Bill Donovan, Father Duffy or Mary Pickford--any or all of them may be there.[35]

The Round Table world was, in Woollcott's eyes, a kind of American Paris: "If you loiter in Neysa McMein's studio, the world will drift in and out." (37)

In her autobiography, screenwriter Anita Loos [78] didn't quite agree with Woollcott's version of the "world":

> I found Neysa's studio in a rundown old building on West 57th Street. Its big main room was a pale yet dirty beige and, although sparsely furnished, it gave an impression of being cluttered because of a jumble of coats, overshoes, sporting gear, and bundles.[36]

Loos thought that "Neysa's unkept appearance seemed phony and even a little conceited," and the majority of the Round Table regulars did not impress her:

> Although self-styled intellectuals, they were concerned with nothing more weighty than the personal items about themselves that were dished up in gossip columns; their conversation was a rehash of easy forms of exhibitionism in which they had recently indulged, such as parlor games and croquet tournaments. . . . as a group, they behaved with that overly casual air which is an attempt of the unsophisticated to appear at ease.[37]

After one meeting with the group, Loos dismissed them as being without interest, except for Parker:

> When I was introduced to Dorothy, she greeted me with an almost
> caressing enthusiasm that was the reverse of the self-consciously casual air
> that permeated Neysa's salon. But I sensed that her over friendliness
> could only be a sardonic comment on the fact that she had no belief at all
> in friendship and knew herself to be a lone wolverine. I doubted that she
> found any true companionship among members of the Round Table, and
> felt that she had given in to their advances on the theory that she might as
> well be with them as elsewhere.[38]

Edmund Wilson [114], whom Parker helped to get a job at <u>Vanity Fair</u>, left almost the
same impression of the Round Table members as Loos did:

> I was sometimes invited to join them, but I did not find them particularly
> interesting. They all came from the suburbs and 'provinces', and a sort of
> tone was set--mainly by Benchley, I think--deriving from a provincial
> upbringing of people who had been taught a certain kind of gentility, who
> had played the same games and who had read the same children's books--
> all of which they were now able to mock from a level of New York
> sophistication. I found this rather tiresome, since they never seemed to be
> able to get above it.[39]

Again like Loos's account, Wilson's maintains that he was impressed only with Parker
who "was naturally spontaneously witty, and the conflicts in her nature made her
interesting." Wilson was not the first of Parker's contemporaries who mentions the many
conflicts he saw within and about her, but if the conflicts "made her unreliable and even
capable of a certain treachery," they also made her able to associate "on an equal basis
with such people as Elinor Wylie and the Gerald Murphys, with whom the other
Algonquinites would have been uncomfortable and out of their depth."[40]
    Parker's association with the Round Table certainly helped to promote the social
side of Mrs. Parker who led a life of theatre-going, cocktail parties, speakeasy recreation,
divorce, numerous lovers, an abortion, and at least four suicide attempts. Parker also made
two of the four European trips during her life as "Mrs. Parker." The first one was in
1926, from February to November; the second was from April to January, 1929-1930.
The cliche about the first trip is that the Round Table members simply found a new hotel
in Paris where they could continue their Algonquin frolics without interruption. In an
essay "What of Europe," Robert Benchley begins by writing that "by 'Europe' I mean
three or four hundred square feet of Paris and another good place in Rome."[41] It was
during this trip that Parker first met Hemingway. The second trip was supposed to be a
working vacation, and Parker spent most of her time with the Murphys in Switzerland.[42]
Being Mrs. Parker included being the houseguest of New York's most wealthy and
socially prominent families. According to Marion Meade, Parker was the most sought-
after weekend house guest of the 1920s, along with Fanny Brice (288). James R. Gaines
called the Round Table member's social climbing a kind of "exquisite purgatory" because
the guests had to perform like "seals and flying fish" (142). This group also founded its
own journal of sorts in a new humor magazine called <u>The New Yorker</u>: "If the city of
New York were already convinced that the Rose Room was <u>the</u> locus of sophistication,

The New Yorker did nothing to dissuade them" (Gaines 144).

Whether one despised the group or envied the members in it, the Algonquin Round Table was certainly an American literary phenomenon that cannot be overlooked. The real danger is in under- or over-rating its members and their accomplishments. It really is unimportant if the legend of the Round Table began with the quips directed against Woollcott. What is important is that those quips set the pattern for classic Round Table humor. First, they were witty because they were quick and totally appropriate for the situation. Second, the quips against Woollcott deflated pomposity, even if the target was the guest of honor and New York's most influential drama critic. Third, the quips were cruel only because they were true, and the truer the jest, the funnier it was. They could be told, appreciated, get a laugh, and no one was hurt.

Three of Parker's classic lines illustrate the special conditions under which the Round Table humor flourished. The target for the wit could be an outsider, and who was better than the President of the United States? When it was reported that Calvin Coolidge was dead, Parker asked "How could they tell?" (Meade 231). The target might well be an insider.

> Under the influence of strong waters--she was not playing at the time--Tallulah [Bankhead] did a few splits, threw a few bottles, and otherwise became so uproariously lighthearted that a committee of four gentlemen was appointed by the hostess to escort her away from there. As the clamor of their departure faded down the hall, Dottie poked her elfin face between the portieres of an adjoining room.
> 'Has Whistler's Mother left yet?' she inquired.[43]

At lunch the next day, Bankhead "gazed ruefully" at herself and said "The less I behave like Whistler's mother the night before, the more I look like her the morning after." She and Parker remained friends until Parker's death in 1967. Finally, the target could just as easily be Parker herself. Asked about a manuscript that was due, Parker (supposedly) wired a telegram that she was "too fucking busy and vice versa."[44] Or, when asked why she never had a home, only hotel rooms, Parker replied that she needed "only a place to lay my hat and a few friends."[45]

Parker's contemporary, and fellow humorist, Cory Ford begins his book The Time of Laughter [80] with the warning that "memory has a way of oversimplifying the past" but he remembered that "Quoting Mrs. Parker became the town's leading indoor sport." Mrs. Parker was "small and attractive, with dark bobbed hair and melting eyes and the innocent mien of a schoolgirl. She seemed as demure as a kitten, but the unwary soon learned that her sheathed claws were lightening fast and could leave a painful scratch."[46]

This persona of Mrs. Parker has been fictionalized eight times between 1923 and 1984: Gertrude Atherton wrote a book called Black Oxen (1923) that satirized the entire Round Table crowd; Donald Ogden Stewart created the character of Mrs. Roger Barbee in The Crazy Fool in 1925; in 1932, George Oppenheimer created Mary Hilliard in Here Today and Philip Barry created Lily Malone in Hotel Universe. In 1934, Charles Brackett's Entirely Surrounded had Daisy Lester, and Kaufman and Hart's Merrily We Roll Along had Julia Glen.[47] The character of Paula Wharton in Ruth Gordon's 1944 play Over Twenty One was based on Parker. Dorothy Parker appears, unfavorably, as Dorothy Parker in Edwin Corley's 1975 Shadows, a novel about Hollywood. Nathaniel Benchley's 1982 novel Speakeasy has Parker portrayed as Dorothy Peters; finally, George

Baxt's delightful murder mystery The Dorothy Parker Murder Case was published in 1984.

No matter how much of a social creature Mrs. Parker was, or that her reputation as a wit was constantly growing, a vital part of Mrs. Parker was that she was also a writer. No amount of hype or appearance of not working could replace the fact that between 1920 and 1934, Parker produced a substantial amount of work. In addition to her monthly dramatic reviews in Ainslee's between 1920 and 1923 [F.1], Parker wrote prose squibs, long essays, and poetry for The Saturday Evening Post between 1921 and 1923 [F.8]. The first book with her name on the title page was published in 1920, High Society [A.1]. Her first short story was published in The Smart Set in December of 1922, "Such a Pretty Little Picture" [B.2]. By 1924, Parker was contributing almost weekly to the old New York Life [F.5]. In 1924, Parker and Elmer Rice co-authored the play Close Harmony [A.4].

An important date in Parker's life is 16 August 1925. Readers who liked the gossip and latest work of the Round Table could have turned to F. P. A.'s "Conning Tower" that Sunday morning and read "News Item": "Men seldom make passes / At girls who wear glasses." In the same group of poems, readers could also read Parker's summary of suicide methods, "Resume" [F.2.a]. If re-quoting Mrs. Parker's speakeasy lines became the leading indoor sport of the 1920's, then so did repeating the lines from these poems. And just one year earlier, "One Perfect Rose" had appeared in Life. Exactly when or how the idea of collecting her poetry into a book came about is not precisely known. What is known is that in December of 1926, Parker's first exclusive book of poetry appeared, Enough Rope [A.6]. After this book became a best seller, Parker never went more than 22 months without a new collection of poems or prose appearing until 1933: 1928, Sunset Gun (poetry) [A.7]; 1930 Laments for the Living (prose) [A.7]; 1931 Death and Taxes (poetry) [A.8]; and 1933, After Such Pleasures (prose) [A.9]. While contributing stories and poetry to The New Yorker, Parker also had her--almost--weekly "Constant Reader" [F.7.c] book reviews between October of 1927 and April of 1929; she contributed ten more between 1931 and 1933 [F.7.d]. While Benchley was in Hollywood making his film debut in short films, Parker substituted for him as a drama critic between February and April of 1931. These reviews and the Constant Reader essays contain the persona of Mrs. Parker at its best.

In 1934, Parker left her beloved New York and moved to California to write screenplays. She would move back and forth between Hollywood, New York, and Pennsylvania during the next thirty years, and return to New York for the final time in 1964. These thirty years were hectic ones for her: they were dominated by her leftist political associations that kept her alive as a public figure, but this period also was one in which she continuously denounced the first forty years of her life.

It's impossible to date precisely when "Mrs. Parker" was begun, and it's equally impossible to date precisely when this persona died for Dorothy Rothschild Parker Campbell. Frank Case called the Round Table a "pleasant and mellow" memory by 1936 or 1937. Tennis had come between F. P. A. and the hotel. Heywood Broun had moved to Connecticut; Woollcott had moved to the "extreme edge" of the East River. Parker, Benchley, Connelly, and Sherwood were in Hollywood.

Parker began renouncing the Round Table legend and her reputation as "Mrs. Parker" as early as 1934. In a Los Angeles Times interview [D.7], Parker was quoted as saying "Why, I'm not even an amateur humorist. I am very serious, and quite hurt when people laugh at some of my most earnest endeavors."[48] After she returned from her fourth trip to Europe in 1937, Parker wrote for New Masses [E.11] that "The only group I have ever been affiliated with is that not especially brave little band that hid its nakedness of heart and mind under the out-of-date garment of a sense of humor."[49] She continued this renunciation in 1941 when she said she had become famous for "a reputation I didn't want." She told Hubbard Keavy [D.15] for The Dallas Herald that "I do have a reputation as a smarty pants . . .I say hardly any of those clever things that are attributed to me. I wouldn't have time to earn a living if I said all those things."[50]

The most often-cited denunciation of her past is the 1963, seventieth birthday interview. In The New York Herald Tribune Saul Pett [D.25] wrote that Parker remembered fondly some of the individuals who were members of the Algonquin Round Table, but that she didn't much like "the hotel Algonquin Round Table collectively as a fountain of intellect and wit". Parker told Pett that

> People romanticize it . . . This was no Mermaid Tavern. These were no giants. Think of who was writing in those days--Lardner, Fitzgerald, Faulkner and Hemingway. Those were the real giants. The Round Table was just a lot of people telling jokes and telling each other how good they were. (13 October 1963: 20)

Parker said that when Woollcott would go into ecstasy about "Valiant Is the Word for Carrie", she had had enough. When Gloria Steinem [D.26] asked for an interview in 1965, Parker who was 71, agreed to talk with her, "But not about that damned Algonquin; I'm fed to the teeth with Algonquin."[51] She told Wyatt Cooper that the whole thing had been made up by people who hadn't been there, and she was surprised that the legend was growing rather than diminishing; her largest complaint wasn't that there was nothing going on, but that there was only "a bunch of loudmouths showing off, saving their gags for days, waiting for a chance to spring them. . . . It's just that there was so much praise" (110). It's important to remember that these remarks were made between 1934 and 1967, so that they were not just final remarks made in bitterness.

As mentioned above, 1934 was a major turning point in Parker's life. She not only began denouncing her old friends and reputation as a humorist but also left New York to begin a career as a screenwriter in Hollywood. She took with her her second husband Alan Campbell. Parker and Campbell had met through mutual theatre friends in New York. They were married in either 1932 or 1933.[52] As a stock actor Campbell was certainly not rich and given Parker's inability to handle money, the two were broke. In the summer of 1934, they were living in Denver, Colorado while Campbell was acting there. The New York Times reported that she and Campbell were to arrive at Paramount Studios--she as a writer and Campbell as both actor and writer--in September.[53] In a letter to Alexander Woollcott, Parker wrote

> The Paramount contract, or Kiss of Death, has come. It is for ten weeks, and it seems the only way to get out from under that suffocating mass of debt which my doting husband calls Dottie's dowry. . . So, when the Elitch Gardens season closes September first--having hung up an untarnished record of not one respectable production--we pack up the Bedlingtons and take again to that god damned nineteen-twenty-nine model Rosinante of the Colonel's.[54]

Parker referred to Campbell as "The Colonel" because he was a native of Virginia, the son of a tobacco farmer.

Parker and Campbell arrived in Hollywood , according to Fred Guiles [111], "in a state of semi-destitution to go on a combined salary beginning the following Monday at $5,000 a week for the two of them. . . . George Oppenheimer loaned them his home."[55] Though their salaries did not always remain so high, they were still averaging $2,000 a week in 1942 before Campbell joined the Army (Meade 289). It was truly a rags to riches story according to Richard Lauterbach [44] in his article "The Legend of Dorothy Parker": "They borrowed the money to buy a second-hand flivver and drove to the coast. They soon drove a Packard and lived in a mansion."[56]

In her 1953 speech "Hollywood, The Land I Won't Return To" [E.8] Parker made the following comment about the money she had earned:

> I used to get money [as a screenwriter] as I told you. It isn't real money.
> It isn't. I think it's made of compressed snow. It just melts in your
> hands.[57]

Some of the money was spent on gifts to friends. Lillian Hellman in "Dorothy Parker" [94] writes that Parker had given her a Picasso gouache and a Utrillo landscape as gifts.[58] They also bought a country estate in 1936. Located in Bucks County Pennsylvania, the 112 acre estate was bought for $4,500. It was sold in 1947 after they divorced, but in the meantime they spent over $98,000 improving it. This was during the Depression when the average family's income was only $1,500 a year.[59] In the fall of 1940, they rented a mansion on North Palm Drive in order to have a proper place for entertaining. It was used only once to host a party for Bea Ames Stewart who, after divorcing Donald Ogden Stewart, married Leo Tolstoy's grandson.[60]

Another act Parker and Campbell performed with their newly found wealth was to host "a huge buffet dinner in their mansion" for the Scottsboro Boys. Eight of the nine black men charged with the rape of two white women in Alabama in 1931 had been sentenced to death. The International Labor Defense had hired New York's most successful defense attorney Sam Leibowitz to seek an appeal. Parker called people who would be sympathetic and raised "several thousand dollars" towards their defense. Guiles cites this incident as Parker's "first step in becoming a political activist" for underdog causes.[61] But Guiles was wrong in calling this action the first step; there had indeed been a lot of practice before.

In 1920 and 1921, while Parker was drama reviewer for Ainslee's, she had criticized the play Come Seven by Octavus Roy Cohan. She wrote that "The actor's portrayal of the negro race goes only as deep as a layer of burnt cork, and so, one cannot help but feel, does the author's. . . . The characters who appear in it are not of the colored race, but of the blackface race--the typical stage negroes, lazy, luridly dressed, addicted to crap shooting, and infallibly mispronouncing every word of more than three syllables."[62] In 1921, Parker praised Charles Gilpin's performance in The Emperor Jones but laments that

> In no way are our producers more wasteful of genius than in their
> disregard of the Negro actors. What has become of Opal Cooper, who
> some seasons ago appeared with the Negro Players? Since that time, his
> opportunities have probably consisted of an offer to play one-fourth of a

quartet in an uptown cabaret, and a chance to don a white cotton wig and say 'Gord bress you, Marse Robert,' as an old family retainer in a heart-interest drama with its scene laid below the Thomas Dixon line.[63]

During her Round Table years, Parker's most political friend would have been Heywood Broun, a dedicated Socialist. But Frank Case's sardonic comment in 1938 was that Broun's socialism consisted of the type that "neatly divides mankind into two classes: the righteous who draw wages and the wicked who pay wages." (61) As Margaret Case Harriman wrote in The Vicious Circle, F. P. A. did wage a war championing postmen "against illegible or obscure house numbers in New York" (78), but as she wisely argued, the politics of the Round Table members was that "unshakable belief in the sacred right of any man to embrace whatever politics he desired" (67). It follows naturally enough that Parker would have been involved in the 1927 Sacco and Vanzetti trial. Seen as a huge miscarriage of justice by Parker and Benchley, they joined the international body of protesters in Boston in 1927. Parker was arrested, but her political activism did not resurface again until 1934 with her fundraising activities on behalf of the Scottsboro Boys. A full-blown consciousness would not come until 1937.[64]

In August of 1937, Parker left for her fourth trip to Europe. Paris was the site for the World Exposition, and Parker renewed acquaintances with the Murphys. She saw Leland Stowe who, as foreign correspondent for the New York Herald Tribune, had just returned from covering the civil war in Madrid. She and Campbell went there for ten days, partly in Madrid and partly in Valencia. It was bombed four times during their stay. They returned to Paris, then home in October. Their return was covered by Dixie Tighe [D.11] in the New York Post:

> As a result of a brief trip to Spain, Dorothy Parker, who long used wit as a shield, has come home to arm herself with more sober weapons. . . . There were tears in the shining eyes of Miss Parker when she disclosed last night on the French Liner Champlain that the tragedy of Spain had tempered her wit and urged her into a desire to raise funds for the American hospitals in Spain.[65]

Tighe reported that Alan, ever in the background, made sure a bar was set up for his friends.

About a month later, Parker's essay "Incredible, Fantastic . . . and True" [E.11] appeared in New Masses. The essay begins with a credible statement: "I want to say first that I came to Spain without an ax to grind. I didn't bring messages from anybody, nor greetings to anybody."[66] The war had not been real to her: "I read in our larger newspapers that here was a civil war, with opposing factions neatly divided into Reds and Whites--rather as if they were chessmen"; but it became real as she watched two girls, who had seen their father killed, try "to get past the guards, back to the still crumbly, crashing house to find their mother. There was a great pile of rubble, and on the top of it, a broken doll and a dead kitten . . . ruthless enemies to fascism." (16) It was then that Parker knew that "ridicule may be a shield, but it is not a weapon." Two weeks later, in December, Parker had become chair of the women's division of the North American Committee to Aid Spanish Democracy. The New York Herald Tribune reported part of her speech that she made during the ceremonies installing her at the Hotel New Yorker:

I was there during a so-called 'lull' which meant that only occasional bombs burst on the city. I was scared green: but I was the only person in Spain who was scared. Every one else was busy, gay and courageous. Theatres and shops were open. Old women sat with their knitting behind their baskets of flowers in stalls. You could buy anything in Madrid-- except food. Food had to go to the soldiers. Children and nursing mothers were the only persons in the city who could have eggs.[67]

Newsweek reported that Parker's visit to Valencia had "unhinged her renowned flippancy on a subject she had never touched before."[68] The report cited her New Masses writing and her short story "Soldiers of the Republic" (New Yorker 5 February 1938: 13-14). It is the tale of two tourists in Valencia who listen to soldiers on leave who, by pooling their money, were able to afford cigarettes. The speaker gives them hers, but thinks "Darling of me to share my cigarettes with the men on their way back to the trenches. Big Lady Bountiful. The Prize Sow." (14). About this story, Alexander Woollcott wrote to Rebecca West that "it comes nearer to telling the reader exactly what she is like than anything else she ever wrote."[69] It's important to note here that Parker certainly personalized this struggle. She kept loathing herself about a situation over which she had no control. It certainly helps to explain Parker's vehemence for organizing and doing what she could to help. Not the least of helping was making sure her days as Mrs. Parker were over. She wrote "The Custard Heart" [B.41] which was a new story for her collected stories Here Lies in 1939. It's the story of Mrs. Lanier who must face meeting poor and ragged people on her chauffeured way to the dressmaker's in "recurrent sorrows of living." It's her "grieved bewilderment" that made "the perfection of her career, the sublimation of wistfulness."

In November of 1938, Parker spoke at Madison Square Garden in a mass meeting which raised over $4,000 to protest Nazi outrages. She maintained that FDR's words were the best said ones on the subject, that the Neutrality Act gave no aid to the victims, only to the aggressors.[70] Parker attended a party in Washington for Loyalist Spain. She sat on a piano, crying and begging for support: "If you had seen what I saw in Spain, you'd be serious too." She once again said that humor was no longer her way of life: "I don't see how you can help being unhappy now. The humorist has never been happy, anyhow. Today he is whistling past worse graveyards to worse tunes."[71] Parker's second, and final, essay in New Masses, "Not Enough", details how Parker thought she was not doing enough to help the underprivileged: "I found there were things I could do actually to fight the things I loathe."[72] She and Donald Ogden Stewart formed the Hollywood Anti-Nazi League. By 1939, it had grown to over 4,000 members. Parker took the conditions personally. When she spoke in June of 1939 to the Third American Writers' Conference [E.33], she said that "Writers could not find themselves until they find their fellow man. Moon, death, and heartbreak were personal matters, but the songs of my time are dead."[73] After America entered the war, Parker spoke to the Los Angeles division of Business and Professional Women. She said that the U.S.O. was the one place their "help may best be put," but she also cites herself as not doing enough to help.[74]

Yet, New York's War Fund raised over $1.3 million in 1944 and Parker as an active member said

it wasn't accomplished by anything as quick and graceful as a miracle. It was done by hard, persistent, grueling work. Knowing what you have done makes me proud to be a member of the human race, and particularly proud to belong to the women's division of it.[75]

Parker also served as a member of the National Council of American Soviet Friendship and on one occasion presented to the wife of the Russian Consul children's books to be delivered to devastated areas as part of the effort by the Women's Council for Post-War Europe.[76]

In his book Writers in Hollywood, 1915-1951, Ian Hamilton demonstrates that Parker was certainly not unique in her leftist politics and extreme views. Before the New York writers invasion of Hollywood in the 1930's, there was a Screen Writer's Guild that had existed since 1914 when Anita Loos, D. W. Griffith, and others had established a Photoplay Author's League that was more a social club than a political party. The League certainly had the purpose of protecting writers from unfair treatment, and Louis B. Mayer proposed that a "writers' division" be established in the Academy of Motion Pictures Arts and Sciences. Depending upon where one's sympathies were, this writers' division of the Academy was part of a perfect system or it was a company union. Hamilton cites Parker as saying "Looking to the Academy for representation was like trying to get laid in your mother's house. Someone was always in the parlor, watching."[77]

The writers in Hollywood were united in their desire to have control over their material. Parker recalled in 1959 that "everyone there wrote. Everyone wrote. I never saw such a thing. The nice man at the gates would write. The producer would write-- that was much worse."[78] Writing for the movies was something new. Plots and stories were given to individuals or teams--like Parker and Campbell--whose job it was to construct scenes and to insert dialogue. Because no one person or team usually wrote an actual, finished script, screen credit for writing was much coveted as recognition for one's efforts. And considering the writers whom Hollywood studios attracted with large salaries, it isn't surprising that they wanted control over their material: from New York came Parker, Benchley, Donald Ogden Stewart, and John O'Hara; there were newspaper men like Ben Hecht and Charles MacArthur; stage writers like George Kaufman and Lillian Hellman; and, novelists like Fitzgerald, Faulkner, and Dashiell Hammett.[79]

From the studios' point of view, if writers wanted control over their material, they were always free to leave, along with their huge weekly salaries. It was this kind of logic that drove Parker to distraction, and it was the basis for her insisting that the studio system was a fascistic system. Thus, she and Donald Ogden Stewart were active in recruiting writers to join the Screen Writers' Guild.

But it wasn't only for control over their material that Parker and Stewart organized. They were also concerned that the average wage for most writers--those who were not famous names--was about $40 a week with no security. When she talked about these issues in 1959, Parker said the Screen Writers' Guild

> was extremely badly needed, because there were people who were not getting any money, because it was all mixed up, people were coming in and getting nothing. The greatest money they could have was $40 a week, and then bang, it would stop. A screenwriter might be employed, say for two weeks in a year and they can say 'the hell with him.' That isn't good, you know. That's all we tried to do, to get a certain level of employment there.[80]

But the studios did not take the activities of the Screen Writers' Guild lying down. They intimidated writers and found others who were willing to join a new league called the Screen Playwrights in 1936. It was an effort on the part of major studios to improve the lot of writers in screen crediting, wages, and contracts. According to Ian Hamilton, it brought an effective end to the Screen Writers' Guild (100-01).

In her book The Hollywood Writers' War, Nancy Lynn Schwartz cites John Brite, who wrote the screenplay for Public Enemy, as saying that membership in the Screen Writers' Guild was a kind of "graylist." Members of the Screen Writer's Guild and Screen Playwrights might be friends in elevators, but not officially: "The commissaries all over town were like armed camps."[81] A letter from Brite to New Masses says that he was "proud of the New Masses which gives [Parker's] talent such a ready forum":

> We in Hollywood are so happy for Dorothy Parker. So happy for her gallant desertion of the lost generation. Happy for her joining in the leadership against the fascist bloodsuckers. Her pioneering in the Hollywood Anti-Nazi League, the Motion Picture Artists' Committee for Spain (about to initiate an international drive for Christmas toys and milk for Spanish children) excites and cheers us forward.[82]

In its 28 February 1938 issue, Newsweek called New Masses "class conscious" (26), but on 7 March 1955, called it "a deadly serious Communist weekly" (25). Whatever the intention of the magazine, Parker's writing there is not evidence to support the idea that she was ever active in any organization whose purpose was to overthrow the government of United States. If a simple dichotomy can be made around that illusive abstraction the "toiling masses," then anyone who wanted to control them was called a fascist by a communist who wanted to rule. According to Larry Ceplair and Stephen Englund in their book The Inquisition in Hollywood, if a communist stood for class conflict leading to revolution and defense of the Soviet Union, then many of the "Hollywood liberals" of the 1930's were not communists, but anti-fascist. They found rallying points in supporting the Republic in the Spanish Civil War, praising unions like the CIO, calling for the containment of Hitler, Mussolini, and Tojo, and for championing civil rights for the poor and minorities in the United States (70). Communists--those people who supported the overthrow of the United States Government and who defended Stalin's Soviet Union--were not adverse to using public figures like Parker; yet, dedicated Communists considered her and her colleagues as "mutant strains": they were intellectual and aloof and could not mesh their own struggles with those "toiling masses" (71). Hollywood liberals, simply, had goals different from dedicated Communists. If more than fifty years later, all the labeling, accusing, and organizing seems tiring, one must remember the conditions Parker found in Hollywood when she arrived there in 1934. Schwartz illustrates how non-political actors and writers were reluctant to become involved with those who were, but once a group of non-politicals--including Groucho Marx and Richard Rogers--who were tired of lunches consisting of helpings of anti-fascist philosophy "tried to move their forty-member lunch club to one of L. A.'s beach clubs; they couldn't get in. All the beach clubs were restricted against Jews" (46).

After returning from Spain in 1937 which had prompted her essay "Not Enough," Parker answered a letter from Sheelagh Kennedy, a member of the North American Committee to Aid Spanish Democracy; in the letter, Parker wrote "I want with all my heart to aid Spanish Children" (Meade 435). She became the National Chair for that organization. During the next ten years, Parker leant her name to more than thirty organizations for various causes. Marion Meade obtained the FBI report on her. It is now in Meade's papers at Columbia. The North American Committee to Aid Spanish Children was called a "communist front" organization, and the FBI questioned her about her activities in it; the extent of her activity was to secure pledges from people willing to help buy milk, including Archibald MacLeish, Clifford Odets, and Laurence Olivier. The FBI report states that Parker was "associated" with the following communist front organizations: the Joint Anti-Fascist Refugee Committee, the Hollywood Anti-Nazi League, the Hollywood League for Democratic Action, the League of Women Shoppers, the United Spanish Aid Committee, and the National Committee to Win the Peace. That report also states that Parker was "vague" about her participation in the Civil Rights Congress and the History Today and Tom Mooney committees; yet, she had actively participated in the Veterans of the Abraham Lincoln Brigade and the Voice of Freedom Committee.

Parker was first publicly cited as a communist in 1949. The California State Senate Committee on Un-American Activities maintained that she along with Pearl Buck, Lillian Hellman, Katharine Hepburn, Lena Horne, Dashiell Hammett, Gene Kelly, Frederick March, Gregory Peck, and Edward G. Robinson had followed or appeased the Communist Party line over a "long" period of time.[83] In 1951, Martin Berkeley who had himself been an active Communist Party member between 1937 and 1947 while he was a screenwriter had seen a new light and had actively begun fighting Communism in something called the Screen-Writers Guild Anti-Communist All Guild Committee. Berkeley estimated that "untold millions of dollars" had been diverted into Communist Party coffers through organizations like the Joint Anti-Fascist Refugee Committee.[84] He specifically cited Parker and Campbell as vocal and active members in acquiring funds.

In 1955, Parker was called to testify at a New York joint legislative committee concerning her activities and politics. When asked directly if she were a Communist, Parker invoked the Fifth Amendment.[85] She was asked what happened to the $1.5 million that the Joint Anti-Fascist Refugee Committee had collected while she was the National Chair, because the New York committee estimated that, at best, only about ten percent of the money could be accounted for.[86] The irony, of course, is that Parker could never handle her own finances, let alone large sums that had to be accounted for. Parker had never been inactive in championing underdog causes but it wasn't until she went to Hollywood in 1934 that a full blown political consciousness came about. She wrote in 1939 that her awareness of inequality had begun early, in 1898 when she was five years old:

> I was in a brownstone in New York, and there was a blizzard, and my rich
> aunt--a horrible woman then and now--had come to visit. I remember
> going to the window and seeing the street with the men shoveling snow;
> their hands were purple on their shovels, and their feet were wrapped with
> burlap. And my aunt, looking over my shoulder, said, 'Now isn't it nice
> there's a blizzard. All those men have work.' And I knew then that it
> was not nice that men could work for their lives only in desperate weather,
> that there was no work for them when it was fair.[87]

In 1962, after having been blacklisted and called before committees, Parker was not sorry for her activities. She told Lois Battle [D.21] in the UCLA <u>Daily Bruin</u>

I can understand the fear and the economic pressures but--after all, what are you going to gain without a controversy? That's not a good reason for keeping out of anything. Acceptance is what hurts you in all forms. There's a concerted dullness in not taking chances. You get soft and don't stand up on your hind legs. When the day comes that you can accept injustice, anywhere, you've got to kill yourself.[88]

And in her final years in New York while she was in failing health, Parker remembered her life in the thirties and forties as "progressive days. We thought we were going to make the world better--I forget why we thought it, but we did." (Cooper 113)

People who met Parker after 1930 had in reality two people to meet, the legend and the woman behind it. Lillian Hellman met the "famous Mrs. Parker" in 1931 in New York. In a gesture "meant to be both funny and serious," Parker bowed and kissed Dashiell Hammett's hand and "embarrassed [him] into a kind of simper." (232)[89] Hammett found her increasingly disgusting and finally refused even to be in the same room with her, but she and Hellman re-met in 1937 and remained friends until Parker's death in 1967. S. J. Perelman [150] began his reminiscence by writing "Dorothy Parker was already a legend when I first met her in the autumn of 1932." She reduced this, then, unknown playwright to a simpering idiot, but the next day, Walter Kerr phoned Perelman

> to apologize for her conduct; I swore that if I ever met the woman again, I'd skewer her with one of her own hatpins. That evening I received a dozen magnificent roses from her accompanied by a note steeped in remorse. It was the beginning of a friendship that survived the next thirty-five years, with intermittent lapses.[90]

When Joseph Bryan III was introduced by Alan Campbell, she "ordered" him to collaborate with her on a new play. They were to meet the following day in her apartment, but beyond not remembering their plans, she failed or refused--or whatever--to allow the doorman to admit him; yet they remained friends for the next thirty years. (102) Sheilah Graham [96] relates the same basic story. After being assigned to interview Parker for the New York Daily Mirror in 1934, Graham came away feeling pleased with herself for having "made an impression--'I want to see you again. Please remember to call me. Promise you will'--on one of the great wits of the day." (138)[91] But when Parker refused to return Graham's calls, she realized that she had made no impression and had invited only Parker's contempt.

One of the cliches about Mrs. Parker was that if someone left a party before she did, he or she was bound to be the object of her next crack. It was, as a matter of fact, a badge of honor among certain people not to have been the butt of one of Parker's jokes. Graham, finally, didn't care because "this was Dottie--nice to your face, cruel behind your back." (140) Archibald MacLeish wrote to Ernest Hemingway in February of 1930 that he had always

> been afraid of her because I thought she was the kind who would be affectionate to you with her right hand and murder you with her left. But she was so fine in talking about the Murphys and you and all her friends and so damn wise and so intelligent about people that she took me in about eight minutes. She may be serving me up cold at this minute for all

I know but I doubt it and if she is it doesn't matter.[92]

Lillian Hellman maintained that this "embrace-denounce" syndrome began when Parker

> found it amused or shocked people, because in time, when she found it
> didn't amuse me, she seldom played it. . . . If she denounced everyone
> else, I had a right to think that I was included, but now I think I was
> wrong about that, too. So many people have told me that she never did
> talk about me, never complained, never would allow gossip about me, that
> I have come to believe it. (234)

Yet, Truman Capote [162] relates that when he had known Parker, he remembered "she
had never a good word to say behind one's back (anyone's)--'The trouble with Lillian
Hellman is she thinks she's Dashiell Hammett--when she only looks like him.'" (224)[93]
Were one offended by this quality, he or she could never have liked Parker.

Being offended and hurt by one of her arrows would win only her contempt; to
top it would win her friendship. Joseph Bryan, III recalled in 1985 that she was truly
"wonderful company," but

> life with her was life on thin ice. You never knew when she would turn
> on you and denounce you as a fascist, an anti-Semite, a warmonger, a
> geoplanarian, a neo-Malthusian, or something equally ridiculous. Almost
> any epithet would serve. It didn't need even a smidgen of justification.
> The barb of her wit made it stick where it hit, and the victim was tagged
> forever after. (112)

Parker and Alan Campbell were married, divorced, remarried, separated and
reconciled during the twenty-nine years they knew each other. Sheilah Graham wrote that
in Hollywood, "Everyone believed Dorothy was carrying Campbell" (145); she also wrote
that Parker liked to deny what Campbell reported her as saying so that Alan would look
like an idiot (144). Wyatt Cooper relates the same action even if the circumstances were
different:

> One night Miss Cathleen Nesbitt and I were invited for dinner, and, when
> we arrived, I recognized the glassy, unfocused look in Alan's eyes as a
> signal that we were headed for trouble. Drinks stretched on and on, with
> Alan making unsteady trips to the kitchen from time to time to check the
> progress of a roast. Dottie was fine--his bad behavior brought out her
> best--she was entertaining and amusing. . . .(112)

Perelman wrote that Parker's hatred of Hollywood caused her and Campbell to buy their
Bucks County Pennsylvania farm:

> 'We haven't any roots, Alan,' she would admonish him after the fourth Martini.
> 'You can't put down any roots in Beverly Hills. But look at Laura and Sid--
> they've got roots, a place to come home to. Roots, roots.' (175)

Campbell confided to Cooper that he

despaired of ever totally pleasing her. When World War II began, she went about muttering that any man worth his salt would be in there fighting. Then when he enlisted, she bitterly accused him of deserting her in perilous times. (112)

Cooper who knew Campbell first and became a confidant of Parker's during her final years was able to conclude that in spite of their alcoholic and childish behavior towards each other, they shared common beliefs about "justice, civil rights, and equal opportunities. They were civilized persons." (113) Yet, William C. Rogers, a classmate of Alan's from Virginia, wrote to the editor of Esquire, that Parker and Campbell seemed to him as tragic as Zelda and Scott Fitzgerald, if tragedy meant "people you know going to hell."[94] Meade most fully sums up their relationship: "The more she relied on Alan, the more bitterly she resented him and the stronger became the denials that she needed him." (306)

As reported above, Parker had had an abortion in 1924. Then while she was married to Campbell for the first time, she had two miscarriages and in 1940 had a hysterectomy (Meade 263-98). John Keats, Parker's first biographer, talked to Mr. and Mrs. Robeson Bailey. Bailey, a college instructor from Smith, and his wife were hosts to the Campbells, for a week while Alan was stationed near them during World War II. Mrs. Bailey remembered that Parker's single contribution during the week was a handful of ration points: Parker had no "feminine small-talk about keeping house or raising children. Nor did she speak of her family or Alan's." (242) Cooper reports that children fascinated Parker, but "A certain degree of mistrust was apparent in her manner, as if waiting for the little tykes to betray themselves and confirm her darkest suspicions." (114) Joseph Bryan wrote that his own children were upset over the 1947 divorce because "They liked Dottie, but they loved Alan" (110). He played with children but Parker "would entertain them, but her principal audience was always herself." (110) Yet, Heywood Hale Broun [120] told that "he was largely ignored by his parents' circle of friends, except for Mrs. Parker. 'She always stopped to ask me how I was. None of the others ever noticed a six-year-old boy, but she always did.'"[95]

In May of 1936, Parker wrote a rebuttal [E.36] of Richard Schayer's remark about screenwriting ("It is a soft racket"). "To Richard--With Love" tells that she went to Hollywood because she needed the money: "Those 1924 debts were beginning to crowd up on me, and I came. Where should I have been, if I hadn't? Why, in the gutter, of course."[96] She may well have thought, as she had about her job with Vanity Fair, that screenwriting would allow her the leisure to write, along with $5,200 a week. But she discovered that screenwriting--aside from its "crossword puzzle" relationship to literature (Lauterbaugh 145)--was hard, demanding work:

> You aren't writing for the love of it or the art of it or the hell of it or whatever; you are doing a chore assigned to you by your employer and whether or not he might fire you if you did it slackly makes no matter. You've got yourself to face, and you have to live with yourself. You don't--or, at least only in highly exceptional cases--have to live with your producer." (8)

Parker also discovered a "great truth" about her ability to write:

--one of those eternal, universal truths that serve to make you feel much
worse than you did when you started And that is that no writer, whether
he writes from love or for money, can condescend to what he writes. You
can't stoop to what you set down on paper; I don't know why you can't
but you can't. No matter what form it takes, and no matter what the
result, and no matter how caustically comic you are about it afterward,
what you did was your best. And to do your best is always hard going.
(8)

In 1944, Richard Lauterbach maintained that Parker received satisfaction only from her
scenario for The Little Foxes. The rest was hack work, which paid well, but resulted in
little of permanent value.[97] What talent should have been expounded upon her writing
was dissipated in verbal wit:

But somehow she can no longer kid herself. Her contribution to 20th
Century Culture, unless she should reverse her field, is the elevation of the
wisecrack from the speak-easy barroom to the level of Bartlett's Familiar
Quotations. (146)

This was precisely the same conclusion that Taffy Herrmann [135] reached in 1979 in her
article "The Wonder Wags" who

start out in life as pianists, actresses, writers--serious dedicated artists.
Somewhere along the way, they learn they can amuse people with their
clever comments; and though they may still pursue their original careers,
the temptation to live by their wit alone grows stronger with time. How
much easier to shine in a cafe or at a party than to spend solitary hours
perfecting a short story or a sonata. The wag learns to compromise, and
slowly, and often tragically, his art suffers. A deep frustration follows,
possibly the real reason so many Wonder Wags come eventually to rely
on pills and alcohol.[98]

This certainly describes the major cause for the decline in the quantity of Parker's stories
and poems after 1934, but Wilfred Sheed [133] in his review of Keats's biography
maintained that a "purer vocation" than that of a wit would have allowed Parker to "have
done a little better: but she tried much harder than she let on, and my guess is she
squeezed out all she could."[99]
      There was a rumor about a novel as early as August 1925 when John Farrar in the
Bookman's "The Gossip Shop" wrote that Parker was "about to write a novel." (617) She
had been given a contract and an advance on one by Viking's editor Harold Ginzburg,
but as Woollcott wrote in 1934,   what Parker showed him "consisted largely of
undestroyed carbons of old articles of hers, padded out with letters from her many
friends." (148) What Viking did get in 1939 was Here Lies, twenty-four stories from her
two earlier collections with a new one called "The Custard Heart." The back of the title
pages reads that the volume "contains all of Dorothy Parker's short stories excepting a
few which she did not wish to retain among her collected prose." But Parker did collect
her work once more in 1943 for Viking's Portable series. She had written two additional
stories by then, "The Standard of Living" [B.43] for The New Yorker and "The Lovely

Leave" [B.44] for <u>Women's Home Companion</u>. It was the final time she collected her work.

One excuse Parker used for not writing was that editors would not take her work unless it was humorous:

> But my work is dismissed, and on the strength of what seems to me a curious adjective-'unpleasant.' The last editor, who may as well be nameless because he has all the other qualities of a bastard told me that if I changed my piece to make it in favor of Franco, he would publish it. 'God damn it,' he said, 'why can't you be funny again?'"[100]

The Genevive Taggard papers in the New York Public Library contain the extant correspondence between Parker and Ellen Lang, the fiction editor of <u>Women's Home Companion</u>, who had published "The Lovely Leave" in December of 1943. A March 1944 cable from Lang asks about another story for the magazine; another one in April asks if Parker's silence is anger or a result of work, to which Parker "It means I'm working my head off." To make a long story short, three more cables and one note to Parker ask about the story, its progress, and a possible completion date. On 13 December 1944, Parker wired Lange with "Sorry about two things. Didn't finish the story and won't be back until Saturday." Another note dated 3 October 1945 had asked Parker if she would, at least, do a title for a book. Written in a red ink over the message by Lang or a secretary are the words "No use now. Prs. of Viking says she doesn't answer <u>him</u>." The last note from Lang is dated 22 August 1946: "I waited for five years for the first [story]; this time three." It's apparent that Lang sincerely wanted to help Parker publish however she could, but she couldn't write the stories for her. Parker would write only six additional stories by 1958, ending her thirty-six year short story career with "The Bolt From the Blue" in <u>Esquire</u>.

Between 1947 and 1953, Parker co-authored three plays. The first, <u>The Coast of Illyria</u> [A.15], was with Ross Evans, a man twenty four years younger than herself whom she took up with after her divorce from Campbell in 1947. Joseph Bryan remembers Evans as "a pleasant, shambling hobbledehoy with huge, lump-toed Army boots that instantly inspired our children to call him 'Li'l Abner'" (117). In his introduction to the play, Kinney writes that Parker gave Evans "primary credit for helping her research the play and for going to the library of the countless books which she said she consulted." (29) The play was produced once in Dallas in 1949 but never went to Broadway. Parker and Evans did have the short story "The Game" published in <u>Cosmopolitan</u> but were unable to get work as screenwriters. They moved to Cuernavaca, Mexico, where Evans deserted her for a shopkeeper (Meade 339).

Parker re-married Campbell in 1950, but by 1952 she was separated from him, living in New York and collaborating with Arnaud d'Usseau on <u>Ladies of the Corridor</u> [A.16]. According to Meade, it was Mrs. Susan d'Usseau who was not only a "rigid taskmaster" but also the one who "succeeded in keeping her sober" (350). The play was produced at the Longacre Theatre and staged by Harold Clurman [105] who said of Parker that she was "seldom far from hysteria." (219) The play closed after forty-five performances, and was thus not a success. Parker told Capron in 1956 that <u>Ladies of the Corridor</u> was "the only thing I have ever done in which I had great pride." (79) Parker's second collaboration with d'Usseau, and her final play, was <u>The Ice Age</u> [A.17]. It was never produced and remains in typescript at Columbia University.

Between 1956 and Campbell's death in 1963, he and Parker kept in contact but lived apart until 1961 when they moved to Los Angeles. Campbell had become a pathetic figure, "reduced to trading on his likability in order to live" (Meade 374). Cooper doesn't exactly romanticize this period, but he does try to make it as palatable as possible:

> Loneliness and guilt were almost like physical presences in the space between them, and they spoke in short, stilted and polite sentences with terrible silences in between, and yet there was a tenderness in the exchange, a grief for old hurts, and a shared reluctance to turn loose. (111)

Kinney is less sympathetic when he writes that in spite of "momentary bright spots," "they lived on alcohol and unemployment checks" (71). Campbell died on 14 June in a former bedroom he had partitioned from the rest of the house. The coroner's report listed the death as a probable suicide; Parker did not attend the funeral in Virginia nor arrange a service in Los Angeles (Meade 399).

In 1964, Parker returned to New York for the final time. Parker's final sustained writing effort was reviewing books for Esquire between 1958 and 1963 [F.3]. These reviews recall Parker's Constant Reader essays, and show that she indeed had not lost her ability to express an opinion worthy of consideration. Her first essay was "A Christmas Guide to the Best Fiction of 1957." In it, she wrote

> The nowadays ruling that no word is unprintable has, I think, done nothing for beautiful letters. . . . the effect is not one of shock, but something far more dangerous--tedium. . . . Obscenity is too valuable a commodity to chuck all over the place; it should be taken out of the safe on special occasions only.[101]

These reviews also show that Parker retained her critical acumen; in "Sex--Without the Asterisks," Parker defends Lolita:

> Lolita, as you undoubtedly know, has had an enormous share of trouble, and caused a true hell of a row. . . . I do not think that Lolita is a filthy book. I cannot regard it as pornography, either sheer, unrestrained, or any other kind. . . [Nabokov's] command of the language is absolute, and his Lolita is a fine book, a distinguished book--all right, then--a great book.[102]

And in reading these essays, one cannot forget that it is Mrs. Parker who is writing them. Although Sheilah Graham praised Parker in Beloved Infidel, Parker calls that book "the possible all-time low in American Letters":

> It may occur to some of us that there has been rather too much digging up of Fitzgerald's bones, but I doubt if we have ever known such greedy gnawing of them.[103]

And Parker berates Graham, who did not even know Zelda Fitzgerald, for writing only of "the more violent expressions of that poor lady's desperate illness." She concludes by asking readers "to sit and think of Miss Graham and her collaborator [Gerold Frank] joyously dividing their thirty pieces of silver." Parker could talk ill of her friends, but others could not. She had deplored Samuel Hopkins Adams's biography <u>Alexander Woollcott: His Life and His World</u> because she felt that Adams had trivialized the man [E.1]. Parker could write that Woollcott's prose was "deplorable" or that he had no critical discernment, but she had known and loved the man as a friend: "he was as close to essential as one friend can be to another."[104]

The <u>Esquire</u> reviews were not pleasant for Parker to write. <u>Esquire</u>'s publisher Arnold Gingrich recalled that getting the monthly reviews from Parker was a "high-forceps delivery."[105] Cooper wrote that she read the books she reviewed, talked "brilliantly" about them, but would lie to <u>Esquire</u> about her column: " 'I can't imagine why it hasn't arrived. I sent it days ago,' when she hadn't written a line of it." (112) Cooper is certainly accurate when he cites a fear of inadequacy as part of the reason these columns were so difficult for her to write, and there are others, like alcoholic avoidance. Another part of the reason is that her eyesight was fading, nearing blindness before she died. Another part of her difficulty was that bursitis made difficult the simple actions of holding a book and typing. Parker was, after all, in 1958, sixty-five years old.

In 1958, Edmund Wilson was asked by James Thurber to discuss with him the book he was writing about Harold Ross and <u>The New Yorker</u>.[106] They arranged to meet for lunch at the Algonquin at 1:00 pm. Wilson had also invited Parker, but knowing about her habitual tardiness, they left word at the front desk for her to join them in the dining room. She arrived on time, for once, but, as Wilson tossed off with a phrase, she "was not recognized by the man behind the desk" and had to hunt for her friends. (<u>The Fifties</u> 530). If Dorothy Parker was not recognized at the Algonquin Hotel, then things had changed.

For her sketch of James and Helen Thurber, Miss Frances Glennon prepared much by interviewing and letter writing to them. In response to one of her letters, Thurber wrote in a 1959 postscript

> I loathe the expression 'What makes him tick.' It is the American mind, looking for simple and singular solution, that uses the foolish expression. A person not only ticks, he also chimes and strikes the hour, falls and breaks has to be put together again, and sometimes stops like an electric clock in a thunderstorm.[107]

By the time Parker had moved to New York in 1964, she had not quite stopped, but her life certainly needed some kind of coherence that she seemed unable to supply for herself. Alan Campbell had performed most of the necesary duties of life for her, like cooking, laundering clothes, and cleaning up after the dogs. At its worst, her life degenerated into a grotesque existence:

> Joseph Bryant, III, came to call at the Volney, only to be called 'a Jew-hating Fascist son of a bitch' by a drunken old woman. Another friend recalled that he and a motion picture actor had the same experience. He said they came to pay homage to a lady, only to find a crone sitting, surrounded by bottles, who looked up at them blearily from a rug strewn with dog feces. 'You're Jew-Fascists,' this apparition said. 'Get out of here.' (Keats 302)

But there is no need to assume all the days of her final years were spent in such horrible conditions. Gloria Steinham's 1965 interview reported that Parker looked "frail but gay in a red plaid skirt and red embroidered Mexican blouse," and that in spite of photographs that made her look old, "the dark, soft hair falling over her forehead in bangs . . . and her quicksilver mobility of expression make her seem younger [than her seventy-one years]" (118e). And in the same year, Michael Stern's interview in the New York <u>World-Telegram and The Sun</u> reports that in spite of her small, frail appearance, "her handshake is firm, her voice is strong, her dark hair still is made up into jaunty forehead fringe, and she is feeling much better, thank you" (3 August 1965). And, as Wyatt Cooper's article shows, Parker was able to muster, as often as not, a regalness that was hers alone.

Cooper wrote that Parker was "genuinely pained by the unhappy aspects of life, but the pain never stopped her from staring disaster square in the face." (61) While staying with the Murphys in Switzerland, Parker wrote a long letter to George Oppenheimer. Fitzgerald had been to visit them. He was then staying near Montreux, in France, Scottie was living with a governess in Brittany, and Zelda, whom Fitzgerald had not been allowed to visit, was in a sanatorium in Geneva:

> I know they got to be awful pests and all that, but I always get sentimental about the Fitzgeralds. I can't help seeing them as they were when they first came to New York, ten years ago--when they were just married, and he had just had his crazy success with <u>This Side of Paradise</u>, and they were the golden lad and golden girl, if ever I saw them. And this is so damn dreary, for a conclusion....Ah, hell. If I were a God, I'd <u>be</u> a God.[108]

With her eyes fully open, Parker could still retain compassion for the unfortunate.

Marc Connelly wrote in his book of memoirs <u>Voices Offstage</u> [87] that Parker had, in addition to her "biting wit," an "unsentimental compassion".[109] These are illustrated well by a story recorded by Peter Feibleman [184]. Once at a weekend gathering, Hellman and Parker had been invited to a party honoring Helen Keller. Parker refused to go, but Hellman went and soon returned, sick at the crying and sentiment among the famous guests: "Leonard Bernstein had played the piano and Helen Keller had held Lennie's hands while he played; then Lennie had cried and the other famous guest had cried . . . ." Hellman's disgust was displayed by heavy sighing. "It's your own fault, dear," Dorothy said quietly, without looking up, "didn't I tell you she was a conwoman and a dyke?" Hellman appreciated Parker's biting wit, but then

> Dorothy put a finger in her book to mark the place and glanced up sadly for an instant.
>   'I have something terrible to tell you about myself, Lilly,' she said.
> 'I hate the blind.'[110]

But it wasn't the blind person or even the blind generally whom Parker hated. She hated the fact that blindness exists. Parties honoring courage and achievement are fine, but such parties and the sentiments they evoke do not change the hell of being blind.

She had told Saul Pett in 1963, "I'm seventy and feel ninety. If I had any decency, I'd be dead. Most of my friends are" (20). This is a perfect example of what Brendan Gill [194], in his book <u>A New York Life</u>, called "the note of mingled apology and mockery" that he found in Parker (150). Gill met her for the first time at the home of Charles Addams; to Gill, "a late comer in her life, she was--and could only be Mrs.

Parker":

> The posture she assumed that afternoon at the Addamses' was an
> especially painful one for a new acquaintance to be forced to observe, and
> of course she had assumed it for that reason among others: perhaps I was
> being punished for not yet having failed, or perhaps for supposing that,
> because I had written a few short stories for <u>The New Yorker</u>, I was a
> success. She knew better--she who had helped, after all, to invent <u>The</u>
> <u>New Yorker</u>, she who had been the most formidable wit at the Algonquin
> Round Table. There were, it appeared, certain truths for me to bear in
> mind.[111]

There was always that huge chasm that separated Dottie from Mrs. Parker. As the
all-powerful Mrs. Parker, she knew at the very least how to react to any situation: use the
wit to slaughter any potential enemy and to keep any feelings at bay. Lillian Hellman's
account of Parker's actions on the day that Campbell's body was removed from their
California home illustrates this perfectly:

> Among the friends who stood with Dottie on those California steps was
> Mrs. Jones, a woman who had liked Alan, had pretended to like Dottie,
> and who had always loved all forms of meddling in other people's
> troubles. Mrs. Jones said, 'Dottie, tell me, dear, what I can do for you.'
> Dottie said, 'Get me a new husband.'
> There was a silence, but before those who would have laughed could
> laugh, Mrs. Jones said, 'I think that is the most callous and disgusting
> remark I ever heard in my life.'
> Dottie turned to look at her, sighed, and said gently, 'So sorry. Then
> run down to the corner and get me a ham and cheese on rye and tell them
> to hold the mayo.' (248)

As Dottie, she seems to have had little idea who she truly was, and her friends even less.
Lois Battle reported in 1962 that Parker hesitated when asked to talk about herself, but

> a smile began in her luminous brown eyes. 'I'm a mongrel; my father was
> a Rothschild; my mother was a goy; and I went to the Catholic school
> around the corner.' (1)

When John Keats was struggling with trying to reconcile the vastly different opinions he
had encountered, he contacted George Oppenheimer, a man who had long admired her
work, who had known her since 1930, and whose play <u>Here Today</u> had a central character
modeled upon her. Oppenheimer wrote to Keats, "Dottie was many things to many
people, more of an enigma than any person I have ever known."[112]

Peter Feibleman who had known Parker through his acquaintance with Lillian
Hellman contrasted the two women: Hellman had enjoyed the company of men, but

> Dorothy was a prim mouselike little thing with a soft voice--a pretty
> woman who could blush at will. If a good-looking man walked into the
> room she turned all pink and simply and batted her eyes and gave every

indication of being at a loss for words; but inside her something yawned
and I always had the feeling she didn't like men much. (101)

This was certainly one Dorothy who can be contrasted with Joseph Bryan's recollection
of a Dottie who

> was always tousled, and a little--well, <u>dingy</u>. Moreover, she was addicted
> to dirndls, a costume that made her seem both dumpy and dowdy. Not
> that this ever bothered her. Her idea of dressing up for the evening was
> to add a tulle scarf to whatever she'd been wearing all day. If it is true that
> women dress to impress other women, this explains Dottie's indifference
> to fashion. She didn't care a damn what women thought of her or her
> appearance. What <u>men</u> thought, yes, but not women. She didn't like
> women. (104)

If Parker appeared inconsistent, it may well be just that--an appearance. She was adept
at playing roles, but she was also incredibly consistent in being who she was--even if that
meant appearing irrational to others. After her affair with John McClain was broken up--
including a half-hearted suicide attempt--Parker called Frank Sullivan to whom she
explained and demanded

> Nobody knows I'm here. Now, you're the one person I'd like to see. You
> come up. Say nothing to anyone. Come to the Plaza this afternoon and
> have a drink with me. (Keats 161)

Once when F. P. A. was on vacation, Frank Sullivan had been assigned to take over his
Conning Tower column. Parker, knowing that Sullivan was worried about filling up a
daily column, sent him two poems.[113] Thus, it's believable when Sullivan told Keats

> You always sprang to the call when Dottie needed you, and I went to the
> Plaza that afternoon about five o'clock, and there must have been at least
> ten people in the room. You know, they were all the only people she
> wanted to see--and she'd moved from a quiet hotel [the Lowell] to one of
> the busiest hotels in New York to get away from it all--five blocks away!
> (162)

A. E. Hotchner [169] reports that after she had been abandoned by Ross Evans, she flew
from Mexico to New York and checked into the Plaza:

> She said she didn't have a penny to her name and that she didn't know
> what to do since she could no longer write screenplays or short stories. I
> asked her how she planned to pay for the opulent suite she occupied, but
> all she said was that she hoped to 'manage,' her usual vagueness where
> money matters were concerned. . . . I watched her pour more Scotch into
> her glass . . . I was there only a short time when a contingent of three of
> her lady friends came boisterously into the bedroom, clucking condolences.
> Dorothy obviously had summoned everyone in her address book to
> commiserate with her tragedy. It was my impression that she was

enjoying her misery.[114]

The adjective unconventional is too pale to fully incorporate how singularly she acted, but to label her behavior perverse would vitiate its precise value. The most that can be said without fear of contradiction is that Parker behaved in a way uniquely her own. Woollcott's 1934 portrait of Parker is the seminal, biographical study because he not only so memorably asserts the duality one finds in Parker--"You see, she is so odd a blend of Little Nell and Lady Macbeth" (149)--but he also asks the one question that may never be satisfactorily answered by his hypothetical student who in the year 2034 must "write a theme on what manner of woman this dead and gone Dorothy Parker really was." (144) It's safe to write that Dorothy Parker was bound to fail in her own eyes. If a person can be known by the enemies she chooses, then Parker, who saw her life as a failure, can be seen only as heroic from an historical perspective. Her enemies were not human, but those qualities and conditions that will never be erased from the human condition: sloth, self-doubt, stupidity stemming from ignorance and prejudice, and finally, those forces and conditions of life over which the individual has little or no control. Parker herself suffered from the first two, was driven into a rage by the third, and fought against while seeing herself and her friends as personal victims of the fourth.

Parker died on 7 June 1967; her body was cremated on the 9th. Her ashes were mailed to the legal firm of Oscar Bernstien and Paul O'Dwyer in New York, where they remained until 1988. In April of 1988, O'Dwyer reported to Liz Smith of the New York Daily News that he wanted to find a place for the ashes. After the situation was made public, suggestions of what to do with the ashes abounded: from spreading them over the Hudson, passing them out in small packets at a performance of a play, placing them in a niche in the Algonquin Hotel, to mixing them with paint for a memorial portrait.[115] O'Dwyer was pleased with Dr. Benjamin Hooks' suggestion that the ashes be interred in a memorial garden at NAACP national headquarters in Baltimore. Parker had left her estate to Martin Luther King, a man whom she'd never met but greatly admired. Following his assassination in 1968, Parker's estate passed directly to the NAACP.

On Thursday, 20 October 1988, the formal dedication of the Dorothy Rothschild Parker Memorial Garden took place. After a reverent but joyous ceremony with distinguished speakers and music, Parker's ashes were sealed in a sunken column of concrete, encircled by three courses of brown brick. Hardwood mulch surrounded the area around the brick, and the mulched area was defined by bushes. The remainder of the area is a natural pine garden. That evening, Laurel Ollstein presented her one-woman play based on Parker's life, Laughter, Hope, and a Sock in the Eye, the title taken from Parker's poem "Inventory."

Notes

1. John Keats, <u>You Might As Well Live</u> (New York: Simon and Schuster, 1971), 15-30; Arthur Kinney, <u>Dorothy Parker</u> (Boston: Twayne, 1978), 25-27; Leslie Frewin, <u>The Late Mrs. Dorothy Parker</u> (New York: Macmillan, 1986), 18-40; Marion Meade, <u>Dorothy Parker: What Fresh Hell is This</u>? (New York: Villard Books, 1988), 3-34.

2. Jane Helen Pearl, "Dorothy Parker Herself: A Psychobiography of the Artist," Diss. Northwestern University, 1982, 28. Pearl cites 1900 as the approximate beginning date for Parker at the Blessed Sacrament Academy.

3. John Keats avoids dates altogether; Kinney cites 1911 as the year Parker left Miss Dana's, but he gives no source for his date. He was incorrect in stating that J.Henry Rothschild died "a year" after Parker left Miss Dana's school (27). Parker herself maintained that she hadn't even finished high school when she was interviewed by Mary Ann Callan: "Students Appalling to Dorothy Parker," The Los Angeles <u>Times</u> 28 April 1963; sec. C: 4.

4. Pearl, 16.

5. In June of 1911, <u>Cosmopolitan</u> published a picture of an actress named Dorothy Parker, page 82. But this photograph couldn't possibly be the Parker of literary fame, simply because Dorothy Rothschild did not become Dorothy Parker until 1917. There are three portraits of Parker. The one by Neysa McMein (1923) is reprinted in Meade. The second was done by Georg Theo Hartmann and appeared in the June 1927 <u>Arts and Decoration</u> (52). Kinney used this as the frontispiece for his book. The other is Gabriel Pascalini's, reproduced in <u>Esquire</u> July 1968 (56).

Paul Hyde Bonner painted the "Thanatopsis Pleasure and Inside Straight Club," including Parker. It is reproduced on the back of the dust jacket of the British edition of Meade's biography. Al Hirschfield's famous caricature of the Round Table is often reproduced. He twice specifically caricatured Parker, once about the famous MEN being painted on her office door; the other is an older Parker having a drink. It was reproduced on the dust jacket of the Canadian edition of <u>Constant Reader</u>. Gluyas Williams, whose caricatures of Robert Benchley are famous, once caricatured Parker and her friends; this is reproduced in Ford's <u>The Time of Laughter</u>, 41. Carl Rose made pen sketches to illustrate Dorothy Parker stories in Cerf's <u>Try and Stop Me</u>. Milt Gross drew a quick sketch of Parker to illustrate her essay "The Thoughts of an Author at Work," <u>Life</u> 16 September 1924: 9. Peggy Bacon's charcoal sketch is reproduced in Max Eastman's <u>Enjoyment of Laughter</u>, and Eva Herrmann's pen and ink caricature appeared in <u>The Bookman</u> 68 (January 1929), 435. The most recent sketch is Everett Peck's, reproduced on the cover of <u>The Portable Curmudgeon</u>, 1987. The UPI and AP press files contain, of course, the largest collection of photographs. Edward Steichen's famous photographic portrait of Parker and her dog, Robinson, is often reproduced. An elegant photographic portrait taken by George Platt Lynes is now owned by Viking, and reproduced in Gaines's <u>Wit's End</u>, 213.

6. Caroline Seebohm, The Man Who Was Vogue (New York: Viking, 1982): 60.

7. 15 November 1916: 128.

8. Arthur Kinney, Dorothy Parker (Boston: Twayne, 1978): 30, 170-76.

9. Vanity Fair September 1915: 32.

10. Vogue 15 February 1917: 55.

11. Vogue 15 November 1917: 124.

12. Always in Vogue (Garden City, NY: Doubleday, 1954): 135.

13. Vogue 15 September 1944: 197.

14. Vanity Fair May 1919: 6.

15. Vanity Fair October 1918: 51.

16. Vanity Fair January 1919: 39. Parker wrote one more small essay about the war under the name Helen Wells. The remainder of the essays under this name are personal, humorous essays about fashionable topics like the theater, house parties, and literary weekend guests. She also wrote a Hymn of Hate called "Slackers."

17. 13 January 1920: 3.

18. The New York World: 12 January 1920.

19. The Worlds of Robert E. Sherwood (New York: Harper and Row, 1965): 136-42.

20. Hirschfield's caricature of this is reproduced in Harriman, 18.

21. The Saturday Evening Post 7 October 1939: 65.

22. "A Wink at a Cock-Eyed World." UCLA Daily Bruin 16 February 1962.

23. "National Institutions." September 1920: 156-59.

24. "Standing Room Only." March 1921: 154-59.

25. "The Primrose Pathology." May 1921: 159.

26. "The Season Chooses Its Exit." August 1922: 159.

27. Anything Goes (New York: Times Books, 1987): 77. One should also see Carl Van Doren's article "Day In and Day Out." Century 107 (December 1923): 308-

315.

28. New York: Frederick A. Stokes, 60-62.

29. The complete title of this book is The Command is Forward: Tales of the A. E. F. Battlefields as They Appeared in 'The Stars and Stripes'. New York: The Century Company, 1919. If one likes Woollcott's style and choice of subjects, then he shall certainly enjoy this book.

30. Case, 8; see also Parker's essay "As The Spirit Moves," The Saturday Evening Post 22 May 1920: 8-9, 108, 111.

31. There were others included in the inner sanctum of the Round Table: Irving Berlin, Howard Deitz, Edna Ferber, Deems Taylor, Frank Sullivan, Neysa McMein, Charles MacArthur, and one or more of the Marx Brothers. When they were around, the following were welcome guests of the group: Noel Coward, Thorton Wilder, Beatrice Lillie, the Lunts, S. N. Behrman, Ring Lardner, Art Samuels, Frank Crowinshield, Herman Mankiwicz, Paul Robeson, Tallulah Bankhead, and William Faulkner. Edwin McDowell cites William Faulkner who, according to Jack Tibby, one of the founding editors of Sports Illustrated, said he always felt welcome as a guest at the Round Table, but he was there primarily because he "just liked to be close to Dorothy Parker." The New York Times Book Review 13 June 1982: 34.

32. The Algonquin Wits (New York: Citadel Press, 1968): 136.

33. James R. Gaines Wit's End (New York: Harcourt, 1977): 29.

34. See Hemingway's poem "To a Tragic Poetess." 88 Poems (New York: Harcourt, 1979): 88-89.

35. "Neysa McMein." Enchanted Aisles (New York: Putnam's, 1924): 36-37.

36. A Girl Like I (New York: Viking, 1966): 147.

37. Loos, 147-48.

38. Loos, 149.

39. The Twenties (New York: Farrar, Straus, & Giroux, 1975): 44-45.

40. Wilson, 47.

41. Benchley Lost and Found (New York: Dover, 1970) 155.

42. Meade's accounts of these trips are the fullest. Parker and Sara Murphy took a short trip to Paris between October and December of 1932. One should also see Calvin Tompkins's Living Well Is the Best Revenge (New York: Viking, 1971).

43. Margaret Case Harriman <u>The Vicious Circle</u> (New York: Rinehart, 1951): 225.

44. Scott Meredith <u>George S. Kaufman</u> (New York: Doubleday, 1974): 489.

45. Cory Ford <u>The Time of Laughter</u> (Boston: Little, 1967): 52.

46. Ford, 52; Ford (1902-1969), a New York newspaper and magazine writer, used the penname "John Riddell" when he parodied current books. Ford reviewed <u>Sunset Gun</u> under the name of Riddell in <u>Vanity Fair</u>. Ford is profiled in Joseph Bryan's <u>Merry Gentlemen (And One Lady)</u>, 199-225.

47. In <u>Merry Gentleman</u>, Joseph Bryan writes that Julia Glen is "Dottie as ever was!" and that Daisy Lester is "Dottie's own voice." (103-04)

48. 9 September 1934. The two major files of newspaper and miscellaneous clippings about Parker are the collections in Lincoln Center and at the Los Angeles <u>Times</u>. In both files, the collectors were not so careful as they might have been. Dates are seldom a problem, but section and page numbers are, more often than not, missing. I have included as much information as possible.

49. 23 November 1937: 15.

50. 7 December 1941.

51. "Dorothy Parker." <u>New York Journal</u> 1965: 118e.

52. Alan Campbell's death notice in 1963 cites the date of their first marriage as 1933, The New York <u>Times</u> 15 June 1963; sec. 2; 24. Yet, in the Los Angeles <u>Times</u> (28 May 1947), notice of the divorce cites 1932 in Raton, New Mexico as the date and place of marriage. The charge for seeking the divorce was mental cruelty, Los Angeles <u>Times</u>, 22 May 1947. The marriage was also reported to have taken place before a justice of the peace in Westbury, Long Island in October of 1933, the New York <u>Herald Tribune</u> 16 June 1934.

53. Saturday, 11 August 1934; sec. L: 11.

54. Undated Letter. 3783 Meade Street, Denver, Colorado. Harvard Ms. See Kinney, <u>Massachusetts Review</u> (Autumn 1989): 487-515. Kinney's annotations and editing of these letters are excellent. A long letter from Parker to Benchely appeared in <u>Esquire</u> August 1989: 144-47.

55. <u>Hanging On In Paradise</u> (New York: McGraw-Hill, 1975): 85.

56. <u>Esquire</u> October 1944: 144.

57. <u>Seven Arts</u> 3 (1955): 135.

58. Hellman sold these in 1965 in order to pay for Parker's hospital bills. "Dorothy Parker," in Three by Lillian Hellman (Boston: Little, 1979): 243.

59. John Keats Dorothy Parker (New York: Simon, 1970): 201-02. One should also read S. J. Perelman's "Dorothy Parker." Here he talks about Parker's always chiding Campbell about the need for roots.

60. Guiles, 175.

61. Guiles, 88-89.

62. "Words and Music." October 1920: 157.

63. "Standing Room Only, and Very Little of That." March 1921: 158.

64. Meade's account of the role Parker took in the Sacco and Venzetti trial is the most complete, pages 178-86. As part of the central contradictions in Parker's life, one should read the article in the New York Times of 7 February 1934, 1 and 11. Parker, Benchley, and Woollcott supported a waiters' strike but their involvement consisted of bons mots and escaping before the police could arrest them.

65. 22 October 1937: 17.

66. New Masses 23 November 1937: 15.

67. 4 December 1937: 3.

68. 22 February 1938: 26.

69. 21 February 1938. The Letters of Alexander Woollcott. Eds. Beatrice Kaufman and Joseph Hennessey. New York: Viking, 1944: 204.

70. The New York Times 22 November 1938: 6.

71. Time 16 January 1939: 55.

72. 27 June 1939: 21.

73. Her speech was published under the title, "Sophisticated Poetry--And the Hell With It." New Masses 27 June 1939: 21.

74. The Los Angeles Times 13 April 1942.

75. The New York Times 17 November 1944: 23.

76. The New York Times 12 November 1944; sec. 2: 43.

77. New York: Harper and Row, 1990, 93.

78. "Dorothy Parker." This interview was conducted by Mr. and Mrs. Robert. C. Franklin for Columbia University Popular Arts Project, 1959: 3.

79. Larry Ceplair and Stephen Englund The Inquisition in Hollywood (Garden City, NY: Anchor Press, 1980): 431-33.

80. Franklin, "Dorothy Parker": 6-7.

81. New York, Alfred A. Knopf, 1982: 76.

82. 7 December 1937: 17.

83. The New York Times 9 June 1949: 5.

84. The New York Times 20 September 1951: 25.

85. The Los Angeles Times 26 February 1955.

86. Newsweek 7 March 1955: 25-26.

87. New Masses 14 March 1939: 3.

88. 16 February 1962.

89. Nancy Caldwell Sorel recounts this meeting in The Atlantic Monthly "First Encounter" series, July 1985: 76.

90. "Dorothy Parker." In The Last Laugh (New York: Simon and Schuster, 1981): 171-73.

91. "The Grim Weeper." In The Garden of Allah (New York: Crown, 1970): 138.

92. Letters of Archibald MacLeish 1907-1982. Ed. R. H. Winnick. Boston: Houghton, 1983, 232.

93. "Three Women." Esquire December 1987: 224. This was written in 1983 but not published until 1987. Hellman died in 1984.

94. William C. Rogers, Letter to the editor of Esquire, 19 June 1968. George Oppenheimer Papers, Lincoln Center, New York.

95. David Smith, "Dorothy Parker and Friends." The Los Angeles Times 4 May 1976; sec. 4: 1.

96. The Screen Guild's Magazine May 1936: 8.

97. Warren argues differently in her dissertation. It is best finally to judge filmscripts by their own, unique merits, rather than by pre-conceived and literary standards.

98. <u>Cosmopolitan</u> November 1979: 319.

99. <u>The Good Words and Other Words</u> (New York: Dutton, 1978): 162.

100. "Not Enough," <u>New Masses</u> 30.12 (14 March 1939): 4. After reading this, Helen Bugbee wrote to Parker and encouraged her to continue writing; Parker answered her letter and included the piece she could not have published, entitled "Who Might be Interested." The letter and the story were published for the first time in <u>Mother Jones</u> February/March 1986: 40-42.

101. December 1957: 60.

102. October 1958: 103.

103. February 1959: 18.

104. Rev. of <u>Alexander Woollcott</u> by Samuel Hopkins Adams. The Chicago <u>Sun Book Week</u> 10 June 1945: 1.

105. <u>Nothing But People: The Early Days at Esquire, A Personal History 1928-1958</u>. New York, Crown, 1971, 301.

106. <u>The Years With Ross</u> was published in 1959. Parker reviewed this book for <u>Esquire</u> September 1959: 18.

107. 24 June 1959. <u>Selected Letters of James Thurber</u>. Ed. Helen Thurber and Edward Weeks. Boston: Little, 1980, 121.

108. Unpublished and undated letter. Lincoln Center, New York.

109. New York: Holt, 1968: 215.

110. <u>Lilly</u> (New York: William Morrow, 1988): 101-02.

111. New York, Poseidon, 1990: 146-47.

112. 24 November 1969. Unpublished letter. Lincoln Center, New York.

113. Nancy Seely, "Dorothy Parker." The New York <u>Post</u> 10 June 1967: 31.

114. "Dorothy Parker is at the Plaza in Dire Straits." <u>Choice People</u> (New York: William Morrow, 1984): 63.

115. Robert Liebman. "Personal View." <u>The [London] Sunday Times</u> 29 May 1988: G4.

2. Primary Bibliography

Parker's work is divided into six sections: A. Books; B. Short Stories; C. Screenplays; D. Published Interviews; E. Miscellaneous Work; F. Individual Pieces.

A. Books

Parker's name appeared on the title pages of seventeen books during her life time. Her play The Coast of Illyria and a selection of her "Constant Reader" essays was published after her death. Her play The Ice Age remains unpublished. Those books Parker co-authored appear with the names of the other authors. Books exclusively by Parker appear by their titles. Each citation is followed by bibliographic information and a list of reviews. The citations are in chronological order.

1. Parker, Dorothy, George S. Chapell, and Frank Crowinshield. High Society: Advice as to Social Campaigning and Hints on the Management of Dowagers, Dinners, Dubutantes, Dances, and the Thousand and One Diversions of Persons of Quality. New York: G. P. Putnam's Sons, 1920.

   Only one edition of this early coffee-table book was ever printed. Its main features are pen and ink sketches by the English satirist "Fish," and its prose precepts by all three authors. Some had appeared in Vanity Fair with Parker's name, but the book makes no distinction in telling who the authors are of the other pieces.

   Rev. of High Society. The New York Times Book Review 26 December 1920: 8-9.

2. Parker, Dorothy, Heywood Broun, et al. Nonsensorship: Sundry Observations Concerning Prohibitions, Inhibitions, and Illegalities. New York: G. P. Putnam's Sons, 1922.

This collection of lively "about the town" verse and prose by the Round Table members has Parker's Hymn of Hate, "Reformers," 95-98. The book has a caricature of Parker hating reformers by Ralph Barton.

Broun, Heywood. "As to 'Nonsensorship' and the ways of Censors." Rev. of Nonsensorship. The New York World 10 September 1922: E6.

Gorman, Herbert. "Mass Attack on the Censor." Rev. of Nonsensorship. The New York Times Book Review: 10 September 1922: 9, 16.

3. Parker, Dorothy, and Franklin Pierce Adams. Men I'm Not Married To / Women I'm Not Married To. Garden City, NY: Doubleday, Page and Company, 1922.

Parker and Adams published this small book with each other's half inverted, so that there are two front covers. Parker's poem "Men I'm Not Married To" appeared first in the Saturday Evening Post 17 June 1922: 13, 42.

4. Parker, Dorothy, and Elmer Rice. Close Harmony, or The Lady Next Door. New York: Samuel French, 1929.

This play was copyright as Soft Music in 1924, but it was performed under the title Close Harmony.

Anderson, John. The Post 1 December 1924: 1.
Benchley, Robert. Life 18 December 1924: 18.
Broun, Heywood. The World 1 December 1924: 6.
Krutch, Joseph Wood. The Nation 24 December 1924: 686-87.
Littell, Robert. New Republic 24 December 1924: 20.
Woollcott, Alexander. The Sun 1 December 1924; Sec. xx: 4-5.
Young, Stark. The New York Times 2 December 1924: 23.

5. Parker, Dorothy, et al. Bobbed Hair. New York: G. P. Putnam's Sons, 1925.

This detective novel was written "by Twenty Authors"; Parker's part is chapter vii: 101-05.

The New York Times Book Review 5 April 1925: 16-17.

6. <u>Enough Rope</u>. New York: Boni and Liveright, 1926.

Dedicated to Elinor Wylie, this is Parker's first, exclusive, published book. It contained 90 poems that had originally appeared in <u>Life</u>, <u>Vanity Fair</u>, <u>The New Yorker</u>, and "The Conning Tower" of the New York <u>World</u>. It was first printed in December of 1926 and by January of 1933 had gone through its twenty-fourth printing. The book was also published as #6 in a new paper-back series, Pocketbooks, Incorporated in New York in May of 1939. By March of 1941, this edition was in its ninth printing. It is identical to the first edition. In New York, the Sundial Press reprinted <u>ER</u> in 1940. This edition went through only one printing and is identical to the Boni and Liveright edition.

Anonymous Reviews

<u>The Booklist</u> April 1927: 304.
<u>The Bookman</u> 65.1 (March 1927): 80-81.
<u>The Independent</u> 5 February 1927: 169.
<u>The Nation</u> 25 MAY 1927: 589.
The New York <u>Times Book Review</u> 27 March 1927: 6.
<u>The Saturday Review of Literature</u> 18 December 1926: 460; January 1927: 492; 12 February 1927: 586.
<u>Wisconsin Library Bulletin</u> March 1927: 77.

Signed Reviews

Alceste. <u>The New Yorker</u> 8 January 1927: 84.
Crouse, Russel. The New York <u>Evening Post and Literary Review</u> 22 January 1927: 16.
Luhrs, Marie. <u>Poetry: A Magazine of Verse</u> 30.1 (April 1927): 52-54.
Taggard, Genevive. The New York <u>Herald Tribune Books</u> 27 March 1927: 7.
Wilson, Edmund. <u>The New Republic</u> 19 January 1927:256.

7. <u>Sunset Gun</u>. New York: Boni and Liveright, 1928.

This book, originally entitled <u>Songs for the Nearest Harmonica</u>, was due to be published in May of 1928. It was reviewed that way by John Riddle in <u>Vanity Fair</u> in May of 1928, page 134. However, it did not appear until June with the title <u>Sunset Gun</u>. Dedicated "For John," the book contained 56 poems from <u>The Bookman</u>, <u>The New Republic</u>, <u>The Nation</u>, <u>The New Yorker</u>, <u>Life</u>, <u>McCall's</u>, <u>Yale Review</u>, and "The Conning Tower" of the New York newspapers <u>The World</u> and <u>The Post</u>. By April of 1934, <u>Sunset Gun</u> had gone through its thirteenth printing. It was reprinted exactly the same as its first printing by the Sundial Press in 1939. It became #76 in the Pocketbook Series in 1940.

Anonymous Reviews

The Independent 14 July 1928: 45.
The New York Times Book Review 1 July 1928: 10.
The Saturday Review of Literature 2 June 1928: 940.
The Woman's Journal September 1928: 34.

Signed Reviews

B., B. F. The Boston Evening Transcript 30 June 1928: 3.
Benet, William Rose. The Saturday Review of Literature 9 June 1928: 943.
Busy, Gretta. The New York Herald Tribune Books 15 July 1928: 7
North, Sterling. Poetry: A Magazine of Verse 33.3 (December 1928): 96.
Riddle, John. Vanity Fair May 1928: 134.
                    August 1928: 93.
Robinson, Henry M. The Bookman 68.1 (September 1928): 96.
Walton, Edith. The New Republic 27 June 1928: 155.
Whipple, Leon. The Survey 63.1 (November 1928): 168.
White, E. B. The New Yorker 9 June 1928: 88-89.

8. Laments for the Living. New York: The Viking Press, 1930.

Dedicated to Adele Quarterly Lovett, Laments for the Living is thirteen pieces of fictitious prose sketches and stories from The American Mercury, The Bookman, The Pictorial Review, and Vanity Fair. It was first issued in June of 1930 and had gone through ten printings by September of 1936. It appeared under the same title in Paris in 1932 in the series Modern Masterpieces in English, #5, published by Crosby Continental Editions. In London, it was published by Longman's. It was re-issued in 1947 in Cleveland by World Publishing Company in the Tower Books Series.

Anonymous Reviews

The Booklist October 1930: 65.
The Nation 16 July 1930: 75.
The New Yorker 21 June 1930: 78.
The New York Times Book Review 15 June 1930: 7.
Outlook and Independent 18 June 1930: 269.
The Saturday Review of Literature 21 June 1930: 1152.
Times Literary Supplement 23 October 1930: 860; 19 July 1930: 1216.

Signed Reviews

Butcher, Fanny. The Chicago Daily Tribune 21 June 1930: 6.

Graham, Gladys. The Saturday Review of Literature 5 July 1930: 1172.
Matthews, T. S. The New Republic 17 September 1930: 133.
Roscoe, Burton. Arts and Decoration September 1930: 71.
Ross, Mary. The New York Herald Tribune Books 15 June 1930: 7.
Weeks, Edward. The Atlantic Monthly December 1930: 30.

9. Death and Taxes. New York: The Viking Press, 1931.

Parker's last volume of original poetry, Death and Taxes contained forty-one
poems. It was dedicated to "Mr. Benchley." It went through nine printings by
December of 1935. The book was also re-issued by the Sun Dial Press in 1939
and in 1940.

Anonymous Reviews

The Booklist 28.1 (September 1931): 19-20.
The Forum August 1931: xii.
The Nation 23 September 1931: 315.
The New Republic 12 August 1931: 315.
Wisconsin Library Bulletin October 1931: 220.

Signed Reviews

Adams, Franklin P. The New York Herald Tribune Books 14 June 1931: 7.
Brooks, Walter R. Outlook and Independent 24 June 1931: 251.
Butcher, Fanny. The Chicago Daily Tribune 13 June 1931: 12.
Canby, Henry Seidel. The Saturday Review of Literature 13 June 1931: 891.
Hutchinson, Percy. The New York Times Book Review 14 June 1931: 4.
Kresensky, Raymond. The Christian Century 28 October 1931: 1345.
Rosenburg, Harold. Poetry: A Magazine of Verse 39.9 (December 1931): 159-
    61.

10. After Such Pleasures. New York: The Viking Press, 1933.

Parker's second collection of fictitious prose, these eleven stories came from
Harper's Bazaar, The New Yorker, and Cosmopolitan. Dedicated to Ellen and
Philip Barry, After Such Pleasures went through five printings by March of 1935.
It was also published by Longman's in London in 1934. The Sun Dial Press
printed it once in 1940.

Anonymous Reviews

The Booklist 30.5 (January 1934): 150.
The Forum January 1934: v.
The Nation 20 December 1933: 715.
The New York Times Book Review 29 October 1933: 3.

Signed Reviews

B. M. F. Boston Evening Transcript 20 January 1934: 3.
Brickell, Herschel. The North American Review January 1934: 94.
Butcher, Fanny. The Chicago Daily Tribune 28 October 1933: 16
Gannett, Lewis. The New York Herald Tribune 27 October 1933: 15.
Matthews, T. S. The New Republic 15 November 1933: 24-25.
Nash, Ogden. The Saturday Review of Literature 4 December 1933: 231.
Nobbe, George. The Brooklyn Daily Eagle Sunday Review: 3 December 1933:
     19.

11. Not So Deep As A Well: Collected Poems. New York: The Viking Press, 1936.

Dedicated to Franklin Pierce Adams, the volume of collected poetry contained 178
poems from Parker's three previous volumes. Parker had deleted fourteen poems
from the original three books and added five new ones. It was published
simultaneously in Toronto by MacMillan in 1935. By March of 1940, Not So
Deep had gone through six printings. It was also published in London in 1937 by
Hamish Hamilton. In 1944, it was republished by the Modern Library in New
York under the title The Collected Poetry of Dorothy Parker.

Anonymous Reviews

The Booklist 33.5 (January 1937): 16.
The Christian Science Monitor 9 December 1936: 16.
Time 7 December 1936: 88-89.

Signed Reviews

Benet, William Rose. The Saturday Review 12 December 1936: 5.
Edman, Irwin. The Nation 19 December 1936: 736-38.
Hazlitt, Henry. The New York Times 11 December 1936: 25.
Keith, Joseph. Prairie Schooner 11 (Spring 1937): 85.
Kronenberger, Louis. The New York Times Book Review 12 December 1936:
     28.
Redman, Ben Ray. The New York Herald Tribune Books 20 December 1936:
     15.

Wills, A. <u>Life and Letters Today</u> 16.8 (Summer 1937): 168-69.

12. <u>Here Lies: The Collected Stories of Dorothy Parker</u>. New York: The Viking Press, 1939.

   Dedicated to Lillian Hellman, <u>Here Lies</u> was published not only by Viking in 1939 but also by Longman's in London and by the Literary Guild of America in New York. The book was re-issued as <u>The Collected Stories of Dorothy Parker</u>. It was prefaced by "A Note on the Author" by Franklin P. Adams. The twenty-four stories in <u>Here Lies</u> were taken from her two earlier collections and contained two previously published but uncollected stories, and the never before published story, "The Custard Heart."

Anonymous Reviews

   <u>The Booklist</u> 35.18 (15 May 1938): 307
   <u>The Christian Science Monitor</u> 17 June 1939: 10.
   <u>Times Literary Supplement</u> 25 November 1939: 687.
   <u>Wisconsin Library Bulletin</u> June 1939: 114.

Signed Reviews

   Britten, Florence H. The New York <u>Herald Tribune Books</u> 7 May 1939: 3.
   Curtiss, Mina. <u>The Nation</u> 15 July 1939: 76-78.
   Fadiman, Clifton. <u>The New Yorker</u> 29 April 1939: 120-21.
   Johnson, Edgar. <u>Kenyon Review</u> 1.3 (Summer 1939): 348-51.
   McCarty, Norma. The New York <u>Times Book Review</u> 30 April 1939: 6.
   McKenney, Ruth. <u>The Saturday Review of Literature</u> 29 April 1939: 7.
   Mair, John. <u>The New Statesman and Nation</u> 21 October 1939: 583-84.
   Plomer, William. <u>The Spectator</u> 17 November 1939: 708.
   Poore, Charles. The New York <u>Times</u> 29 April 1930: 15.
   Rufus [sic]. <u>The Canadian Forum</u> June 1939: 97.
   Springer, Ann. The Boston <u>Evening Transcript</u> 27 May 1939: 2.

13. <u>The Portable Dorothy Parker</u>, 1944; revised and enlarged by Brendan Gill. New York: Viking, 1973.

   The most important book in the Parker canon, <u>The Portable Dorothy Parker</u> was selected and arranged by Parker herself. It was only one in a series of "portables" issued by Viking Press. The same year it was published, it was also distributed by the Editions for the Armed Services publishers in New York. The book was published in 1944 as <u>The Indispensable Dorothy Parker</u> by the Book Society. The original preface was written by William Somerset Maugham. This book remained in print and unchanged until 1973 when the "revised and enlarged" edition appeared. It contained a new preface by Brendan Gill and was published in London by Duckworth as The Collected Dorothy Parker. This 1973 edition is still being printed today; except for specialists, the reading public knows Parker's work only through this edition.

1944 Reviews

The Booklist 15 June 1944: 353.
Kirkus Reviews 1 May 1944: 202.
North, Sterling. The Chicago Sun Book Week 21 May 1944: 2.
Weeks, Edward. The Atlantic Bookshelf July 1944: 125.
Wilson, Edmund. The New Yorker 20 May 1944: 67-68.

1973 Reviews

Choice 10.7 (September 1973): 982.
Clive, James. New Statesman 27 April 1973: 623-24.
Coleman, John. The Observer Review 15 April 1973: 38.
Times Literary Supplement 6 April 1973: 395.

14. The Portable F. Scott Fitzgerald. Selected by Dorothy Parker. New York: The Viking Press, 1945.

Parker selected and arranged this edition of Fitzgerald. It is introduced by John O'Hara. The reviews of this book do not mention Parker.

15. Parker, Dorothy and Ross Evans. The Coast of Illyria. 1948. Introd. Arthur Kinney. Iowa City, IA: University of Iowa Press, 1990.

This play was first produced by the Margo Jones' Theatre '49 company. The play remained in manuscript until Professor Kinney edited and published it in 1990.

Reviews

Atkinson, Brooks. The New York Times 13 April 1949; sec. L: 27.
Rosenfield, John. The New York Times 5 April 1949; sec. L: 37.
Time 18 April 1949: 78.
Variety 13 April 1949: 48.

16. Parker, Dorothy and Arnaud d'Usseau. The Ladies of the Corridor. New York: The Viking Press, 1954.

This was the last of Parker's plays produced during her lifetime. It ran on Broadway, was well-reviewed, but it was a commercial failure. In his edition of The Coast of Illyria, Professor Kinney has included scenes from this play that were dropped from the production.

Anonymous Reviews

America 7 November 1953: 157-58.
Newsweek 2 November 1953: 65.
Theatre Arts January 1954: 20.
Theatre Critics' Reviews 14.2: 244-46. [A reprinting of the opening night reviews from seven New York newspapers.]
Time 2 November 1953: 82.

Signed Reviews

Atkinson, Brooks. The New York Times 1 November 1953; sec. 2: 1.
Bentley, Eric. The New Republic 9 November 1953: 21.
Bracken, Eric. The New York Times 18 October 1953; sec. x: 1, 3.
Brown, John Mason. Saturday Review of Literature 12 December 1953: 47.
Gibbs, Wolcott. The New Yorker 31 October 1953: 58-60.
Hayes, Richard. The Commonweal 27 November 1953: 197-98.
Kirchway, Freda. The Nation 7 November 1953: 378.

17. Parker, Dorothy and Arnaud d'Usseau. The Ice Age. c. 1953.

This is an unpublished, unproduced playscript at Columbia University.

18. Candide: A Comic Operetta Based on Voltaire's Satire. New York: Random House, 1957.

Parker's name appears on the title page as contributing to the lyrics. [pp. 127-31]

19. Short Story: A Thematic Anthology. Eds. Dorothy Parker and Frederick B. Shroyer. New York: Scribners, 1965.

Kirsch, Robert. Los Angeles Times 24 November 1965; sec. 4: 4.

20. Constant Reader. New York: The Viking Press, 1970.

Published in England as <u>A Month of Saturdays</u>, this collection of Parker's 46 book reviews for the <u>New Yorker</u>, that she signed "Constant Reader," is not complete, and even those included are sometimes abbreviated.

Anonymous Reviews

<u>Booklist</u> 1 January 1971: 345.
<u>Kirkus Review</u> 15 July 1970: 787.
<u>Publisher's Weekly</u> 13 July 1970: 152.
<u>Saturday Review</u> 28 November 1970:
<u>Times Literary Supplement</u> 16 April 1971: 442.

Signed Reviews

Eatenson, Ervin. <u>Library Journal</u> 15 October 1970: 34.
Greer, Germaine. <u>Spectator</u> 10 April 1971: 502.
Nardi, Marcia. <u>The Christian Science Monitor</u> 7 December 1970: 15.
Roberts, Ray. <u>Books and Bookmen</u> 16 April 1971: 51-52.

B. Short Stories

Parker's prose fiction may be the most important part of her canon. The stories are listed in their chronological order. The titles are given as they originally appeared.

1. "Sorry, The Line is Busy." Life 21 April 1921: 560.

2. "Such a Pretty Little Picture." The Smart Set 69.4 (December 1922): 73-78.

3. "Too Bad." The Smart Set 71.3 (July 1923): 79-85.

4. "Mr. Durant." The American Mercury 3.9 (September 1924): 81-87.

5. "The Wonderful Old Gentleman." Pictorial Review January 1926: 25-26, 56, 58.

6. "Dialogue at Three in the Morning." The New Yorker 13 February 1926: 13.

7. "The Last Tea." The New Yorker 11 September 1926: 23-24.

8. "Oh, He's Charming." The New Yorker 9 October 1926: 22-23.

9. "Travelogue." The New Yorker 30 October 1926: 20-21.

10. "Lucky Little Curtis." Pictorial Review February 1927: 26-29.

11. "The Sexes." The New Republic 13 July 1927: 203-04.

12. "Morning." Life 7 July 1927: 9, 32.

13. "Arrangement in Black and White." The New Yorker 8 October 1927: 22-24.

14. "A Telephone Call." The Bookman 66.5 (January 1928): 500-02.

15. "A Terrible Day Tomorrow." The New Yorker 11 February 1928: 14-16.

16. "Just a Little One." The New Yorker 12 May 1928: 20-21.

17. "The Mantle of Whistler." The New Yorker 18 August 1928: 15-16.

18. "The Garter." The New Yorker 8 September 1928: 17-18.

19. "Long Distance." Vanity Fair October 1928: 61.

20. "You Were Perfectly Fine." The New Yorker 23 January 1929: 17-18.

21. "Big Blonde." The Bookman 68.6 (February 1929): 639-50.

22. "The Cradle of Civilization." The New Yorker 21 September 1929: 23-24.

23. "But the One on the Right." The New Yorker 19 October 1929: 25-27.

24. "Here We Are." Cosmopolitan March 1931: 32-35, 98.

25. "Lady With a Lamp." Harper's Bazaar April 1932: 56-57, 102, 104.

26. "Dusk Before Fireworks." Harper's Bazaar September 1932: 36-37, 90, 92, 94, 96.

27. "A Young Woman in Green Lace." The New Yorker 24 September 1932: 15-17.

28. "Horsie." Harper's Bazaar December 1932: 66-67, 118, 120-21, 124.

29. "Advice to the Little Peyton Girl." Harper's Bazaar February 1933: 46-47, 84, 86.

30. "The Diary of a Lady During Days of Panic, Frenzy, and World Change." The New Yorker 25 March 1933: 13-14.

31. "Sentiment . . . ." Harper's Bazaar May 1933: 64-65, 113.

32. "Mrs. Carrington and Mrs. Crane." The New Yorker 15 July 1933: 11-12.

33. "The Little Hours." The New Yorker 19 August 1933: 13-14.

34. "The Road Home." The New Yorker 16 September 1933: 17-18.

35. "Glory in the Daytime." Harper's Bazaar September 1933: 50-51, 122, 124, 126-27.

36. "The Waltz." The New Yorker 2 September 1933: 11-12.

37. "Cousin Larry." The New Yorker 30 June 1934: 15-17.

38. "Mrs. Hofstadter on Josephine Street." The New Yorker 4 August 1934: 20-26.

39. "Clothe the Naked." Scribner's Magazine January 1938: 31-35.

40. "Soldiers of the Republic." The New Yorker 5 February 1938: 13-14.

41. "The Custard Heart." [New for Here Lies]

42. "Spain, For Heaven's Sake!" 1939. Mother Jones February/March 1986: 40-42.

43. "The Standard of Living." The New Yorker 20 September 1941: 24-26.

44. "The Lovely Leave." Woman's Home Companion December 1943: 22-23, 85, 88.

45. "The Middle or Blue Period." Cosmopolitan December 1944: 54-55, 184.

46. "Song of the Shirt, 1941." The New Yorker 28 June 1947: 13-16.

47. "The Game." With Ross Evans. Cosmopolitan December 1948: 58, 90-102.

48. "I Live on Your Visits." The New Yorker 15 January 1955: 24-27.

49. "Lolita." The New Yorker 27 August 1955: 32-35.

50. "The Banquet of Crow." The New Yorker 14 December 1957: 39-43.

51. "The Bolt Behind the Blue." Esquire December 1958: 168-69, 171, 173-74.

C. Screenplays

This chronological listing of each of the movies Parker worked on is followed by selected reviews. Parker may have written the entire screenplay, as in Smashup; she may have co-authored it with Alan Campbell, as in A Star Is Born; or she may have contributed scenes and/or dialogue. An asterisk after the title indicates that Parker received screen credit in some way.

1. Remodeling Her Husband, D. W. Griffith, 1919.

2. Business is Business, with George Kaufman, Paramount, 1925.

3. Here is My Heart, Paramount, 1934.

> The New York Times 22 December 1934: 21.
> Time 31 December 1934: 14.

4. One Hour Late, Paramount, 1934.

5. The Big Broadcast of 1936, Paramount, 1935.

> Canadian Magazine November 1935: 40.
> The New York Times 16 September 1935: 15.
> Newsweek 21 September 1935: 17.
> Time 23 September 1935: 45.

6. Mary Burns, Fugitive, Paramount, 1935.

7. Hands Across the Table, Paramount, 1935.

> Literary Digest 7 December 1935: 24.
> The New Republic 13 November 1935: 18.
> The New York Times 2 November 1935: 13.
> Time 28 October 1936: 54.
> Vanity Fair December 1935: 51.

8. Paris in Spring, Paramount, 1935.

> The New York Times 13 July 1935: 16.
>   21 July 1935; sec. IX: 3.
> Time 18 May 1936: 62.

9. Three Married Men,* Paramount, 1936.

10. The Case Against Mrs. Ames, Paramount, 1936.

   Literary Digest 16 May 1936: 20.
   The New York Times 28 May 1936: 19.
   Newsweek 16 May 1936: 42.
   Time 18 May 1936: 62.

11. Lady, Be Careful,* Paramount, 1936.

   The New York Times 10 October 1936: 21.

12. The Moon's Our Home, Paramount, 1936.

   Literary Digest 25 April 1936: 34.
   The New York Times 28 May 1936: 19.
   Newsweek 16 May 1936: 42.
   Time 18 May 1936: 62.

13. Suzy,* MGM, 1936.

   Canadian Magazine November 1936: 38.
   Literary Digest 25 July 1936: 34.
   The New York Times 25 July 1936: 16.
                  26 July 1936: 4.
   Time 3 August 1936: 29.

14. It Happened in Hollywood, Columbia, 1937.

   The New York Times 2 October 1937: 18.
                  10 October 1937; sec. XI: 5.

15. Nothing Sacred, Selznick International, 1937.

   Life 6 December 1937: 36-39.
    13 December 1937: 70-71.
   Literary Digest 18 December 1937: 33-34.
   Nation 18 December 1937: 696-97.
   The New York Times 26 November 1937: 27.
   Newsweek 6 December 1937: 33.
   Time 6 December 1937: 49.

16. A Star Is Born,* United Artists, 1937.

       Canadian Magazine June 1937: 45.
       Commonweal 14 May 1937: 78.
       Life 3 May 1937: 38+.
       Literary Digest 1 May 1937: 20.
       New Republic 19 May 1937: 47-48.
       The New York Times 25 October 1936; sec. X: 5.
                  9 December 1936; sec. XII: 9.
                  23 April 1937: 25.
                  2 May 1937; sec. XI: 3.
                  3 May 1937; sec. XI: 4.
       Newsweek 1 May 1937: 29.
       Saint Nicholas March 1937: 69.
       Scholastic 8 May 1937: 28.
       Stage March 1937: 60.
        May 1937: 69.
       Time 3 May 1937: 28+.

17. Woman Chases Man, United Artist, 1937.

18. The Awful Truth, Columbia, 1937.

       Commonweal 5 November 1937: 48.
       New Republic 1 December 1937: 102.
       The New York Times 5 November 1937: 19.
                  14 November 1937; sec. XI: 5.
       Scholastic 18 December 1937: 36.
       Stage December 1937: 87.
        May 1938: 26.
       Time 1 November 1937: 45.

19. You Can Be Beautiful, Goldwyn, 1937.

20. Sweethearts, MGM, 1938.

       Canadian Magazine February 1939: 44.
       Commonweal 6 January 1939: 302.
       Life 24 October 1938: 28-29.
       The New York Times 21 August 1938; sec. IX: 3.
                  23 December 1938: 16.
                  25 December 1938; sec. IX: 7.
       Newsweek 2 January 1939: 25.
       Photoplay January 1939: 54.
                  June 1939: 10.

21. Trade Winds,* United Artists, 1938.

       Canadian Magazine February 1939: 44.
       Commonweal 6 January 1939: 302.
       Nation 21 January 1939: 102.
       The New York Times 18 September 1938; sec. X: 3.
                 9 October 1938; sec. X: 5.
                 8 January 1939; sec. IX: 4.
                 13 January 1939: 17.
       Newsweek 2 January 1939: 25.
       Photoplay February 1939: 48.
       Time 26 December 1938: 30.

22. Crime Takes a Holiday, Columbia, 1938.

       The New York Times 28 November 1938: 11.

23. Flight Into Nowhere, Columbia, 1938.

       The New York Times 2 May 1938: 13.

24. The Cowboy and the Lady, Goldwyn, 1938.

       Commonweal 2 December 1938: 161.
       Life 21 November 1938: 38-40.
       The New Republic 14 December 1938: 174.
       The New York Times 20 November 1938; sec. IX: 4.
              25 November 1938; sec. IX: 19.
       Newsweek 28 November 1938: 19.
       Stage September 1938: 26.
       Time 21 November 1938: 53.

25. The Goldwyn Follies, Goldwyn, 1938.

       Commonweal 2 December 1938: 161.
       Life 7 February 1938: 20-23.
       Literary Digest 19 February 1938: 23.
       The New York Times 21 February 1938: 15.
              27 February 1938; sec. IX: 5.
       Newsweek 14 February 1938: 24.
       Stage December 1937: 86.
       Time 7 February 1938: 58.

26. Five Little Peppers and How They Grew, Columbia, 1939.

27. Weekend For Three,* RKO, 1941.

   The New York Times 24 October 1941: 27.

28. The Little Foxes,* Warner Brothers, 1941.

   Commonweal 5 September 1941: 473.
   Life 1 September 1941: 47-50.
   The New York Times 22 January 1941; sec. IX: 4.
              22 August 1941; sec. IX: 3.
   The New Yorker 23 August 1941: 63.
   Newsweek 25 August 1941: 53-54.
   Photoplay September 1941: 44-45+
   Scholastic 22 September 1941: 30.
   Scribner's Commentator November 1941: 105-06.
   Theatre Arts October 1941: 730.
   Time 1 September 1941: 86-87.

29. Pride of the Yankees, RKO, 1942.

   Commonweal 31 July 1942: 352.
   The New Republic 27 July 1942: 118.
   The New York Times 25 January 1942; sec. IX: 5.
              1 March 1942; sec. VIII: 3.
              12 April 1942; sec. VIII: 3.
              12 July 1942; sec. VIII: 3.
              16 July 1942: 23.
              19 July 1942; sec. VIII: 3.
   The New Yorker 18 July 1942: 42.
   Newsweek 20 July 1942: 56+.
   Photoplay October 1942: 6.
   Time 3 August 1942: 74.

30. Saboteur,* Universal, 1942

   Commonweal 15 May 1942: 87.
   Life 11 May 1942: 67-71.
   Nation 23 May 1942: 609.
   The New Republic 18 May 1942: 669.
   The New York Times 1 February 1942; sec. IX: 5.
              8 May 1942: 27.
              10 May 1942; sec. VIII: 3.

The New Yorker 9 May 1942: 67.
Newsweek 4 May 1942: 54.
Theatre Arts May 1942: 318-19.
Time 11 May 1942: 87.

31. A Gentle Gangster, Republic, 1943.

32. Mr. Skeffington,* Warner Brothers, 1944.

Commonweal 9 June 1944: 184-85.
Nation 3 June 1944: 661.
The New Republic 31 July 1944: 133.
The New York Times 26 May 1944: 23.
The New Yorker 27 May 1944:   61.
Newsweek 5 June 1944: 90.
Photoplay September 1944: 21.
Time 5 June 1944: 94+.

33. Smashup: The Story of A Woman,* Universal, 1947.

Commonweal 25 April 1947: 38.
Cosmopolitan March 1947: 67+
Life 14 April 1947: 79-80+.
The New Republic 24 February 1947: 39.
The New York Times 19 May 1946; sec. II: 3.
            23 June 1946; sec. II: 3.
             6 April 1947; sec. II: 5.
            11 April 1947: 31.
            27 April 1947; sec. II: 4.
             1 June 1947; sec. II: 1.
The New Yorker 19 April 1947: 44.
Newsweek 28 April 1947: 95+.
Theatre Arts April 1947: 97.
Time 10 March 1947: 97.
Women's Home Companion March 1947: 10.

34. The Fan,* Twentieth Century-Fox, 1949.

Commonweal 22 April 1949: 46+.
Good Housekeeping May 1949: 10.
The New Republic 19 April 1949: 31.
The New York Times 2 April 1949: 12.
            10 April 1949; sec. II: 1.
Newsweek 18 April 1949: 90.
Photoplay April 1949: 22.
Rotarian July 1949: 50.
Time 11 April 1949: 102.

Woman's Home Companion May 1949: 10-11.

35. Dynamite, Paramount, 1949.

36. Come to the Stable, Twentieth Century-Fox, 1949.

Catholic World August 1949: 387-88.
Commonweal 5 August 1949: 415.
Cosmopolitan July 1949: 12+.
Life 8 August 1949: 48-50.
The New Republic 1 August 1949: 29.
The New York Times 28 July 1949: 19.
          31 July 1949; sec. II: 1.
The New Yorker 6 August 1949: 38.
Newsweek 8 August 1949: 68.
Rotarian January 1950: 40.
Theatre Arts August 1949: 106.
Time 1 August 1949.
Vogue 1 August 1949: 87.
Woman's Home Companion August 1949: 10-11.

37. Queen for a Day,* United Artists, 1951.

Library Journal 1 May 1951: 785.
The New York Times 19 November 1950; sec. II: 5.
Newsweek 30 April 1951: 82.
Saturday Review 21 April 1951: 28.

38. The I Don't Care Girl, Twentieth Century-Fox, 1953.

National Parent-Teacher February 1953: 37.

39. The Good Soup, Twentieth Century-Fox, 1961.
     [This Film was never produced.]

D. Published Interviews

Parker's interviews are an important addition to her canon. In them she talks about herself, her reputation, and her work. They are listed in chronological order.

1. Halasz, George. "Always Hampered by Money." The Brooklyn Daily Eagle 18 November 1928.

2. "Dorothy Parker Here; Her New Book On The Way." The New York World 1 February 1930: 3.

3. Wettergren, Gunilla. "Dorothy Parker Went to Hollywood for her Sins, but Escaped, She Tells Swedish Interviewer." The New York World Telegram 15 September 1932: 3.

4. "Literati Jeers: Ten Beautiful Words of Funk." The New York Herald Tribune 12 December 1932.

5. Martindale, James. "Dorothy Parker for LaGuardia." The New York Evening Post 27 October 1933: 12.

6. "Dorothy Parker Reveals She's a Bride of 8 Months." The New York Herald Tribune 16 June 1934.

7. Whitaker, Alma. "Dorothy Parker, Our Only Woman Humorist, Denies It." The Los Angeles Times 9 September 1934.

8. Thirer, Irene. "Priestess of Caustic Quip Talks Movies." The New York Post 24 April 1937.

9. Tazelaar, Marguerite. "It Seems That Hollywood Gags Dorothy Parker, not Vice Versa." The New York Herald Tribune 25 April 1937.

10. "Literary Cult Hails Return of Leader." The New York American 2 May 1937.

11. Tighe, Dixie. "Dorothy Parker Returns from Spain With Tears in her Soul." The New York Post 22 October 1937: 17.

12. "Dorothy Parker Heads Women Aiding Madrid." The New York Herald Tribune 4 December 1937: 3.

13. "Miss Parker Never Poses." The New York Times 8 January 1939; sec. 9: 4.

14. "'Read but not Seen' Condemns Most Plays, but not this One." The New York Herald Tribune 22   June 1941.

15. Keavy, Hubbard. "Dorothy Parker Deflates Herself." [Baltimore] The Sun 4 January

1942.

16. "Movie-Inquiry Witnesses Are Guests at Rally." The New York Herald Tribune 2 November 1947: 9.

17. Morehouse, Ward. "'Give Me New York!' Says Miss Parker." The New York World Telegram and Sun 16 October 1953; sec. 2: 28.

18. Drutman, Irving. "Ladies of the Corridor." The New York Herald Tribune 18 October 1953; sec. 4: 1, 4.

19. Capron, Marion. "Dorothy Parker." Paris Review 13(Summer 1956): 72-87.

20. Franklin, Robert C. "Dorothy Parker." Columbia University Popular Arts Project. Oral History Research Office, Columbia University, 1959.

21. Battle, Lois. "A Wink at a Cock-Eyed World." UCLA Daily Bruin 16 February 1962.

22. Schumach, Murry. "Dorothy Parker Discusses TV." The New York Times 6 May 1962; sec. 2: 17.

23. Townsend, Dorothy, "Dorothy Parker Sets Up L. A. Shop." The Los Angeles Times 18 June 1962; sec. iv: 1, 4.

24. Callan, Mary Ann. "Students Appalling to Dorothy Parker." The Los Angeles Times 28 April 1963; sec. C: 1, 4.

25. Pett, Saul. "Various Views of the Aging Mrs. Parker." The New York Herald Tribune 13 October 1963: 20.

26. Steinem, Gloria. "Dorothy Parker." New York Journal 1965: 118e, 118n, 118o.

27. Stern, Michael. "The Undaunted First Lady of Wit. Illness has Failed to Dull the Edge of Dorothy Parker's Shining Talent." The New York World Telegram and Sun 3 August 1965.

E. Miscellaneous Work

This alphabetical listing of incidental essays, poems, and critical prose spans Parker's writing career from 1923 until her final published work, a prose portrait of Oscar Levant in 1966.

1. "About the 'Town Crier' and His World: Turning a Microscopic Eye on Alexander Woollcott." Rev. of Alexander Woollcott and his World by Samuel Hopkins Adams. The Chicago Sun Book Week 10 June 1941: 1.

2. "At the Dog Show." Cosmopolitan May 1934: 62-63, 114.

3. "Bric-A-Brack." The Bookman 66.1 (September 1927): 33.

4. "Destructive Decoration." House and Garden February 1942: 33-35, 88.

5. "From the Ladies." A poem in Julie Goldsmith Gilbert's Ferber: A Biography. Garden City, NY: Doubleday, 1978. 185.

6. The Happiest Man. Incomplete Playscript. Lincoln Center Library, New York City.

7. "Higgledy Piggledy." In William Somerset Maugham's Introduction to the Portable Dorothy Parker. New York: Viking, 1944.

8. "Hollywood: The Land I Won't Return To." Seven Arts 3 (1955): 130-140.

9. "The Homebody." The New Republic 3 August 1927: 282.

10. "Humor Takes in Many Things." Rev. of The Road to Miltown by S. J. Perelman. The New York Times Book Review 20 January 1957: 1, 36.

11. "Incredible, Fantastic . . . And True." New Masses 23 November 1937: 15-16.

12. Introduction. The Seal in the Bedroom and Other Predicaments by James Thurber. New York: Grosset and Dunlap, 1950.

13. ---. Spanish Portraits. New York: Georgian Press, n.d. [ca. 1938].

14. ---. Thunder Over the Bronx by Arthur Kober. New York: Simon and Schuster, 1935.

15. ---. Watch on the Rhine by Lillian Hellman. New York, 1942. Privately Printed.

16. "Interior." The Nation 30 November 1927: 598.

17. "Landscape." The Bookman 66.3 (November 1927): 271.

18. "Letter from Dorothy Parker to Ogden Nash." The Saturday Review of Literature

17 January 1931: 544.

19. "The Maid Servant at the Inn." The Bookman 66.4 (December 1927): 340.

20. "Miss Brass Tacks of 1943." Mademoiselle May 1943: 85, 144-46.

21. "New York at 6:30 pm." Esquire November 1964: 96.

22. "Not Enough." New Masses 14 March 1939: 3-4.

23. "A One Woman Show." Everybody's Magazine March 1921: 33-34.

24. "Oscar Levant." In Double Exposure by Roddy McDowall. New York: Delacorte Press, 1966.

25. "Our Cousins." The Diary of Our Own Samuel Pepys by Franklin P. Adams. Vol. 2. 1926-1934; 1121. New York: Simon and Schuster, 1936.

26. "Prayer for a New Mother." The Bookman 68 (January 1929): 376.

27. Preface. Thurber's Men, Women, and Dogs: A Book of Drawings by James Thurber. New York: Harcourt, 1943.

28. Speech. Esquire Symposium on Writing, October 1958. R. G. Davis Collection. Rare Book and Manuscript Library, Columbia University, New York.

29. Rev. of For Whom the Bell Tolls by Ernest Hemingway. PM 20 October 1942: 42.

30. Rev. of The Lake by Dorothy Massingham and Murray MacDonald. The New York Journal American 27 December 1933.

31. "Salute." Mademoiselle November 1943: 77, 132.

32. "Society Goes to a Play." The New York World 6 February 1922: 9.

33. "Sophisticated Poetry--And the Hell With It." New Masses 27 June 1939: 21.

34. "Take My Vows." The Yale Review n.s. 20 (September 1932): 139.

35. This Is My Best. Ed. Whit Burnett. New York: The Dial Press, 1942. 206.

36. "To Richard With Love." The Screen Guilds' Magazine May 1936: 8.

37. "The Trough of Plenty." Rev. of Why Women Cry by Elizabeth Hawes, and Snoot, If You Must by Lucius Beebe. The Saturday Review 11 December 1943: 11.

38. "Upon My Honor." Poem Attributed to Parker. Jesse L. Lasky. Whatever Happened

to Hollywood. New York: Funk and Wagnalls, 1975: 30.

39. "When Is a Benefit?" The New York Times 24 February 1924; sec. 7: 2.

40. "When I Painted Luis Firpo." Neysa McMein as told to Dorothy Parker. The New York World 9 September 1923: 10.

41. "Who Is that Man?" Vogue July 1944: 67, 138-39.

F. Individual Pieces from Magazines and Newspapers

Individual poems and essays are detailed in this section. The arrangement is
alphabetical by the titles of magazines and newspapers. Parker contributed both prose and
poetry to some magazines, and that distinction is so noted. The listing within each
subsection is chronological.

1. Ainslee's

After Parker was fired from Vanity Fair in January of 1920, she began working
as drama critic for Ainslee's. The title of the column was "In Broadway Playhouses."

May	1920:	154-57.	"Springtime on the Rialto"
June/July	1920:	155-58.	"Advance Models in Summer Shows"
August	1920:	155-58.	"Plays in the Past and Presence Tense"
September	1920	156-59.	"National Institutions"
October	1920:	154-57.	"Words and Music"
November	1920:	155-58.	"Season's Greetings"
December	1920:	155-59.	"Laurels and Raspberries"
January	1921:	156-59.	"Hang the Expense"
February	1921:	156-59.	"First Thoughts on Second Nights"
March	1921:	154-59.	"Standing Room Only, and Very Little of That"
April	1921:	155-59.	"Night and Day Shifts"
May	1921:	155-59.	"The Primrose Pathology"
June	1921:	157-60.	"Nights Off"
July	1921:	155-59.	"Oh, What a Pal Was Mary!"
August	1921:	156-59.	"Exit the Season. Laughingly"
September	1921:	156-59.	"Fair to Middling"
October	1921:	155-59.	"The Banalities of 1921"
November	1921:	154-59.	"Comic Relief!"
December	1921:	156-59.	"Plays and Plays and Plays"
January	1922:	155-59.	"Take Them or Leave Them"
February	1922:	155-59.	"Hard Times"
March	1922:	155-59.	"For Auld Lang Syne"
April	1922:	156-59.	"And Still They Come"
May	1922:	155-59.	"The Force of Example"
June	1922:	155-59.	"Back to Methuselah, or Thereabouts"
July	1922:	155-59.	"The Comedy Blues"
August	1922:	156-59.	"The Season Chooses Its Exit"
September	1922:	156-59.	"The Dog Days"
October	1922:	157-59.	"Marking Time"
November	1922:	156-59.	"Let 'er Go"
December	1922:	154-58.	"Not So Good"
January	1923:	156-59.	"Better Times"
February	1923:	155-59.	"Three Rousing Cheers"
March	1923:	155-59.	"Storm and Stress"
April	1923:	154-58.	"Nothing from Nothing"

May	1923: 155-59.	"A Lot of New Plays"
June	1923: 156-59.	"Oh, Pretty Well"
July	1923: 156-59.	"The Season Plucks at the Coverlet"

2. "The Conning Tower"

In the 1920s, New York had twelve daily newspapers. Columnists abounded and contributors to the columns were usually not paid. "The Conning Tower" was Franklin Pierce Adams's Daily column for, first, the New York <u>World</u> and then for the <u>Herald Tribune</u>. Adams published not only his notions, but also a lot of light and nonsense verse. He was especially fond of Parker's poetry, and some of her most famous poems were first published here.

A. The New York <u>World</u>

22 February	1923:13.	"How Bold It Is"
20 April	1923: 8.	"Condolence."
22 September	1924:11.	"Ballade of Big Plans"
27 December	1924: 7.	"Light of Love"
20 March	1925:13.	"I Shall Come Back"
9 May	1925:11.	"A Dream Lies Dead"
13 June	1925:11.	"Story of Mrs. W."
26 June	1925:11.	"Little Song"
30 June	1925:11.	"Braggart"
31 July	1925:11.	"Threnody"
3 August	1925:11.	"Epitaph for a Darling Lady"
16 August	1925:11.	<u>Some Beautiful Letters</u>
		"Observation"
		"Social Note"
		"News Item"
		"Interview"
		"Comment"
		"Resume"
18 August	1925:13.	"Convalescent"
20 August	1925:11.	"Testament"
28 August	1925:11.	"Recurrence"
29 August	1925:11.	"August"
20 January	1926:13.	"The Satin Dress"
7 October	1926:15.	"The Dark Girl's Rhyme"
8 October	1926:15.	"The White Lady"
24 November	1926:15.	"To Elsbeth"
18 February	1927:13.	"Verses in the Night"
10 March	1927:15.	"When We Were Very Sore"

23 March	1927:15.	"There Was One"
23 August	1927:13.	"Godmother"
20 January	1928:13.	"Fair Weather"
15 March	1928:13.	"The Whistling Girl"
20 March	1928:13.	"The Last Question"
22 May	1928:13.	"Coda"
17 August	1928:11.	"Excursion Into Loneliness"
		"Return"
4 September	1928:11.	"Garden Spot"
12 December	1928:15.	"Song of Social Life in Hollywood"
25 December	1928:15.	"Purposely Ungrammatical Love Song"
14 January	1929:11.	"Midnight"
15 March	1929:15.	"The Danger of Writing Defiant Verse"
16 August	1929:11.	"Sonnet"
19 November	1929:13.	"Sonnet on An Alpine Mount"
28 April	1930:13.	"Prayer for a Prayer"
29 April	1930:13.	"Verse Demode"
19 June	1930:11.	A Cup of Coffee, A Sandwich, and Yew
		"Prologue to a Saga"
		"Ornithology for Beginners"
		"Lines On Reading Too Much Verse"
		"The Apple Tree"
		"Requiescat"
1 August	1930:11.	"The Little Old Lady in Lavender Silk"
15 September	1930:11.	"For a Woman, Dead Young"
8 January	1931:13.	"Ballade of Unfortunate Mammals"

B. The New York Herald Tribune

3 March	1931:26.	"After a Spanish Proverb"
26 March	1931:20.	"Ballade of a Talked Off Ear"
21 April	1931:30.	"My Own"
7 May	1931:20.	Pastoraliana
		"Sanctuary"
		"Cherry White"
		"Sweet Violets"
		"The Willow"
15 October	1931:21.	"Song in the Worst Possible Taste"
21 April	1932:30.	"Sight"
13 April	1933:15.	"The Lady's Reward"
23 October	1933:13.	"Prisoner"

3. Esquire

Parker's last sustained writing effort was reviewing books for Esquire between 1957 and 1962. This monthly feature was originally entitled "Dorothy Parker on Books," but as her reviews became sporadic, the title became "Book Reviews" followed by her name.

December	1957:	60-66.	"The Best Fiction of 1957"
May	1958:	41-42.	"Second Thoughts on Some Major Themes"
June	1958:	32-34.	"Corruption, Mr. Keefe and Other Distractions"
July	1958:	18,20.	"Four Rousing Cheers"
August	1958:	16,18.	"Hammock Reading with a Slice of Humor"
September	1958:	12,14.	"This September Song: Too Much Is Too Much"
October	1958:	102-03.	"Sex--Without the Asterisks"
November	1958:	30,32.	"Three Banners From the Passing Parade"
December	1958:	46-48.	"A Curtsey or Two, and A Bow with a Lunar Arrow"
January	1959:	20,22.	"They Done It: Murder as Treated by the Best"
February	1959:	16-18.	"The Veiled Surface, Minus Fronds and Dreams."
March	1959:	18,20.	"An End to Beating about the Bush."
April	1959:	31,33.	"Acclaim for Four Finds: Glittering, Charming, Fascinating, Fine."
May	1959:	164-66.	"A Sweet Little Murderess, A Selfish Little Lady, and a Little Group."
June	1959:	166-68.	"Two Autobiographies, One to be Continued."
July	1959:	26-27.	"At Least one of these is for you, Whoever You Are."
September	1959:	18,20.	"A Valentine for Ross, Lauds for a Translator, and Other Matters."
October	1959:	26,30.	"Calling a Spayed a Spayed; Out of a Lump--Five Specials."
November	1959:	26,28.	"Characters, Characters, but few of them walk out of these Pages."
December	1959:	104-05.	"Characters Outrageously Funny--and just Outrageous."
February	1960:	20,22.	"The World of Wars and Other Skirmishes."
March	1960:	58,60.	"Flynn-flam, etc."
April	1960:	36.	"Excursions and Side Trips: Seven Selected Adventures."
July	1960:	18,20.	"The Shadow and the Substances."
August	1960:	16,18.	"The Irish Scene: Dublin of the Uprising; a Village of Any Time."
September	1960:	36,40.	"Summer Leafing, Some of it Green."
October	1960:	45-46.	"Looking for Love? You'll Find it in the Bookstores."
November	1960:	51-52.	"Reading Fare: Deep-dish Humble Pie."
December	1960:	90-92.	"Lovely Lady and Lively Ghost."
March	1961:	48,50.	"The Way to Exercise is not Always Through Sitting Down and Reading."
April	1961:	40,42.	"There, at the bottom of the Pile: A Stimulating and Endearing One."
May	1961:	12,14.	"The One Perfect Mystery."
June	1961:	34,38.	"From Tabloids to Collette, to Yates, and on to a Bum Voyage."
July	1961:	28-29.	"Sparklers for July, Two Burn Brightly."

September 1961:	32,34.	"From Miller to Mitford, with a stop for a Norris."
October 1961:	54,56.	"Unforgettable Experiences."
November 1961:	73-74.	"The Story of the Lindbergh Case."
December 1961:	72-73.	"Clock without Hands Belongs in Yesterday's Ivory Tower."
January 1962:	133.	[No Title]
April 1962:	31-32.	"Something for Everyone, Including the Animal Kingdom."
May 1962:	33-34.	"A Couple of Blue Roses for the Library Garden."
June 1962:	64.	"Six Collections of Short Stories and a Lovely Novel."
July 1962:	129-30.	"The Pyramid, Other Monuments, and Needles in Haystacks."
September 1962:	62.	"A Magnificent Time and Its People."
December 1962:	40.	"Shudders: Quiet and Cumulative; Fine and Fascinating; and Others."

4. The Ladies Home Journal

Parker contributed only four essays to this magazine. They are interesting because the satirical portraits she first draws here receive fuller attention in her prose fiction.

July	1920:	4,88.	"Our Tuesday Club."
August	1920:	4,121.	"A Dinner Party Anthology."
September	1920:	32,194.	"A Summer Hotel Anthology."
October	1920:	37,124.	"The Education of Gloria."

5. The New York <u>Life</u> (1883-1936)

<u>Life</u> was a national magazine of humor. Parker's poetry and prose squibs appeared almost weekly from 1920 until 1927. Managing editor Thomas Masson wrote the first important biographical sketch of Parker in 1931.

A. Poetry

23 September	1920:	527.	"Our Own Home Talent."
18 November	1920:	902.	"I Hate Bores."
2 December	1920:	1039.	"With Best Wishes."
3 February	1921:	160.	"Invictus."
7 April	1921:	487.	"Song of the Open Country."
28 April	1921:	596.	"The Passionate Freudian to His Love."
5 May	1921:	636.	"I Hate Drama."
2 June	1921:	790.	"I Hate Parties."
30 June	1921:	933.	"Love Songs."
7 July	1921:	3.	"Idyl."
21 July	1921:	10.	"I Hate Movies."
28 July	1921:	8.	"To My Dog."
18 August	1921:	1.	"Absence."
15 September	1921:	3.	"Lyric."
6 October	1921:	3.	"Song for the First of the Month."
27 October	1921:	1.	"Fulfilment."
24 November	1921:	3.	"Lynn Fontanne."
8 December	1921:	7.	"To Marjorie Fambeau."
15 December	1921:	1.	"Christmas, 1921."
		3.	"Marilyn Miller."
22 December	1921:	12.	"I Hate Books."
12 January	1922:	1.	"Fragment."
19 January	1922:	12.	"Playing Safe."
		24.	"The Sheik."
26 January	1922:	22.	"The Flapper."
2 February	1922:	2.	"Chantey."
9 February	1922:	11.	"Moral Tales for the Young."
16 February	1922:	16-17.	"Life's Valentines."
2 March	1922:	4.	"Nocturne."
9 March	1922:	3.	"The Far-Sighted Muse."
		22.	"The Drab Heroine."
16 March	1922:	3.	"Paging Saint Patrick."
23 March	1922:	5.	"Mood."
		12.	"Triolets."
30 March	1922:	8.	"I Hate the Younger Set."
6 April	1922:	5.	"To Myrtilla, On Easter Day."
13 April	1922:	24.	"The Glad Girl."
		5.	"Rondeau Redouble."

27 April	1922:	3.	"Plea."
		24.	"The Boy Savant."
4 May	1922:	7.	"Moral Tales for the Young."
11 May	1922:	9.	"Poem in the American Manner."
18 May	1922:	1.	"Thoughts."
1 June	1922:	19.	"Fantasy."
		21.	"Renunciation."
22 June	1922:	1.	"Woodland Song."
		9.	"Rondeau."
29 June	1922:	1.	"Day Dreams."
		22.	"The Great Lover."
20 July	1922:	23.	"Folk Song."
27 July	1922:	23.	"Standardized Song Sheet for Get-Together Meetings."
17 August	1922:	10.	"I Hate Summer Resorts."
5 October	1922:	7.	"Song in a Minor Key."
19 October	1922:	25.	"Memories."
9 November	1922:	11.	"Promise."
4 January	1923:	13.	"One Perfect Rose."
1 March	1923:	7.	"Rondel."
23 March	1923:	24.	"The Western Hero."
29 March	1923:	8.	"Triolet."
19 April	1923:	9.	"Wanderlust."
3 May	1923:	9.	"Song."
10 May	1923:	8.	"I Hate Wives."
14 June	1923:	7.	"Finis."
21 June	1923:	9.	"Ballade of a Not Insupportable Loss."
15 November	1923:	8.	"I Hate Husbands."
3 January	1924:	12.	"Song of a Hopeful Heart."
31 January	1924:	3.	"Verses for a Certain Dog."
20 March	1924:	11.	"Song."
24 April	1924:	20.	"Song for an April Dusk."
26 June	1924:	12.	"Ballade at Thirty-Five."
7 August	1924:	3.	"Portrait of a Lady."
14 August	1924:	6.	"Rosemary."
18 September	1924:	3.	"Ballade of a Complete Flop."
2 October	1924:	9.	"Now At Liberty."
16 October	1924:	7.	"Folk Song."
23 October	1924:	20.	"Love Song."
13 November	1924:	12.	"I Hate College Boys."
27 November	1924:	7.	"Lullaby."
22 January	1925:	12.	"Song of Perfect Propriety."
26 February	1925:	15.	"Balto."
9 April	1925:	10.	"Biographies."
20 August	1925:	3.	"Wail."
8 April	1926:	11.	"Songs Just a Little Off Key."
19 August	1926:	9.	"Songs Slightly Tainted by Sex"
26 August	1926:	5.	"Neither Bloody Nor Bowed."
2 September	1926:	13.	"The Thin Edge."

9 September	1926:	5.	"Chant for Dark Hours."
30 September	1926:	13.	"The Leal."
7 October	1926:	8.	"Godspeed."
14 October	1926:	15.	"Faute de Mieux."
21 October	1926:	17.	"The Trusting Heart."
28 October	1926:	13.	"Fighting Words."
11 November	1926:	12.	"Inventory."
18 November	1926:	15.	"The Temptress."
2 December	1926:	28.	"For a Much Too Unfortunate Lady."
		45.	"Words of Comfort, To Be Scratched on a Mirror."
9 December	1926:	9.	"Pictures in the Smoke."
3 February	1927:	9.	"The Dramatists."
24 February	1927:	5.	"Partial Comfort."
24 March	1927:	13.	"The Accursed."
2 June	1927:	13.	"A Pig's-Eye View of Literature."
9 June	1927:	13.	"The Red Dress."
14 July	1927:	15.	"Story."
28 July	1927:	13.	"The Counsellor."
1 September	1927:	11.	"Ballade of a Well-Earned Weariness."
8 August	1930:	5.	"The False Friends."

B. Prose

2 September	1920:	428.	"Famous Last Words."
17 March	1921:	380.	"Words and Music."
24 March	1921:	433.	"A Resume of Any Mother's Conversation."
21 April	1921:	560.	"Sorry, The Line is Busy."
9 June	1921:	829.	"Things I Don't Want to Do Before I Die."
23 June	1921:	903.	"Active Depressants."
30 June	1921:	942.	"Where To Go Tonight."
7 July	1921:	6-7.	"Once More Mother Hubbard, As Told by F. Scott Fitzgerald."
14 July	1921:	11.	"The Bridge of Sighs."
18 August	1921:	25.	"The Illiterati."
25 August	1921:	1.	"Figures in American Folklore." [1]
		12.	"The Rocking Chair Talkers."
1 September	1921:	12.	"Figures in American Folklore." [2]
29 September	1921:	4.	"The Beauty Parlor Lizards."
10 November	1921:	20.	"The 'Howdy Neighbor' Club."
17 November	1921:	22.	Rev. of Norma Sheridan by Kathleen Norris.
1 December	1921:	18.	"A Christmas Fable."
12 January	1922:	3.	"Both Sides of the Footlights."
26 January	1922:	4.	"Formulae for the Great American Short Story." [1]
16 February	1922:	5.	"Formulae for the Great American Short Story." [2]
23 February	1922:	8.	"The Liars."
6 April	1922:	35.	"The Contents of the Easter Issue of Any Humorous

			Magazine."
4 May	1922:	8.	"At the Spring Academy."
25 May	1922:	10.	"An Open Letter to Our Burglars."
22 June	1922:	3,32.	"Good, Clean Sport."
21 September	1922:	22.	"The Aftermath of Vacation."
5 October	1922:	7.	"Things I Wonder About at the Theatre."
21 December	1922:	24,31.	"The Christmas Dinner: A Playlet of the Annual Family Reunion."
20 March	1924:	25.	"Can a Woman Combine Business and Home-Making?"
5 June	1924:	5.	"The Proud Parents at Graduation Ceremonies."
13 August	1924:	47.	"Greetings From Bay City."
28 August	1924:	9.	"Read What These Experts Have to Say about Bobbed Hair."
16 September	1924:	9.	"In the Throes: The Thoughts of An Author at Work."
7 July	1927:	9.	"Morning."
21 July	1927:	7-8.	"Week's End."
1 December	1927:	56.	"A Piece About Christmas."

6. McCalls

January	1928:	4.	"My Home Town."
February	1928:	8.	"The New York Type."
March	1928:	4.	"The Curtain Rises at 8:30 Sharp."
April	1928:	8.	"Spring Song."
May	1928:	8.	"Toward the Dog Days."

7. The New Yorker

Parker's prose fiction from this magazine is included in the section of short stories. Parker was named as one of the original editors by Harold Ross, but her editorial contributions were slight, according to Ross's wife Jane Grant.

A. Poetry

28 February	1925:	5.	"Cassandra Drops into Verse."
26 September	1925:	10.	"Rainy Night."
1 May	1926:	18.	"Song of the American Resident in France."
15 May	1926:	16.	"Rhyme of an Involuntary Violet."
25 September	1926:	21.	"Songs of a Markedly Personal Nature." [6 poems]
8 January	1927:	20.	"A Fairly Sad Story."
19 February	1927:	28.	"The Enemy."
5 March	1927:	26.	"To A Favorite Granddaughter."
12 March	1927:	28.	"Afternoon."
19 March	1927:	28.	"Songs Not Encumbered by Reticence." [3 poems]
26 March	1927:	26.	"The Second Oldest Story."
2 April	1927:	23.	"Swan Song."
9 April	1927:	31.	"Thought for a Sunshiny Morning."
23 April	1927:	27.	"Parable for a Certain Virgin."
2 July	1927:	26.	"Daylight Saving."
23 July	1927:	25.	"Frustration."
17 September	1927:	25.	"Bohemia."
12 November	1927:	28.	"Songs for the Nearest Harmonica." [4 poems]
7 January	1928:	21.	"Songs for the Nearest Harmonica." [5 poems]
26 May	1928:	20.	"Songs for the Nearest Harmonica." [6 poems]
18 June	1928:	22.	"To A Lady Who Must Write Verse."
4 May	1929:	22.	"Tombstones in the Starlight."
14 August	1929:	14.	"Little Words."
24 August	1929:	14.	"The Evening Primrose."
			"If It Be Not Fair."
14 December	1929:	27.	"The Beloved Ladies, For Philip Barry." [4 poems]
26 March	1938:	20.	"Threat to a Fickle Lady."
4 March	1944:	22.	"War Song."

B. Incidental Prose

21 February	1925:	13-14.	"The Theatre."
28 February	1925:	13.	"The Theatre."
		15-16.	"A Certain Lady."
19 September	1925:	35.	"Why Not She-Fiends."
7 July	1928:	28-30.	"G. B. S., Practically in Person."
1 September	1928:	28-32.	"Out of the Silence."
30 November	1929:	28-31.	"The Artist's Reward."

C. Drama Reviews
[Substituting for Robert Benchley]

21 February	1931:	25-26,28.	"Kindly Accept Substitutes."
28 February	1931:	22-23.	"In, Or Around Desperate Straits."
7 March	1931:	33-34.	"Willow, Willow, Waley."
14 March	1931:	30,32,36,38.	"Just Around Pooh Corner."
21 March	1931:	28,30,32,34.	"No More Fun."
28 March	1931:	30-32,34.	"A Very Dull Piece."
4 April	1931:	32,34.	"A Few Minutes of Your Time."
11 April	1931:	30,32.	"Valedictory"

D. "Constant Reader" Book Reviews

1 October	1927:	86-89.	"The Highly Recurrent Mr. Hamilton--Al Smith, and How He Grew--Bad News of May Sinclair."
8 October	1927:	94-97.	"Mr. Colby's Second Novel--The Private Papers of the Dead--The Philosopher Takes a Long Look at Himself."
15 October	1927:	105-09.	"An American Du Barry--A Biography of Henry Ward Beecher."
22 October	1927:	98-101.	"Re-enter Margot Asquith--Something Young--A Masterpiece from the French.
29 October	1927:	92-95.	"A Book of Great Short Stories--Something About Cabell."
5 November	1927:	90-92.	"The Professor Goes in for Sweetness and Light--Short Stories from One Who Knows How to Do Them--Sketches, Mostly Unpleasant--a Biography of a Much-talked About Lady."
12 November	1927:	112-13.	"Mr. Morely Capers on a Toadstool--Mr. Milne Grows to be Six."

19 November 1927: 116-17. "Adam and Eve and Lilith and Epigrams--Something More
                                    About Cabell."
26 November 1927: 04-06. "Madame Glynn Lectures on 'It,' with Illustrations."
 3 December 1927: 22-23. "The Most Popular Reading Matter."
10 December 1927: 22-24. "The Socialist Looks at Literature--A Lyricist Looks at His
                                    Neighbors."
17 December 1927: 109-11. "The Short Story, Through a Couple of Ages."
31 December 1927: 51-53. "Mrs. Post Enlarges on Etiquette."
 7 January   1928: 77-79. "More Troubles for Colonel Charles A. Lindbergh."
14 January   1928: 69-71. "Poor, Immortal Isadora."
28 January   1928: 75-77. "Re-enter Mrs. Hurst, Followed by Mr. Tarkington."
 4 February 1928: 74-77. "A Good Novel, and a Great Story."
11 February 1928: 78-80. "Literary Rotarians."
18 February 1928: 76-79. "Excuse It, Please."
25 February 1928: 79-81. "Our Lady of the Loud-speaker."
10 March   1928: 81-83. "Unfinished Endeavors."
17 March   1928: 102-03. "The Complete Bungler."
24 March   1928: 93-94. "Ethereal Mildness."
31 March   1928: 97-100. "A Very Dull Article, Indeed."
 7 April   1928: 107-07. "Mr. Lewis Lays It on with a Trowel."
14 April   1928: 97-100. "Mrs. Norris and the Beast."
21 April   1928: 104-07. "These Much Too Charming People."
19 May   1928: 92-94. "Hard-Boiled Virgins are Faithful Lovers."
26 May   1928: 104-06. "Mr. See Sees it Through."
25 August   1928: 60-62. "Back to the Book Shelf."
15 September 1928: 100-03. [Untitled]
29 September 1928: 86-88. "How it Feels to be One Hundred and Forty-Six."
20 October   1928: 98-99. "Far From Well."
17 November 1928: 108-10. "Wallflower's Lament."
16 March   1929: 106-07. "And Again, Mr. Sinclair Lewis."
27 April   1929: 104-06. "Hero Worship."
24 January   1931: 62-64. "Home is the Sailor."
31 January   1931: 57-59. "Mr. Vanderbilt, and Other Entertainers."
21 February 1931: 56-58. "Kiss and Tellegen."
14 March   1931: 78-82. "Two Lives and Some Letters."
 4 April   1931: 84-86. "Collapse of a High Project."
25 Aprl   1931: 91-93. "Oh, Look--Two Good Books."
30 May   1931: 64-66. "Words, Words, Words."
25 July   1931: 55-57. "The Grandmother of the Aunt of the Gardener."
10 October   1931: 72-73. "Sex Marks the Spot."
18 March   1933: 64-66. "Not Even Funny."

8. The Saturday Evening Post

A. Long Articles

22 May	1920: 8-9,108,111.	"As the Spirit Moves."
20 August	1921: 10-11,66,68.	"Apartment House Anthology."
17 June	1922: 13,42.	"Men I'm Not Married To."
21 October	1922: 10,25-26.	"Our Own Crowd."
12 April	1923: 14,156.	"Professional Youth."
1 September	1923: 10-11,38,41.	"You Must Come See Us."

B. Prose Squibs in "Short Turns and Encores"

29 July	1922: 16.	"On Any Hotel Porch."
12 August	1922: 24.	"Over the Teacups."
26 August	1922: 24.	"The Justly Proud Mothers."
2 September	1922: 24.	"Speaking of Husbands."
9 September	1922: 28.	"See Any Hat Shop."
16 September	1922: 26,86.	"Popular Short Stories."
6 January	1923: 24.	"The Overweight Alibis."
24 February	1923: 26.	"The World's Dullest Anecdotes."
7 April	1923: 141.	"Safe Remarks for Use in Times of Stress."
21 April	1923: 109.	"Things That Every Woman Believes."

C. Poetry

29 July	1922: 16.	"Rosemary" [as Helen Wells]
	46.	"Song"
19 August	1922: 22.	"Grandfather Said It"
30 September	1922: 105.	"Somewhat Delayed Spring Song."
7 October	1922: 28.	"Sonnet"
14 October	1922: 30.	"To A Lady"
11 November	1922: 84.	"Rondeau"
18 November	1922: 26.	"Song of the Conventions."
	93.	"Song"
27 January	1923: 24.	"Ballade of Understandable Ambitions"
24 February	1923: 75.	"Song of a Contented Heart"
3 March	1923: 28.	"Song of the Wilderness"
21 April	1923: 109.	"Triolet"
12 May	1923: 181.	"Paean"
19 May	1923: 162.	"Song"
9 June	1923: 28.	"And Oblige"
16 June	1923: 105.	"Triolet"

9. Vanity Fair

Both Vanity Fair and Vogue were part of the large Conde Nast publishing empire. Parker began her publishing career with Vogue in 1914.

A. Poetry

September	1915:	32.	"Any Porch"
January	1916:	118.	"The Bridge Fiend"
June	1916:	126.	"A Musical Comedy Thought"
August	1916:	61.	"Women: A Hate Song"
October	1916:	120.	"The Gunman and the Debutante"
February	1917:	65.	"Men: A Hate Song"
May	1917:	64.	"Actresses: A Hate Song"
August	1917:	39.	"Relatives: A Hate Song"
December	1917:	83.	"Slackers: A Hate Song"
October	1917:	46.	"Bohemians: A Hate Song"
December	1918:	48.	"Oh, Look!--I Can Do It Too"
May	1919:	6,8.	"Our Office" [A Hate Song]
July	1919:	37.	"Actors: A Hate Song"
February	1926:	44.	"The Trifler"; "Paths"
March	1926:	70.	"I Know I Have Been the Happiest"
April	1926:	64.	"Meeting Place"; "The Small Hours"
August	1926:	44.	"A Very Short Song"
September	1926:	58.	"A Portrait"
October	1926:	73.	"The New Love"
November	1926:	83.	"The Immortals"

B. Prose

October	1916:	51,122.	"Why I Haven't Married: Sketches of My Seven Deadly Suitors."
December	1916:	83.	"The Christmas Magazines and the Inevitable Story of the Snowbound Train."
March	1918:	100b.	"The Fakirs--and Their Dance: Shattering a Few Time Honored Illusions About Artists."
April	1918:	57,90.	"Are You a Glossy?"
		69,97.	"A Succession of Musical Comedies: The Innocent Diversions of a Tired Business Woman."
May	1918:	58,89.	"How to Know the Glossies.
		49.	"The New Order of Musical Comedies: Helpful Hints on What to do with Your Left-Over Farces."
June	1918:	47,84.	"The Dramas That Gloom in the Spring."
		57,88.	"If I Were A Movie Manager."
July	1918:	29,81.	"Mortality in the Drama."

August	1918:	29,66.	"The Star Spangled Drama."
September	1918:	23.	"Are You A Glossy?"
		46,86.	"Is Your Little Girl Safe?"
October	1918:	56,104.	"The Fall Crop of War Plays."
November	1918:	23.	"The Seven Who Were Not Hanged."
		53,98.	"The New Plays."
December	1918:	39,84.	"The New Plays."
January	1919:	33,70.	"Plays of War and Peace."
February	1919:	39,94.	"The Midwinter Plays."
March	1919:	36,92.	"All's Quiet Along the Rialto."
April	1919:	41,100.	"The New Plays."
May	1919:	41,94.	"Signs of Spring in the Theatre.
		21.	"So, This is New York."
June	1919:	41,100.	"The New Plays."
		47,94.	"Good Souls."
July	1919:	33.	"The Close of a Perfect Season."
August	1919:	23,66.	"The First Shows of Summer."
September	1919:	29,98.	"Trying It on the Dog-days."
October	1919:	41,112.	"The New Plays--If Any."
November	1919:	37,84.	"The Union Forever."
December	1919:	60-61.	"On the Trail of a Wife."
		37,108-10.	"The First One Hundred Plays are the Hardest."
January	1920:	62-63.	"Our Great American Sport."
		39,94.	"The Oriental Drama."
February	1920:	41,102.	"The Anglo-American Drama."
March	1920:	41,128.	"Optimism and the Drama."
		68-69.	"The Throes of First Love."
January	1927:	71.	"The Paris that keeps Out of the Papers."
October	1928:	61.	"Long Distance."
February	1934:	27,57.	"A Valentine for Mr. Woollcott."

C. Under the pen name "Helen Wells"

October	1918:	51.	"Fun--For the Boys on Leave."
January	1919:	39.	"They Won the War."
February	1919:	41.	"It All Comes Under the Head of Peace."
May	1919:	47,94.	"What is Worse than a House Party?"
July	1919:	20.	"Afternoons in Bohemia."
August	1919:	33.	"How To Write Musical Comedy Lyrics."
September	1919:	33,110.	"The Autobiography of Any Movie Actress."
October	1919:	47,118.	"The Actors' Demands."
November	1919:	47,118.	"The Life Beautiful."
December	1919:	43,116.	"Is There a Humorist in the House?"
January	1920:	59.	"Who's Who in the Audience?"
February	1920:	49.	"The Non-Professional Critics."

10. <u>Vogue</u>

15 November 1916: 128.   "The Lady in Back."
15 February 1917: 54-55.   "Love Fashion, Love Her Dog."
15 April   1917: 54,129. "Interior Desecration."
 1 June   1917: 56,138. "Life on a Permanent Wave."
15 June   1917: 36-37.   "Here Comes the Groom."
15 October   1917: 51,144. "Each Thought a Purl, Each Purl a Prayer."
15 November 1917: 57,124. "When You Have Come to the End of a Perfect Day."

3. Secondary Bibliography

Writing about the life of Dorothy Parker inevitably leads to writing about her work. The reverse is also generally true. Since a distinction between biographical and critical writing is especially difficult to make, I have listed published writing about Parker year by year. The citations are listed alphabetically by authors' names under each year, and the entire bibliography is numbered consistently. The annotations of these sources will distinguish the particular focus of the writer.

The biographical sources listed below consist of books, articles, chapters in books, and anecdotes. The three book-length biographies are each followed by a list of reviews. I have not included those reviews that give only bibliographic information. John Keats's You Might As Well Live [97] is both a life and times biography. It appeared in 1970, the same year that a selection of Parker's New Yorker book reviews was published under the title Constant Reader [A.20], so many of these reviews criticize both books. There really is no consensus from the reviewers about Keats's book. Kenneth Tynan thought the book was a mixture of nonsense and sentimentality: by writing both a history and a biography, Keats had succeeded in doing neither. Yet Richard Schickel and Edward Weeks maintained that Keats was as sympathetic as he could have been.

There was no substantial biographical writing about Parker for the next sixteen years. However, Parker appeared in dozens of autobiographies and memoirs, like Ruth Gordon's My Side [116], where there is a brief portrait of Parker holding court in her bedroom at the Swope estate, or Harold Clurman's All People are Famous [105] in which he claims the Parker he knew was always on the verge of hysteria while The Ladies of the Corridor was in preparation.

Although Leslie Frewin's biography The Late Mrs. Dorothy Parker [179] was published in England in 1986, it appeared in America at about the same time as Marion Meade's What Fresh Hell Is This? in 1988 [186]. No reviewer gave Frewin's book any higher praise than a half-hearted OK. Most were sympathetic with Frewin over the difficulty of his chosen subject, but the vast majority agreed with Maureen Freely: "What Frewin has done to poor Dorothy Parker in the name of popular biography is to take every opportunity to make her look silly, stupid, and helpless."

After reading Meade's biography, one can see that Parker needed no help in appearing silly and helpless, but she was never stupid. John Updike called Meade's biography shoddy, and Alden Whitman rated it as uneven. But as they had done with Frewin, reviewers sympathized with Meade about the difficulty of her subject. As Meade's biography shows, Parker's life was one of emotional and financial excesses, and as Michiko Kakutani aptly wrote in his review, a string of very catchy and, finally, very unpleasant anecdotes. David Wright was disappointed in Meade's conclusions because the facts about Parker's life that Meade so adequately documents reveal a person whom Meade makes nice, but who was not always so very nice. Shena MacKay believed Meade had under-emphasized Parker's talents just as Frewin and Keats had over-emphasized them. More biographies about Parker will be written, and any further biographer will do well to heed Hamlin Hill's advice: "We need a biography of Parker that explores that paradox [i.e., Dorothy Rothschild Parker Campbell and "Mrs. Parker"] and the literature it produced, and the mixed and tormented motives which produce it."

There is a surprisingly small body of good criticism about Parker's work. (Reviews of her books appear after their citations in Chapter 2.) Mark Van Doren's essay "Dorothy Parker" [13] is the first, truly critical analysis, and he pointed out that a major problems in writing about her work is distinguishing between the writer one reads and the personality one hears about. His criticism about Parker's poetry is harsh, and he believed Parker's reputation would rest upon the prose fiction. He maintained that her work through 1934 showed "great promise" but he was still awaiting a major accomplishment. And that has become a constant strain in criticism about Parker, i. e., she has been criticized for what she did not write.

Fred Millet's brief analysis [46] in 1944 praised her technical skill in poetry--as did William Somerset Maugham [45] in her prose--but Millet found Parker's politics distasteful. William Shanahan [92] praised Parker's prose as very fine but argued that she hadn't produced enough ever to have more than a cult following. The same sentiment was expressed by Wilfred Sheed [133] who argued that Parker, in whom he had seen a major talent, had wasted her gifts and did not produce anything of a lasting value. After Keats had written his biography, he too echoed the thought that the personality had been the ruin of the talent [112], just as Richard Lauterbach had argued 29 years earlier [44].

Aside from those critics who didn't like Parker's politics or who lamented about what she should have done, Parker's other critics have been especially lavish in their praise of her talent as a writer. The most important critical study is Arthur Kinney's Dorothy Parker [131]. Kinney is the only critic who has looked at Parker's entire body of work. He labeled her early essays, light verse, and drama as "apprentice work," necessary for her major accomplishments in poetry, prose fiction, and criticism. He calls her the best epigrammatic poet of this century in America, and concluded that "no matter where we come upon her, she leads us back to the best of her poetry, fiction, and criticism and outward to the rest" (p. 137).

One pleasant problem critics have had in writing about Parker's work is deciding whether she should be seen as a humorist--as she was in the 1920's--a satirist, or even a moralist. The terms are not mutually exclusive and the fact that any one of them may be applied shows the large scope of Parker's creativity and the appeal it has. For example, Lynn Bloom [146] thinks that Parker's prose fiction has an over-riding moral cast, but Norris Yates [74] argues that Parker is the kind of satirist who doesn't say how to change the conditions she abhors so much. Margaret Lawrence [21] was one of the first critics to argue that Parker was a sentimentalist, hence her melancholy. James Gray [49] argues for Parker's being classified as a satirist, but instead of seeing melancholy, Gray writes that something positive emerges from the whole.

In the massive amount of writing about American humor, four overviews [10, 85, 99, 126] have been included because they are excellent studies with more than passing reference to Parker and her humor. A major theme of these books is that the 1920s was a major turning point for American humor, and Parker was instrumental in helping to make the change from rural and sentimental humor to urban and cynical humor. Especially good is Allen Churchill's The Literary Decade [99], showing how in their struggle to overcome the genteel tradition, humorous writers had to develop a "smarty" voice and cynical attitude. Critics of Parker's stories always note how important she was in developing America's city voice, especially in her choice of settings.

The evaluation of Parker's poetry depends upon which poems critics have read. Morris Bishop [153] says her light verse is as good as any other, but as Ruthmarie Mitsch [180] argues, Parker's "Iseult of Brittany" is certainly more than light verse. A common characteristic of writing like Mitsch's is a call for a re-evaluation of Parker's work; for another call to re-read Parker, see Bette Richart [69].

The best criticism, and probably the most enlightening way to see Parker's work, has come from the feminist critics. Susanne Bunkers [128] argues that Parker practiced feminism before it was defined as we know it after 1970. The earliest of these feminist writers is Marjnia Farnham [51] who cites Parker's poetry and prose as evidence for the high standards women had set for themselves by 1947. Nora Ephron [103] also argues that Parker was a spokesperson for women, but Ephron fails to explain how. Essays like Maureen Lajoy's [119] and Nancy Walker's [152] argue that "humor" directed against women--through stereotypes by men and from women who accept the stereotypes--is not funny. They use Parker's and others' writing as examples of these stereotypes, but argue that Parker shows only what is, and not what should be, except by implication. Parker's talent was in attacking the stereotypes by not accepting them, according to Emily Toth [151]. Finally Nancy Walker [160] makes clear that the ideal attitude and voice towards the stereotypes should be that of Parker's in her poem "Indian Summer": "And if you do not like me so / To hell, my love, with you."

1922

1. Woollcott, Alexander. "The "'Chauve-Souris.'" <u>Shouts and Murmurs: Echoes of a Thousand and One First Nights</u>. New York: The Century Co., 1922. 247-53.

   The Algonquin Round Table members enacted their own revue called <u>No Siree!</u> the title parodying the very popular Russian entertainment called the "Chauve-Souris." Woollcott explains that the Russian revue was "singers and dancers and clowns who used to contribute to a midnight frolic they enjoyed giving behind closed doors after theatre time at the little Bat Restaurant in Moscow" (247). Instead of frolicking in the Algonquin's Rose Room, the Round Table members frolicked on stage.

1923

2. McMein, Neysa. "The Woman Who is a Design." <u>Arts and Decoration</u> October 1923: 14-15.

   McMein describes in detail what she means by "design": women who are perfect in linear beauty and proportion. She wrote that only about five per cent of all women are a design; she painted a portrait of Parker whose physical beauty made her a perfect design.

3. Van Doren, Carl. "Day In and Day Out." <u>Century</u> 107 (December 1923): 308-15.

   A popular analysis of four Manhattan wits--F. P. A., Christopher Morley, Don Marquis, and Heywood Broun. Through their varied approaches, these "column-conductors, closely as they fit their times, continue a tradition which goes back to one of the earliest moments in the history of human fun--the moment when cities began to demand of their wits more edged, more sophisticated, more varied, and more continuous entertainment than had been demanded among the farms and villages." Parker was a frequent contributor to F. P. A.'s column "the Conning Tower." And F. P. A. was instrumental in establishing her reputation.

1924

4. Woollcott, Alexander. "Neysa McMein." <u>Enchanted Aisles</u>. New York: G. P. Putnam's Sons, 1924. 33-38.

   Woollcott describes the life of the creative artist. McMein's studio was frequented by the Algonquin Round Table members who whiled afternoons away there. According to Woollcott, "If you loiter in Neysa McMein's studio, the world will drift in and out." (37) One should also see his essay "The Passing of the Thanatopsis," where Woollcott predicts the end of the poker club frequented by Round Table members (242-51).

1926

5. Hemingway, Ernest. "To A Tragic Poetess." 88 Poems. Ed. Nicholas Georgianis. New York: Harcourt, Brace, Jovanovich, 1979. 88-89.

Hemingway's poem shows the disgust he felt, not towards Parker, but towards her antics and melodramatic self-pitying. One should also read poem number 66, "Little drops of grain alcohol," where Hemingway mocks Parker's and Benchely's alcoholism (86).

1927

6. Wilson, Edmund. "The Muses Out of Work." The New Republic 11 May 1927: 319-21.

Wilson's early praise of Parker remained high throughout his life. In this essay he wrote "But I believe that, if we admire, as it is fashionable to do, the light verse of Prior and Gay, we should admire Miss Parker also . . . her wit is the wit of her time and place; but it is often as cleanly economic at the same time that it is as flatly brutal as the wit of the age of Pope; and, within its scope, it is a criticism of life. It has its roots in contemporary reality, and that is what I am pleading for in poetry." (321)

1928

7. Jaffray, Norman R. "To A Little Lady." Life 19 May 1928: 32

A poem parodying Parker's own poetry. It is interesting for its view of Parker's poetry by one of her contemporary humorists. Jaffray also parodies her prose in a squib, "Two Dorothy Parker Fans Converse": Life 26 January 1928: 25.

8. Lardner, Ring. "Mr. Lardner's Christmas List." Life 7 December 1928: 27.

Lardner lists in verse the Round Table members whom he will not buy presents for. An especially good brief portrait of Lardner by John Wheeler appeared in The Reader's Digest October 1966: 113-117.

1929

9. Marks, Jeannette. Thirteen Days. New York: M. Albert and Charles Boni, 1929.

Dorothy Parker appears as especially courageous in this account of the international protest in Boston against the execution of Sacco and Vanzetti.

10. Masson, Thomas L. "Dorothy Parker." Our American Humorists, 1931; Freeport, NY: Books for Libraries Press, 1966. 276-84.

A non-critical look at Parker's life when Masson was managing editor of the old

New York <u>Life</u> magazine. Masson maintained that getting Parker "to write anything is one of the most hazardous sports in the world." (277) Masson was the first of a long list of authors who maintained that "No matter what anybody writes about Dorothy Parker, he will be wrong." (281)

1934

11. Dialist. "Radio Dries Up Originality." The New York <u>Evening Post</u> 9 March 1934.

A harsh review of Parker's second radio broadcast, because she re-read "The Waltz" as she had done on her first radio appearance on Woollcott's radio show "The Town Crier."

12. "Guests' Aiding Strike Beaten at the Waldorf; Fists, Bon Mots Fly in Empire Room Fracas." The New York <u>Times</u> 7 February 1934: 1, 11.

Parker, Benchley, and Woollcott aided a waiters' strike against management by leading moral support and wit.

13. Van Doren, Mark. "Dorothy Parker." <u>English Journal</u> September 1934: 535-43.

The first truly critical examination of Parker as an author. Van Doren did not like her poetry: "She may please many people at the moment, but considering what English poetry can be and has been there is not the slightest chance, unless she set out deliberately to improve her product, that she will be numbered among the good. The bulk of her poetry is thin and voiceless, without any accent or undertone suggesting complexity." (539) Her stories "by teaching us how to hate the vices which are really evil, the vices of hypocrisy and coldness, have a salutary, a cleansing power; and I suspect that Mrs. Parker is nowhere more valuable than she is in these contemptuous pages." (542)

14. Woollcott, Alexander. "Our Mrs. Parker." <u>While Rome Burns</u>. New York: The Viking Press, 1934. 142-52.

The single-most important biographical and critical assessment of Parker between 1916 and 1934. Woollcott maintains that the best portrait of Parker is given in the poetry because it is "an incomparable portrait of her done by herself . . . her every lyric line is autobiographical." (145) He offers his famous evaluation of the conflicts one finds in Parker: "The outward social manner of Dorothy Parker is one calculated to confuse the unwary and unnerve even those most addicted to the incomparable boon of her company. You see, she is so odd a blend of Little Nell and Lady Macbeth. It is not so much the familiar phenomenon of a hand of steel in a velvet glove as a lacy sleeve with a bottle of vitriol concealed in its folds. " (148-49)

1935

15. Adams, Franklin P. <u>The Diary of Our Own Samuel Pepys</u>. 2 vols. New York:

Simon and Schuster, 1935.

In addition to his daily column "The Conning Tower," Adams published weekly his <u>Diary</u>, imitating the style and tone of Pepys. This collection is certainly not complete, but it was a selection he made himself. The anecdotes and quotes about and by Parker and other members of the Round Table make fascinating browsing. The index to the volumes is complete so one can easily find individual members Adams quoted or wrote about.

16. Emerson, Dorothy. "Poetry Corner." <u>Scholastic</u> 23 March 1935: 5.

Scholastic included four articles with selections of Parker's poetry and prose. The evaluations Emerson offers are most valuable because they show reactions to Parker while she was a best-selling author. See also 23 May 1936: 9; 13 March 1937: 11; and, 19 March 1938: 5.

17. Hoyt. Nancy. <u>Elinor Wylie: The Portrait of an Unknown Lady</u>. Indianapolis: The Bobbs-Merrill Company, 1935.

According to this brief portrait of Parker's life from 1922 until 1928, Wylie allowed Parker to work in her study. Parker was unfailing a pleasure to be around, especially when she had a "new best beau," which was apparently quite often.

1936

18. Bradley, Scully. "Our Native Humor." <u>North American Review</u> 242.2 (Winter 1936-37): 351-62.

Old American humor presented the writer as a perfect fool. New American humor, especially after World War I with a setting in the city, presented the writer as a perfect neurotic.

19. Dayton, Dorothy. "Dorothy Parker." <u>Mademoiselle</u> March 1936: 18, 47-50.

In spite of its unintentional sexism, Dayton's analysis offers a valuable view of Parker from a 1936 perspective: "But as for Dorothy Parker, the Great Enigma, I say nonsense. I think that she merely is a woman who was able to indulge her moods a little more freely than most women can afford to, who had no patience with hypocrisy and bunk, who said what other people stop at thinking--except that she said it incomparably better--and who wanted precisely what nearly every woman wants." (50)

20. Eastman, Max. <u>Enjoyment of Laughter</u>. New York: Simon and Schuster, 1936.

Parker is quoted on humor, though Eastman does not cite the source: "I don't think that superiority idea is true at all. The funny people you like best are ones you laugh <u>with</u>. There's Benchley, for instance. You live through his troubles with him--they are your own troubles--and that is why you enjoy them so particularly. A humorist, I think, is just balancing on the edge of the dumps." (331) There is a charcoal sketch of Parker by Peggy Barton.

21. Lawrence, Margaret. "Little Girl Pals." The School of Feminity, 1936; Port Washington, NY: Kennicut Press, 1966. 159-180.

Lawrence writes that Parker was "a little girl pal gone professionally critical and professionally witty. She is a Nell Gwyn columnist a with a dash of Vashti added." (173) Parker was a "persistent 'yapper'" because she was, basically, a sentimentalist. Hence, cynicism was the best way to keep feeling always at bay.

22. Sherwood, Robert. "The Lunts." Stage 14 May 1936: 36-38.

Much interested in meeting Parker, the Lunts asked Sherwood to bring her to tea. Sherwood was not sure about the meeting, but he concluded that "I can report only that . . . nothing much happened." (38)

1937

23. Bright, John. "Orchid for Dorothy Parker." New Masses 7 December 1927: 17.

A fellow screenwriter and political activist applauds Parker's efforts: "Her pioneering in the Hollywood Anti-Nazi League, the Motion Picture Artists' Committee for Spain (about to initiate an international drive for Christmas toys and milk for Spanish children) excite us and cheer us forward."

24. DeVoto, Bernard. "The Lineage of Eustace Tilly." The Saturday Review of Literature 25 September 1937: 3-4, 20.

The New Yorker was a culmination of the new attitude of writers and was important because there were no ready-made guidelines for humorists to follow. Eustace Tilly is the cartoon character who appeared on the cover of the first issue of the New Yorker and who appears on anniversary issues.

25. Loggins, Vernon. I Hear America . . . American Literature Since 1900. New York: Thomas Y. Crowell, 1937.

After a brief bibliography, Loggins's assessment of Parker was that she was in a happy and favorable position in American letters: She was both popular and important.

26. Prescott, Orville. "A Lament for the Living." Cue 10 July 1937: 6-7, 34-35.

Who was Parker in 1937? According to Prescott, she was a "bundle of contradictions from start to finish; Mrs. Parker's most conspicuous paradox is her nearly complete lack of ambition combined with one of the greatest literary talents in America." (34) But like other writers, Prescott laments "But there must be a good many who would be glad to offer her a rose (perfect if possible) if only she would return to New York and to the writing of more verses and short stories of the inimitable Parker brand." (35)

27. Woollcott, Alexander. "An Afterword on Dorothy Parker." Woollcott's Second Reader New York: The Viking Press, 1937. 634-35.

Woollcott reprinted three of Parker's stories in his second reader: "The Little Hours," "The Waltz," and "Arrangement in Black and White." He offered this evaluation: "Seemingly Mrs. Parker is at ease only in disparagement, and most of her sketches--"Arrangement in Black and White," for example--are forms of malediction, kin across the years to the antique and satisfying practice of making wax images and then sticking pins into them."

1938

28. "America's Wittiest Woman . . . Goes Hollywood and Turns Anti-Nazi." Look 20 December 1938: 48-49.

Five photographs of Parker in Hollywood and a recounting of the basic facts of her life. The article cites Parker's $5,200 weekly salary.

29. Broun, Heywood. "It Seems to Me." The New York World Telegram 26 January 1938.

Broun, Parker's long-time friend and renowned Socialist, cites Parker's New Masses writing as her "important contribution to the ever current discussion of humor, its uses and abuses."

30. Case, Frank. "That Round Table." Tales of a Wayside Inn. New York: Frederick A. Stokes, 1938. 57-81.

An appreciative account of the Round Table and its members. Of Parker, Case wrote that "she would simply sit, now and then saying something at which the others would laugh and that was the end of that." Still, Parker's remarks were influential in their ability to "dress and fashion the conversation of a whole nation." By 1938, the Round Table had faded into a "pleasant and mellow" memory for Case.

31. Lewis, Therese. "Ten on the Isle." Town and Country August 1938: 30-33, 70.

A highly informative but objective account of Neshobe Island, the island in Vermont that Rounds Table members frequented. The only real requirement for being invited was that one must not be boorish. Parker was a frequent guest who constantly forgot to pay her dues.

32. "Life Goes to a Party." Life 17 January 1938: 38-39.

Although there is little that is new in this article, the pictures of Parker and Campbell at a Greenwich Village New Year's Eve party are interesting.

1939

33. "An Afterword on Dorothy Parker." Enough Rope. New York: Pocketbooks Incorporated, 1939.

This first paper-back edition of Enough Rope contains an anonymous afterword that predicts that Parker will hold the same rank in the history of literature as Samuel Johnson.

34. Gibbs, Woollcott. 'Big Nemo, I." New Yorker 18 March 1939: 24-29; "Big Nemo, II." New Yorker 25 March 1939: 22-27; "Big Nemo, III." New Yorker 1 April 1939: 22-27.

This three-part Profile of Woollcott constantly cites Parker with a repeated emphasis upon her fondness for the man.

35. "People." Time 16 January 1939: 55.

Parker's political activities were a matter of national interest. She's pictured atop a piano, crying while she solicits fund for the Spanish Loyalists: "I don't see how you can help being unhappy now. The humorist has never been happy, anyhow. Today he's whistling past worse graveyards to worse tunes. . . .If you had seen what I saw in Spain, you'd be serious too. And you'd be up on this piano, trying to help those people."

36. "U.S. Citizens Disagree Violently Over U.S. Intervention in Spain." Life 30 January 1939: 10.

Life has a picture of Parker weeping for Spanish Loyalists when neutrality was the official policy of the United States towards the Spanish Civil War. According to the article, 51% of Americans favored the Loyalist cause, but it doesn't report statistics on attitudes towards intervention.

37. Case, Frank. Do Not Disturb. New York: Frederick A. Stokes, 1940.

According to the manager and, later, the owner of the Algonquin Hotel, Parker was smarter than any of the men who constantly surrounded her.

1941

38. Aldrich, R. "Dorothy Parker: A Parody." Prairie Schooner 15 (1941): 208-10.

Aldrich imitates what he considers an excellent prose style. There is not an extended discussion of Parker's style.

39. Daniels, Earl. <u>The Art of Reading Poetry</u>. New York: Farrar and Rinehart, Inc., 1941.

   Daniels is one of the first critics to cite Parker's poetry as poetry, rather than as newspaper fluff. He writes an extended analysis of Parker's poem "The Actress."

1944

40. Adams, J. Donald. "Speaking of Books." The New York <u>Times Book Review</u> 4 June 1944: 4; and, 11 June 1944: 2.

   Adams reacts to Wilson's excessive lamenting about loss in "A Toast and a Tear for Dorothy Parker." The next week Adams writes that he "cannot share [Wilson's] admiration, as least in so far as it includes the story's psychology; in its purely technical competence, ["The Lovely Leave"] is, like nearly everything else in the volume, highly skilled." Of her poetry, Adams writes "Mrs. Parker, of course, brings to her restatements of the old plaint the twist and turns of posture which were peculiar to the time in which she wrote them."

41. Adams, Franklin P. Foreword. <u>The Collected Stories of Dorothy Parker</u>. New York: Random House, 1944. vii-ix.

   "It seems foolish of me to write a foreword to the stories, the satires, the concentrated hatreds of stupidity, pretentiousness, and the hypocrisy contained in this volume. Nobody can write such ironic things unless he has a deep sense of injustice--injustice to those members of the human race who are victims of the stupid, the pretentious, and the hypocritical. These victims, my mathematics assures me, are in the majority. Therefore Dorothy Parker likes more people than she hates. . . . It occurs to me, for the first time, that one who hated the same things, and would have hated the same persons, was Abraham Lincoln." (viii)

42. Crowinshield, Frank. "Crowinshield in the Cub's Den." <u>Vogue</u> 15 September 1944: 162-63, 197-201.

   Parker's former boss, who had to fire her from <u>Vanity Fair</u>, recalled that she, Benchley, and Sherwood made the editorial office a "combined club, vocal studio, crap game, dance-hall, sleeping lounge, and snack bar" rather than an office where "interminable galley-proofs [had to be] read." (163) In addition to commenting upon her physical beauty and quick mind, Crowinshield wrote that with "all her iconoclastic inclinations, she was, and still is, capable of extraordinary kindness, generosity, and loyalty." (198)

43. Kaufman, Beatrice and Joseph Hennessey, eds. <u>The Letters of Alexander Woollcott</u>. New York: The Viking Press, 1944.

   Letters to Parker and Alan Campbell are especially interesting for chatty details of daily life.

44. Lauterbach, Richard E. "The Legend of Dorothy Parker." Esquire October 1944: 93, 139-44.

Although this is not an intimate account of Parker's life, Lauterbach does give an astute analysis of how Parker's reputation as a wit was seriously damaging her development as a writer. It is one of the best accounts of Parker's reputation during her life; it is reprinted in the Appendix.

45. Maugham, William Somerset. Introduction. The Portable Dorothy Parker. New York: The Viking Press, 1944.

Maugham likes Parker's poetry, but he admits he knows little about the techniques of it. He does offer valuable criticism of her fiction. One needs to read the entire piece; in the 1973 re-issue, this introduction was abbreviated.

46. Millet, Fred B. Contemporary American Authors. New York: Harcourt, 1944.

Millet praises Parker's skill in creating anti-climax in her stories, but he wishes she would quit politics and write more.

47. Wilson, Edmund. "A Toast and a Tear for Dorothy Parker." Rev. of Dorothy Parker. New Yorker 20 May 1944: 67-68.

Parker "is not Emily Bronte or Jane Austin, but she has been at some pains to write well, and she has put into what she has written a voice, a state of mind, and era, a few moments of human experience that nobody else has conveyed." (68)

1945

48. Cerf, Bennet. Try and Stop Me. New York: Simon and Schuster, 1945.

A brief but joyous anthology of stories about and by Parker in this collection of humor. It contrasts sharply with his final account (See entry 122).

1946

49. Gray, James. "Dreams of Unfair Women." On Second Thought. Minneapolis: University of Minnesota Press, 1946. 184-200.

Writing about the battle of the sexes as women treat it, Gray praises Parker in this vein: "Yet there is a very sharp difference between Clare Luce and Dorothy Parker: The satires of the former always seem shallow, empty of emotion, devoid of values; those of the latter, though they may be quite as devastating in their treatment of an individual figure, always carry the implication that some positive good, inherent in human nature, has here been trod upon ruthlessly by an insensitive savage." (196) Gray praises Parker's technical skill in prose, especially her diction, but concludes "it is not this glittering gift that makes her work worth reading and re-reading. Rather it is the fact that Dorothy Parker has a mature mind and a will to protect the dignity of man from the assaults of the insensitive." (199)

1947

50. Engle, William. "Dorothy Parker's Rebounding Quips." The American Weekly 15 June 1947: 12.

A recounting of the major facts of Parker's life when she divorced Alan Campbell. The article contains quotes and offers an interesting view of Parker's reputation in 1947.

51. Farnham, Marjnia. "The Pen and the Distaff." The Saturday Review 22 February 1947: 7-8, 49.

An important essay about what women's writing was, where it had come from, and where it was going. Parker is cited as one example of the standards women had achieved.

52. Maurois, Andre. "Ecrivains Americains." Revue de Paris 54 (April 1947): 9-24.

A basically positive analysis of the mood Parker creates in her fiction; Maurois, not surprisingly, calls Parker the "American Collette."

1948

53. Orvis, Mary Burchard. The Art of Writing Fiction. New York: Prentice-Hall, 1948.

Chapter nine, "Characterization" (153-69), argues that Parker is a master of "portrait painting with a special ability for noting and revealing the little ways in which people show what they are." (160) A good analysis of "Mr. Durant" and "Big Blonde": "Both stories reveal the Parker acuteness, the Parker sense of economy, and the Parker flair for focus. There is no loose impression here: no chance for the reader to miss the point." (164)

1949

54. Kramer, Dale. Heywood Broun: A Biographical Portrait. New York: A. A. Wyn, 1949.

Although Parker was not instrumental in Broun's life, she constantly defended the man, both in his politics and his slovenly personal habits.

1951

55. Harriman, Margaret Case. The Vicious Circle: The Story of the Algonquin Round Table. New York: Rinehart, 1951.

This sentimental and personal account from Frank Case's daughter is entirely delightful. It contains sketches of all the important Round Table members and it reproduces the programs from the two revues of the Round Table. It presents the members of the Round Table as they should be, but one must not look below their glittering surfaces.

56. Kramer, Dale. Ross and The New Yorker. Garden City, NY: Doubleday, 1951.

According to Kramer, Parker aided greatly in making a success of the magazine, because "her appearance in its pages coincided with the bloom of her fame." (115) Her work in the New Yorker "distilled her sorrow for the light quaffing of a flippant generation." (116)

1952

57. Bankhead, Tallulah. Tallulah: My Autobiography. New York: Harper and Row, 1952.

Bankhead's fondness for Parker never wavered. She called Parker the supreme "mistress of the verbal grenade," and conceded to Parker's ability to coin "the most acid and accurate" mots.

58. Jensen, Oliver. The Revolt of Modern Women. New York: Harcourt, Brace, and Jovanovich, 1952.

Parker's major accomplishment was her striking against the "old morality" in both her work and in her life.

1953

59. O'Hara, John. Foreword. Appointment in Samarra. New York: Modern Library, 1953.

Originally entitled The Infernal Grove, Appointment in Samarra (1934) became the title of this novel after Parker showed O'Hara Maugham's play Sheppy. O'Hara acknowledges that he learned point of view from Parker's work.

1954

60. Chase, Edna Woolman and Ilka Chase. Always in Vogue. Garden City, NY: Doubleday, 1954.

Chase recounts a typical Parker prank while she worked for the Conde Nast publishing company. A Mr. Albert Lee followed the news accounts of World War I battles quite closely, and kept in the office a map of Europe with pins marking battles. Parker would arrive at work early and re-arrange his pins, much to his consternation.

1955

61. Benchley, Nathaniel. Robert Benchley. New York: McGraw Hill, 1955.

This solid life of Benchley was written without Parker's cooperation, but she is an omnipresent character.

62. Untermeyer, Louis. Makers of the Modern World. New York: Simon and Schuster, 1955.

Parker had a special pique towards Marion Davies, whom everyone else seemed to like. The poem "Upon my Honor" is directed at Davies, but Parker was coy about its authorship.

63. "Where'd the Money Go?" Newsweek 7 March 1955: 25-26.

Parker, as joint national chairperson of the Joint Anti-Fascist Refugee Committee, had helped to raise $1.5 million, but Bernard Tompkins in a New York State joint legislative committee investigation said only 10% of the money had been accounted for. Parker took the Fifth Amendment protection when asked directly "Are you a member of the Communist Party?" Parker did concede she had signed many appeals for funds for many organizations.

1956

64. American Heritage. August 1956.

This special issue of the magazine is devoted entirely to the social, political, and cultural history of the 1920s. It is as informative as it is interesting to see a 1950s view of the 1920s.

65. Harriman, Margaret Case. Blessed are the Debonair. New York: Rinehart, 1956.

Here is a brief appreciation of Parker's wit by an author whom Parker dismissed as a fusspot.

1957

66. Hecht, Ben. Charlie: The Life and Times of Charles MacArthur. New York: Harper and Brothers, 1957.

Detailing the pleasant side of the affair between Parker and MacArthur, Hecht claims the famous "ducking for apples" story was Parker's final comment on the relationship.

1958

67. Lyons, Leonard. "The Lyon's Den." The New York Post 28 August 1958.

This brief article has a Parker anecdote: Another woman, mooing about how wonderfully well her husband treated her, was told by Parker to keep him because "he'll come back in fashion some day."

1959

68. Thurber, James. <u>The Years With Ross</u>. Boston: Atlantic Monthly Press, 1959.

Thurber gives his perspective of Harold Ross and the <u>New Yorker</u>. Parker enters and exits like a character in a comedy of manners.

1960

69. Richart, Bette. "The Light Touch." <u>The Commonweal</u> 9 December 1960: 277-79.

Re-reading Parker's work after a number of years away from it, Richart was amazed at how well Parker's verse held up. She connected Parker's work with that of Phyllis McGinley.

1961

70. Marx, Harpo and Rowland Barber. <u>Harpo Speaks</u>. New York: Bernard Geis, 1961.

A favorite member of Algonquin Round Table, Marx gives his version of what the other members were like. Especially important is the portrait of Woollcott that emerges. Chapters 12--"No Use Talking" (188-211)--and 13--"Buckety-Buckety into the Lake (213-27)--cite Parker and stories about her.

1962

71. Brown, John Mason. "High Spirits in the Twenties." <u>Horizon</u> 4.1 (July 1962): 33-40.

A sentimental, but informative account of Prohibition and the Round Table. Of Parker, Brown writes that "To those she did not like or who bored her, she was a stiletto made of sugar. Her malice came from the disappointments of a romantic rather than the cynicism of the disillusioned." (35)

1963

72. Rice, Elmer. <u>Minority Report: An Autobiography</u>. New York: Simon and Schuster, 1963.

Rice's only collaboration with Parker was on her first play <u>Close Harmony</u>. Rice wrote that "the play's merit lay in Dorothy's shrewd observations and pungent writing." (203) The play was well-reviewed but it was a commercial failure. Rice remembered that Parker "was unfailingly courteous, considerate and, of course, amusing and stimulating. It was hard to believe that this tiny creature with the big, appealing eyes and the diffident, self-effacing manner was capable of corrosive cynicism and devastating retorts. I discovered in the granite of her misanthropy there was a vein of softish sentimentality." (204)

1964

73. Cooper, Morton. "Men Seldom Make Passes / At Girls Who Wear Glasses." Diner's Club Magazine October 1964: 46-47, 68-69.

An appreciative account of Parker's life by a long time admirer, Cooper is as mystified by her as anybody else. He does offer one important observation: "she took only her work, never herself, seriously." (69)

74. Yates, Norris. "Dorothy Parker's Idle Men and Women." The American Humorist: Conscience of the Twentieth Century. Ames, IA: Iowa State University Press, 1964. 262-73.

Men, as well as women, were the objects of Parker's satire. Yeats believes Parker is basically a satirist who shows the need for reform but fails to say how to achieve it in her fiction, yet "Parker's indignation and guilt feelings led her into social crusades and into praise of the fighting peasant of loyalist Spain (in "Soldiers of the Republic"), whom she depicted with an emphasis on simplicity, courtesy, and selflessness that seldom appears in her profiles of idle Americans." (273)

1965

75. Brown, John Mason. The Worlds of Robert E. Sherwood: Mirror to his Times, 1896-1939. New York: Harper and Row, 1965.

An especially detailed account of Sherwood's, Benchley's and Parker's time at Vanity Fair. Parker was not so much of a victim as she like to portray herself.

76. Straumann, Heinrich. American Writers in the Twentieth Century. New York: Harper and Row, 1965.

Perhaps too lavish in his praise of her work, Straumann argues that Parker's major worth lies in her attacking the genteel tradition.

1966

77. Dos Passos, John. The Best Times: An Informal Memoir. New York: New American Library, 1966.

Dos Passos gives glimpses of New York and New York writers of the 1920's who were part of the literary scene but who were not part of the lost generation.

78. Loos, Anita. A Girl Like I. New York: The Viking Press, 1966.

Parker's presence caused tension no matter the circumstances, but Loos writes that only Parker among the Round Table members was an interesting personality away from the group.

79. Oppenheimer, George. The View From the Sixties: Memories of a Spent Life. New York: David McKay, 1966.

A long-time friend, Oppenheimer saw only the Little Nell of Woollcott's observation. He relates the following anecdote during the first three weeks Parker and Campbell were in Hollywood sharing his home: "For three weeks Dottie and Alan, a personable and intelligent man, some years younger than she, spent their honeymoon with me and Peaceful [Oppenheimer's dog], who fell in Love with Dottie at first sight (as who did not). I remember happily a Sunday morning when we were sitting around, lazily trying to read the Los Angeles papers. On the front page of one of them, as a reminder that the circus had come to town, was a large photograph of three elephants, standing on their hind legs. One was wearing a bridal veil perched grotesquely on its head, another had a high silk hat, and the third wore a priest's collar about its neck. Dottie took one look, tossed it contemptuously aside, and said, 'I give it six months.'" (157)

1967

80. Ford, Cory. The Time of Laughter. Boston: Little, Brown, and Company, 1967.

Excellent portraits of the Round Table members by one of their fellow humorists. This book is especially interesting for the details it has of day to day life among the humorists and their times in speakeasies. It also details how Dorothy Parker became Mrs. Parker. For instance, Ford remembered Parker as "small and attractive, with dark bobbed hair and melting eyes and the innocent mien of a school girl" who said to a real estate agent that most apartments were too large because "All I need is room enough to lay my hat and a few friends." (52)

81. "Guinevere of the Round Table." Time 16 June 1967: 94.

Parker's obituary, interesting for the assessment of her at the time of her death.

82. "Queen of the Round Table." Newsweek 19 June 1967: 43.

Parker's obituary and a brief assessment of her place in popular culture.

83. Seely, Nancy. "Dorothy Parker: The Lilt and the Laughter." The New York Post 10 June 1967: 31.

An important obituary because it contains quotations from Parker's life-long friend Bea Ames.

84. Whitman, Alden. "Dorothy Parker." The Obituary Book. New York: Stein and Day, 1971.

This is a reprint of Whitman's New York Times obituary of 8 June 1967: 1, 38.

1968

85. Allen, Everett. "Dorothy Parker. Famous American Humorous Poets. New York: Dodd and Meade, 1968. 99-108.

Although intended for younger readers, these nine pages are a good headnote to the whole of Parker's life.

86. Bier, Jesse. The Rise and Fall of American Humor. New York: Henry Holt, 1968.

An overview of the conditions that allowed the humorists of the 1920's to develop; Bier considers Parker's poetry and prose. He labels Parker, Lardner, Marquis, and Benchley as misogynists.

87. Connelly, Marc. Voices Offstage: A Book of Memoirs. New York: Holt, Rinehart and Winston, 1968.

Connelly reproduces the programs of the revue No Siree! and writes about Parker in the early 1930's in Hollywood. Parker and Frank Sullivan co-wrote a program for The Depression Gaieties, a benefit performance for the Author's League and Stage Relief Funds.

88. Cooper, Wyatt. "Whatever You Think Dorothy Parker Was Like, She Wasn't." Esquire July 1968: 56-57, 61, 110-114.

Acquainted with Parker through Alan Campbell, Cooper knew Parker in Hollywood and he gives the most complete and intimate account of her final years in New York. Based on a series of interviews that were to lead to a biography or an autobiography, this article is the single-most important piece of writing about Parker's later life. It is reprinted in the Appendix.

89. Drennan, Robert, ed. The Algonquin Wits. New York: Citadel Press, 1968.

A collection of the "best of" sort. This book contains brief bibliographies of the major Round Table figures.

90. Grant, Jane. Ross, The New Yorker, and Me. New York: Reynal and Company, 1968.

The first wife of Harold Ross, Grant gives her unique perspective on the development of the New Yorker and on the members of the Round Table. She writes that Benchley and Sherwood often played straight men to Parker's gags. Grant knew of at least of two of Parker's suicide attempts, but she maintains they were only pleas for attention, never serious.

91. Levant, Oscar. The Unimportance of Being Oscar. New York: G. P. Putnam's
     Sons, 1968.

     "Dorothy Parker was an original, as a wit, a person, and a critic. She was a tiny
     woman, fragile and helpless, with a wispy will of iron. She loved dogs, little
     children, President Kennedy, and lots and lots of liquor. Even her enemies were
     kind to her; she brought out the maternal in everyone. At her cruelest, her voice
     was most caressive--the inconstant nymph. She was one of my favorite people."
     (88) "Dottie was usually quite taciturn, what I call a 'spare speaker.' The use
     of the exact and appropriate words--and nothing else--was always her great talent.
     But she was completely dependent on others for the basic necessities. She never
     learned how to boil water for instance, or even how to turn off a TV set." (89)
     "It seemed to me she had a great will to self-destruction." (90)

92. Shanahan, William. "Robert Benchley and Dorothy Parker: Punch and Judy in
    Formal Dress." Rendezvous 3.1 (1968): 23-34.

    Although heaping elaborate praise upon their work, Shanahan argues that Parker
    and Benchley are too minor ever to have more than a cult following.

                                      1969

93. Gish, Lillian and Ann Pichot. The Movies, Mr. Griffith, and Me. Englewood Cliffs,
    NJ: Prentice Hall, 1969.

    Parker first wrote dialogue for silent movies in New York in 1919 before she went
    to Hollywood in 1934. Gish remembered one subtitle Parker wrote: A man in
    a barber shop was having his nails manicured, and the title read "The divinity that
    shapes our ends" (224).

94. Hellman, Lillian. "Dorothy Parker." An Unfinished Woman. Boston: Little, Brown
    and Company, 1969. 218-28.

    More an affectionate memoir than anything else, this chapter leaves the reader
    with a favorable impression of Parker, in spite of documenting her excesses. Yet,
    one must question Hellman's intention because Teichmann, in his biography of
    Hellman, records that she called Parker "that God-damn bitch" because she had
    left her estate to Martin Luther King.

                                      1970

95. Gilmer, Walker. Horace Liveright: Publisher of the Twenties. New York: David
    Lewis, 1970.

    Parker's first exclusive publisher, Liveright took quite a chance in publishing

Enough Rope, but it proved to be one of the company's most successful books.

96. Graham, Sheilah. "The Grim Weeper." The Garden of Allah. New York: Crown
    Publishers, 1970. 138-46.

    As the title of this chapter from her book implies, Graham seems to want revenge
    for Parker's remarks about Graham's Beloved Infidel: "It may occur to some of
    us that there has been rather too much digging up of Fitzgerald's bones, but I
    doubt if we ever have known before such greedy gnawing of them." [Esquire
    February 1959: 18] Nonetheless, Graham does show that even in Hollywood,
    Parker's actions, affections, and spending of money was excessive.

97. Keats, John. You Might As Well Live: The Life and Times of Dorothy Parker. New
    York: Simon and Schuster, 1970.

    The first, book-length study of Parker's life, and still the only source of many
    anecdotes, as noted by Frewin's, Meade's and Kinney's references to it.

    Allum, Nancy. Books and Bookmen June 1971: 50-51.
    Bell, Pearl. The New Leader 2 November 1970: 16-17.
    Coxe, Louis. The New Republic 24 October 1970: 25-26.
    Croce, Arlene. The New York Times Book Review 11 October 1970: 6.
    Darrach, Brad. Life 16 October 1970: 17.
    Epstein, Joseph. Commentary January 1971: 96-98.
    Janeway, Elizabeth. Saturday Review 10 October 1970: 30-32.
    Kazin, Alfred. Vogue December 1970: 100.
    Lasson, Robert. The Chicago Tribune Book World 25 October 1970: 12.
    Murry, Michele. The National Observer 30 November 1970: 25.
    Parker, Dorothy. The Christian Science Monitor 19 November 1970: 13.
    Schickel, Richard. Harper's January 1971: 94.
    Tomalin, Claire. New Statesman 2 April 1971: 426.
    Tynan, Kenneth. The Observer Review 4 April 1971: 4.
    Weeks, Edward. The Atlantic November 1970: 141-42.

98. Thomas, Bob. Selznick. Garden City, NY: Doubleday, 1970.

    Parker was furious with David Selznick that Bud Schulberg and Ring Lardner, Jr.,
    were assigned to rewrite the "Parker-Campbell-Carson re-write of the Wellman-
    Carson" script of A Star is Born. Nothing Sacred had "witty lines" supplied by
    Parker.

                                    1971

99. Churchill, Allen. The Literary Decade. Englewood Cliffs, NJ: Prentice Hall, 1971.

    An excellent survey of how necessary it was for writers of the 1920s to be
    "smarty" in order to overthrow the genteel tradition. See especially Chapter 9,

"When Does Louis Write?" (130-44).

100. Gringrich, Arnold. <u>Nothing But People: The Early Days at 'Esquire'</u>. New York: Crown Publishers, 1971.

Parker's years reviewing books for <u>Esquire</u> (1958-1962) were filled with difficulty for her editor and full of promise for an article about the 1920's but it never went beyond the title, "The Dingy Decade."

101. Rosmond, Babette. <u>Robert Benchley: His Life and Good Times</u>. Garden City, NY: Doubleday, 1971.

Mrs. Benchley was instrumental in helping Rosmond write this biography. Mrs. Benchley's views about Parker are generally favorable, but there is a strong current of reservation.

102. Tompkins, Calvin. <u>Living Well Is the Best Revenge</u>. New York: The Viking Press, 1971.

This book is the story of Gerald and Sara Murphy. It shows how extraordinarily kind they were to the writers whom they gathered about them.

103. Ephron, Nora. "Women." <u>Esquire</u> November 1973: 58, 86.

An appreciation of Parker as a role model for women. Ephron's interesting comment about Parker's work is that the emotions Parker portrays in her poetry are accurate, even if literary and social politics makes them currently unfashionable.

104. Gill, Brendan. Introduction. <u>The Portable Dorothy Parker</u>. New York: The Viking Press, 1973.

A survey of all of Parker's work in this "revised and enlarged" edition of the 1944 <u>Dorothy Parker</u>. Gill, unfortunately, is insensitive to both Parker's life and work.

1974

105. Clurman, Harold. <u>All People are Famous</u>. New York: Harcourt, Brace, and Jovanovich, 1974.

While he was directing Parker's fourth play <u>The Ladies of the Corridor</u>, Clurman remembers that Parker was an unhappy woman with a caustic tongue who was seldom far from hysteria.

106. Dietz, Howard. <u>Dancing in the Dark</u>. New York: Quadrangle, 1974.

The Parker whom Dietz remembers was witty, earthy, and entirely irresistible when she was on her best behavior, especially so when she was surrounded by an

army of adoring men, which was quite often. "It was easy to get a crush on
Dottie Parker as she sent you flattering telegrams on your birthday, your show
opening and whenever she thought you were slipping from her grasp. Her
equipment was witty telegrams, vers de societe and kisses on the lips when you
aimed for her cheek." (76-77) "Dorothy Parker arrived at the Island one day with
a huge suitcase which, when opened, contained only a large picture hat. She spent
a week at Lake Bomoseen practically naked. Her figure was as eloquent as her
verses. (83)

107. Meredith, Scott. George S. Kaufman and His Friends. Garden City, NY:
      Doubleday, 1974.

      Even though they never fully blew up at each other, Parker and Kaufman's
      relationship was always uneasy. In 1925 they collaborated on a screenplay,
      Business is Business.

108. St. Johns, Adela Rogers. Some are Born Great. New York: Doubleday, 1974.

      St. Johns declares that Parker's talent as a writer was used up before she went to
      Hollywood. This appreciative and quite sympathetic review of Parker's life and
      achievements cites Robert Benchley as the most important person in her life. "No
      woman ever showed more guts than Dorothy Parker did in the last years. To sit
      on the sidelines and watch the game in which she had once been the brightest
      star--no woman was ever a brighter one than Dorothy Parker of the Algonquin
      Round Table, every word she spoke, and a lot she didn't, was quoted as one of
      her bons mots. Yet as the last of life went on for her, all downhill, she kept her
      humor and her courage." (107)

109. Tunny, Kieran. Tallulah--Darling of the Gods. London: Secker and Warburg, 1974.

      Bankhead claimed that Parker was made bilious because the same witticisms were
      always quoted; Parker said "One must, even by accident, have said other things
      worth repeating if the lazy sons-of-bitches bothered to find them out."

                                    1975

110. Gill, Brendan. Here at the New Yorker. New York, Random House, 1975.

      A compendium of anecdotes but no extended discussion of Parker. He does credit
      her with establishing "the New Yorker short story."

111. Guiles, Fred Lawrence. Hanging on in Paradise. New York: McGraw-Hill, 1975.

      A definitive but dispiriting look at Parker's years in Hollywood. There is a good
      discussion of other literary figures in Hollywood, like Faulkner and Fitzgerald.

112. Keats, John. "Mrs. Parker Comes to Television." TV Guide 5 April 1975: 8-9.

Written after his biography, Keats previewed the PBS version of <u>Ladies of the Corridor</u>. He maintained that her personality was the major block to her writing, but as he explains "The readers who laughed at her quoted remarks did not always understand the true nature of the wisecrack, a particular form of jest that, piercing pretense, carries a reproof. It is a way of getting at the truth, and if Dorothy Parker's wisecracks are thus reviewed, it will be seen that she viewed the world about her with a scorn that may well have been deserved." (9)

113. Stewart, Donald Ogden. <u>By A Stroke of Luck</u>. New York: Paddington Press, 1975.

Stewart claims it was he who raised Parker's political consciousness during her early Hollywood years.

114. Wilson, Edmund. <u>The Twenties</u>. Ed. and Introd. Leon Edel. New York: Farrar, Straus, and Giroux, 1975.

Wilson's notebooks contain glimpses of Parker through the eyes of a friend and constant admirer of her work. See also his other notebooks: <u>The Thirties</u> (1980); <u>The Forties</u> (1950); <u>The Fifties</u> (1986), and <u>Letters on Literature and Politics, 1912-1972</u> (1977).

1976

115. Douglas, Ann. "Feminists Critics and Cultural History: Dorothy Parker and the 1930's." MLA, New York City, December 1976.

116. Gordon, Ruth. <u>My Side</u>. New York: Harper and Row, 1976.

Gordon narrates a brief portrait of Parker holding court in her bedroom at the Swope estate.

117. Lardner, Ring, Jr. <u>The Lardners: My Family Remembered</u>. New York: Harper and Row, 1976.

Ring Lardner's writing was greatly admired by all of the Round Table members, and his oldest son relates this incident about him and Parker: "Dottie had complained to Ring at a party in the Great Neck days that she couldn't get the solitude she needed for work, and he invited her to come and stay in one of our guest rooms and enjoy absolute privacy. When she came, they left her entirely alone as she presumably wanted, and she couldn't stand it after a week and left. A short time later it was reported back to Ellis [Lardner's wife] that Dottie, asked how things had gone at the Lardners', had said she had to escape because Ring was after her all hours of the day and night." (189) The son maintains the affair never happened.

118. Labrie, Ross. "Dorothy Parker Revisited." <u>The Canadian Review of American Studies</u> 7 (1976): 48-56.

Labrie gives high praise to a "neglected" writer; he argues for an essential unity among all of Parker's work, citing the stories as antidotes to the poems.

119. Lajoy, Maureen. "No Laughing Matter: Women and Humor." Women 5.1 (1976): 6-9.

The humor directed against women--by men and by women themselves--is not in the least funny.

120. Smith, David. "Dorothy Parker and Friends: Reminiscences of the Algonquin." The Los Angeles Times 4 May 1976; sec. 4: 1.

Smith quotes Heywood Hale Broun who describes the elaborate pranks and games of the Round Table members as masks for people who "were afraid of everything. But they were funny and gallant about it."

121. Teichmann, Howard. Smart Aleck: The Wit, World, and Life of Alexander Woollcott. New York: William Morrow, 1976.

Woollcott's life admirably written. Woollcott's fondness for Parker was best exhibited publicly by insult and privately in praise.

1977

122. Cerf, Bennet. At Random: The Reminiscences of Bennet Cerf. New York: Random House, 1977.

Calling Parker "something of a fraud all of her life, a charm girl," Cerf illustrates that Parker was kind to a person's face and devastating behind his back. Cerf's final estimation was that "She was a very dangerous woman." (34)

123. Gaines, James R. Wit's End: The Days and Nights of the Algonquin Round Table. New York: Harcourt, Brace and Jovanovich, 1977.

An excellent, well-documented and illustrated history of the Round Table. It's difficult to call this book definitive because of its unbalanced and overly negative estimations. It's an important book for its details, but is truly the antithesis of Harriman's The Vicious Circle.

124. Mailer, Norman. "Of Small and Modest Malignancy, Wicked and Bristling with Dots." Esquire November 1977: 125-48.

Another account of the Parker contradictions: Mailer writes "She had also a manner that was gentle, full of praise, and treacherous as a scorpion." (132)

125. Toth, Emily. "Dorothy Parker, Erica Jong, and New Feminist Humor." Regionalism and the Female Imagination. 3 (1977/1978): 70-85.

Parker is valuable as a feminist writer for her ability to show "what is," even if she does not say "what should be."

1978

126. Blair, Walter and Hamlin Hill. American Humor: From Poor Richard to Doonesbury. New York: Oxford University Press, 1978.

An excellent overview of urbanity as a reaction to the more traditionally rural American humor.

127. Bruccoli, Matthew J., ed. The Selected Letters of John O'Hara. New York: Random House, 1978.

Parker looms large in helping O'Hara establish his reputation.

128. Bunkers, Susanne L. "I Am Outraged Womanhood: Dorothy Parker as Feminist and Social Critic." Regionalism and the Female Imagination 4.2 (1978): 25-34.

Calling Parker more a satirist than a humorist, Bunkers illustrates how Parker used female stereotypes like "the Bitch and Galatea" not as choices women make to act like, but as examples of their "society's limited visions of acceptable, 'proper,' female roles."

129. Escar, Evan. The Comic Encyclopedia. Garden City, NY: Doubleday, 1978.

Escar calls a rhyming quip based on "Men seldom make passes / At girls who wear glasses" a "Parkerism." I have never seen the term or heard it used, but Escar makes a persuasive case.

130. Gilbert, Julie Goldsmith. Ferber: A Biography. Garden City, NY: Doubleday, 1978.

This is a more than adequate biography of Ferber who was popular among the Round Table members, even if her work was not. She did not enjoy the sniping that the regular members thrived upon.

131. Kinney, Arthur. Dorothy Parker. Boston: Twayne, 1978.

Although the life of Parker has been superseded by Meade, Kinney's study of all of Parker's work is the best scholarship on her to date. This book is invaluable for anyone at all interested in Parker or her work. He published some of her letters with annotations in the Massachusetts Review 30.3 (Autumn 1989): 487-515.

132. Mostel, Kate and Madeline Gilford. 170 Years of Show Business. New York: Random House, 1978.

The wife of Zero Mostel, who delivered Parker's eulogy, remembers Parker as the kindest and nicest woman she knew: "Dorothy was tiny and the softest, loveliest voice I ever heard. Her diction was impeccable, and, of course, her choice of words was precise. And the brain behind all of this was formidable." (129) "After Alan Campbell died, she came back east and we saw her occasionally. She'd come to the house for dinner and fold the napkins in the shape of animals as she'd always done, and she'd do her best toward cleaning up by picking up one dish to dry and rubbing it all the time everybody was washing, drying, emptying garbage. She was darling, but not domestic." (131)

133. Sheed, Wilfred. "The Wit of George S. Kaufman and Dorothy Parker." The Good Word and Other Words. New York: Dutton, 1978. 159-63.

Sheed's harsh criticism is directed towards both writers, but especially towards Parker who, he thinks, largely wasted her talents in verbal wit and screenwriting.

1979

134. Arce, Hector. Groucho. New York: G. P. Putnam's Sons, 1979.

Marx was allowed to sit at the Round Table, but Arce writes that Marx always felt intimidated by the other members.

135. Hermann, Taffy. "The Wonder Wags." Cosmopolitan November 1979: 316-19, 372.

A popular but insightful account of Parker, Oscar Levant, Tallulah Bankhead, Gore Vidal, and Truman Capote, interesting for showing how a "wag's" art suffers due to her or his cleverness in speaking.

136. Hoffman, Kitty. "A History of Vanity Fair: A Modernist Journal in America." Diss. University of Toronto, 1979.

While nothing new about Parker's life is told, the analysis of Vanity Fair as a magazine satirizing the polite world adds a new perspective to Parker's work published there.

137. Logan, Joshua. Movie Stars, Real People, and Me. New York: Delacorte Press, 1979.

Logan knew Parker and Campbell during World War II and a bit afterward: "I'd imagined her to be sharp and somewhat tough, with a kind of acid edge to her voice. Instead, she was a beady-eyed dumpling, the sweetest-voiced of the mama dolls; also there was always a gush of emotion as she delivered barbs as though it killed her to say them." (249) Logan writes that she was sincerely concerned about the soldiers during the war, even if she continually chided Campbell for deserting her.

1980

138. Denis, Brian. <u>Tallulah, Darling: A Biography of Tallulah Bankhead</u>. New York: Macmillan, 1980.

Citing Truman Capote, Brian writes that Parker, who was at home only in midtown Manhattan, claimed "'If I go above Seventy-second Street, I get a nosebleed.'" (236)

139. Ceplair, Larry and Stephen Englund. <u>The Inquisition in Hollywood: Politics in the Film Community</u>. Garden City, NY: Anchor Press, 1980.

An excellent, scholarly study of how "liberals" who were not Communist were blacklisted and kept from screenwriting. Parker was certainly an active, and vocal, member of organizations attempting to rectify injustice.

140. Corwin, Norman. "Corwin on Media." <u>Westways</u> November 1980: 64-65.

Parker was unable not to be witty. It was a natural, spontaneous wit, according to Corwin.

141. Gordon, Ruth. <u>Ruth Gordon: An Open Book</u>. Garden City, NY: Doubleday, 1980.

Philip Barry's play <u>Hotel Universe</u> has a character named Lily Malone who was based upon Parker; Parker was the only American George Bernard Shaw asked Gordon about when they met.

142. Kazin, Alfred. "Boozy Ladies." <u>The Dial</u> December 1980: 21-22.

This is Kazin's preview of the PBS dramatization of "Big Blonde." Kazin writes that Parker's work "was smart, but not shallow; a reader had to pay attention to sentence after sentence, for these came booby-trapped with some unexpected truth about the brevity of man-woman relationships in glittering Manhattan." (21) He concludes by writing "Why did Hazel fail even at suicide? Unlike Marilyn Monroe, unlike Diana Barrymore, only two of the famous people who died of the combination of booze and pills without meaning to. Hazel is uninteresting even to herself. The lack of a fine consciousness is complete. Her boredom is a kind of death. But only a gifted and troubled writer could have made Hazel an example of so telling of something in our national life." (21)

143. McShane, Frank. <u>The Life of John O'Hara</u>. New York: E. P. Dutton, 1980.

Parker was instrumental in helping O'Hara becoming a published author.

144. Teichler, Paula. "Verbal Subversion in Dorothy Parker: Trapped Like a Trap in a Trap." <u>Language and Style</u> 13.4 (Fall 1980): 46-61.

After an extended analysis of "The Waltz," Teichler argues for the need of unborrowed language that will "construct an uncompromised and unique female selfhood."

1981

145. Benedict, Stewart, ed. The Literary Guide to the United States. New York: Facts on File, 1981.

A valuable introduction to the lives and work of the Round Table members.

146. Bloom, Lynn Z. "Dorothy Parker." Critical Survey of Short Fiction. Ed. Frank N. Magil. 7 vols. Englewood Cliffs, NJ: Salem Press, 1981. Vol. 5.

Based only upon the stories published in collections, Bloom's argument is that "To the extent that Dorothy Parker was a satirist she was also a moralist. In satirizing aimless, frivolous or social-climbing lives, she implied a purposeful ideal."

147. ---. "Dorothy Parker." Critical Survey of Poetry. Ed. Frank N. Magill. 8 vols. Englewood Cliffs, NJ: Salem Press, 1981.

Based upon only the collected poetry, Bloom's generalizations are nonetheless good ones to agree with or to disprove.

148. Boyd, William. "The Uses of Normality." New Statesman. 19 June 1981: 24.

Boyd discusses the BBC production of "Big Blonde": "The undue length rather weakened Dorothy Parker's point that Haze was condemned not through any fault of her own but by constantly having to live up to the expectations of the men in her life. They didn't want her to be herself, they only wanted her to be a sport."

149. Mosedale, John. The Men Who Invented Broadway. New York: Richard Marek, 1981.

Parker was a much sought after houseguest among the wealthy in the 1920s and early 1930s. Mosedale tells the following anecdote: "One night the Governor of Maryland was a dinner guest [at the Swope estate] and an overserved celebrant burped loudly. After a moment of silence, Dorothy Parker said sweetly, 'The governor will pardon you.'" (167)

150. Perelman, S. J. "Dorothy Parker." The Last Laugh. New York: Simon and Schuster, 1981. 171-76.

A fragment of an unwritten autobiography, this short but informative article details how the first meeting between an unknown playwright and the legendary Mrs. Parker left him feeling like an idiot. It also has an amusing picture of Parker whining about the need for "roots." So, she and Campbell bought a farm in Bucks County Pennsylvania, in 1936.

151. Toth, Emily. "Female Wits." <u>The Massachusetts Review</u> 22.4 (Winter 1981): 783-93.

Female wit is directed toward what can be changed in the individual, not what is impossible to change, according to Toth.

152. Walker, Nancy. "Do Feminists Ever Laugh? Women's Humor and Women's Rights." <u>International Journal of Women's Studies</u>. 4 (1981): 1-9.

Women writers become self-mocking unawares: they must learn not to mock men's stereotypes of women as noisy, sentimental, and irrational because it reenforces them.

1982

153. Bishop, Morris. <u>Light Verse in America</u>. Aquilla Essays. No. 8. Portree, Island of Skye, Scotland: J. C. R. Green, 1982.

Bishop offers excellent definitions backed up with examples of light verse. He sees no break with light verse of the nineteenth century, the 1920's, or that which follows it.

154. Dresner, Zita Atkin. "Twentieth Century American Women Humorists." Diss. University of Maryland, 1982.

Dresner argues that although Parker's women characters are funny, they are too painful to evoke a grin. They are midway between madcap heiresses and tragic figures. This is a first-rate study of Parker and other women humorists.

155. Grant, Thomas. "Dorothy Parker." <u>Dictionary of Literary Biography</u>. Ed. Stanley Trachtenberg. 27 vols. Detroit: Gale, 1982. Vol. 11.

Inaccurate in some of his facts, Grant nevertheless provides an adequate overview to the whole of Parker's work. He is the first to argue that the word "minor" does not have a pejorative meaning when applied to an artist.

156. Hermann, Dorothy. "Dorothy Parker." <u>With Malice Towards All</u>. New York: G.P. Putnam's Sons, 1982. 73-86.

A review of known facts about Parker's life with additional anecdotal material given by Hermann's interviews with William S. Targ.

157. Pearl, Jane Helen. "Dorothy Parker Herself: A Psychobiography of the Literary Artist." Diss. Northwestern University, 1982.

An admirably argued statement (based on primary sources) that Parker's childhood was so horrible that there was a basic "disconnectedness" that remained with her throughout her entire life. Her wit, work, and "significant others" gave a focus to an otherwise centerless being.

158. Seebohm, Caroline. <u>The Man Who Was Vogue: The Life and Times of Conde Nast</u>. New York: The Viking Press, 1982.

Parker, still Dorothy Rothschild, began her career as a caption writer for <u>Vogue</u>. Her first impression of the lavish <u>Vogue</u> offices were that they looked like a house of prostitution. Her captions were so risque they often times had to be cut from the magazine.

159. Schwartz, Nancy Lynn. <u>The Hollywood Writers' War</u>. New York: Knopf, 1982.

Parker was relentless in her opposition to the fascistic control exercised by the major studio heads.

160. Walker, Nancy. "'Fragile and Dumb': The 'Little Woman' in Women's Humor, 1900-1940." <u>Thalia</u> 5.2 (1982-83): 24-29.

Women must learn to recognize and to fight stereotypes like "the little woman."

1983

161. Broun, Heywood Hale. <u>Whose Little Boy Are You? A Memoir of the Broun Family</u>. New York: St. Martin's/Marek, 1983.

Parker had the unique ability to make others want to be liked by her. Broun relates an anecdote that happened at the Broun family farm. After buying the farm in 1923, the Broun family had frequent Round Table guests, upon whom elaborate tricks would be played. One time Parker--"hoping that a little country quiet would help her through a spell of medically recommended abstinence from alcohol"--was to be the butt. But after much planning, the jokesters took "a look at the fragile face, a gardenia petal bruised by fear," and the joke was ended.

162. Capote, Truman. "Three Women: A Trio of Mighty Women Encountered and Remembered." <u>Esquire</u> December 1987: 223-24.

Written in 1983, this gossipy account of Parker's final years in New York was not published until 1987. The portrait of Parker is that of a "squirrel-like mouse" who "aware of her sorrows seemed seriously ignorant of her humor: 'Why are you laughing at me? Just <u>what</u> did I say?'"

163. Douglas, George H. "Women of the Twenties." <u>Edmund Wilson's America</u>. Lexington: Kentucky University Press, 1983. 44-71.

Douglas agrees with Wilson that Parker's writing declines in quality and quantity after the Depression because the conditions in which she flourished were gone.

164. MacLeish, Archibald. <u>Letters of Archibald MacLeish, 1907-1982</u>. Ed. R. H.

Winnick. Boston: Houghton Mifflin, 1983.

MacLeish called Parker the "natural consequence" of Millay. He wrote to
Hemingway that after a fearful introduction, he was completely under Parker's
spell "in about eight minutes."

165. Puk, Francine Shapiro. "Dorothy Rothschild Parker." American Women Writers.
     Ed. Langdon Lynne Faust. 2 vols. New York: Frederick Unger, 1983.

     Puk calls for a re-evaluation of Parker, arguing that her themes make her writing
     timeless.

1984

166. Arrington, Philip. "Ready, Responding, Composing: A Revisionary Approach."
     Journal of Advanced Composition 5 (1984): 37-49.

     Using the short story "But the One on the Right" as a text, Arrington demonstrates
     how Parker's monologue is capable of several readings.

167. Guilason, Thomas A. "The Lesser Renaissance: The American Short Story in the
     1920's." The American Short Story 1900-1945. Ed. Philip Sterick. Boston:
     Twayne, 1984. 71-102.

     Guilason maintains Parker's fiction is limited in scope, but within its confines, it
     is excellent: "The slick professionalism and smoothness of her ironical stories
     gave Dorothy Parker a certain fame for a time, but her reputation was to rest on
     her clever poetry and her legendary wit. Many of her stories remain superficial
     exercises in pain and depression; they lack the full range of emotions found in
     human beings and in life. As they rehearse her cynical view of the stupidity and
     meanness of the nature of things, they yield to formula, to what became popularly
     known as the Dorothy Parker story." (92)

168. Hellman, Lillian and Peter S. Feibleman. Eating Together: Recipes and
     Recollections. Boston: Little, Brown and Company, 1984.

     This book of recollections about mutual friends contains the details about Alan
     Campbell's death.

169. Hotchner, A. E. "Dorothy Parker is at the Plaza in Dire Straits." Choice People:
     The Greats, Near Greats, and the Ingrates I Have Known. New York: William
     Morrow, 1984. 50-64.

     Here is a bemused picture of the legend. Parker--who had been abandoned by her
     lover Ross Evans, 33, when she was 57--put herself into an expensive suite at the
     Plaza and appeared to be perfectly happy being a victim. Yet, the picture of the
     final years is not amusing: The final six years of her life "were years of lonely
     exile from the life of celebrity wit and flop plays, love affairs and sexual debacles,

Hollywood affluence and New York penury, literary accomplishment and writing paralysis. She had a warmth uniquely hers, and I always felt better after I had seen her even when things were going badly for her. She was gracious and graceful under the most hideous circumstances, and she never blamed anyone for her plight. I just wish she had been happier. She deserved it." (64)

170. Melzer, Sondra Roslyn. "'The Rhetoric of Rage': A Study of the View of Women in Selected Short Stories of Dorothy Parker." Diss. New York University, 1984.

More sociological than critical, Melzer's study argues that patriarchal societies force women to turn inward.

171. Toth, Emily. "A Laughter of Their Own: Women's Humor in the United States." Critical Essays on American Humor. Eds. William Bedford Clark and W. Craig Turner. Boston: Hall, 1984. 199-215.

Women's humor has been directed towards the home, not commerce, politics, or diplomacy. Parker is good at attacking the roles women have been forced to accept.

1985

172. Bryan, Joseph. "Bittersweet." Merry Gentlemen (And One Lady). New York: Atheneum, 1985. 99-118.

Bryan's affectionate portrait of Parker is truly one that makes her seem human, rather than like a character in fiction. Bryan does illustrate the contradictions, but he makes clear that even though one hated himself for laughing with her at someone else's expense, her company was worth it: she was "Dottie and nobody else." This essay is reprinted in the appendix.

173. Bone, Martha Denham. "Dorothy Parker and New Yorker Satire." Diss. Middle Tennessee State University, 1985.

In addition to listing Parker's contributions to the magazine, Bone argues that Parker was fundamental in establishing "the New Yorker satirical style."

174. Edwards, Anne. A Remarkable Woman: A Biography of Katharine Hepburn. New York: Pocketbooks, 1985.

Not content with stealing Alan Campbell from Hepburn, Parker also reviewed Hepburn's performance in The Lake. Parker's famous quip was cruel because, according to Edwards, it was accurate.

175. Sorel, Nancy Caldwell. "Dorothy Parker and Dashiell Hammett." The Atlantic Monthly July 1985: 76.

Parker's first meeting with Hammett was public display of admiration, but

Hammett eventually refused even to be in the same room with her.

1986

176. Ashley, Sally. <u>F. P.A.: The Life and Times of Franklin Pierce Adams</u>. New York: Beaufort Books, 1986.

A popular but informative life of Adams who was probably as instrumental in establishing Parker's reputation as anyone could have been. He fully appreciated Parker's poetic skills, even if he did tend to overrate her accomplishments.

177. Douglas, George H. "Dorothy Parker." <u>Women of the 20's</u>. Dallas: Saybrook Publishers, 1986. 148-229.

Douglas offers no new information about Parker's life, but he does argue persuasively that Parker's best work has remained--and will continue to remain--popular simply because her themes are perennial ones, "the continuing miseries of the human condition--not the socioeconomic sort, but the kind we inflict on ourselves and each other in the struggle of emotional relief." Parker's work continues "to discover us to ourselves."

178. Forster, E. M. <u>Commonplace Book</u>. Ed. Philip Gardner. Stanford: Stanford University Press, 1986.

Forster was agreeably surprised by Parker's extraordinarily high praise of his work.

179. Frewin, Leslie. <u>The Late Mrs. Dorothy Parker</u>. New York: Macmillan, 1986.

The second, full-length life of Parker. It has been the least favorably reviewed of the three. Its major fault is lack of notes identifying sources. Its major strength is showing the conflicts within Parker and the always surprising effect she had upon others.

Broun, Heywood Hale. The Washington <u>Post Book World</u> 17 May 1987: 4.
Burgess, Anthony. <u>Times Literary Supplement</u> 5 February 1988: 132.
Freely, Maureen. <u>Observer</u> 20 August 1987.
Henry, William. <u>Time</u> 15 June 1987: 73.
Hill, Hamlin. <u>American Literature</u> 60.1 (March 1988): 149-50.
Overmyer, J. <u>Choice</u> November 1988: 474.
Rich, Frank. <u>The New Republic</u> June 1987: 37-39.
Wright, William. The Chicago <u>Tribune</u> 24 May 1987; sec. 14: 4-5.

180. Mitsch, Ruthmarie H. "Parker's 'Iseult of Brittany.'" <u>The Explicator</u> 44.2 (Winter 1986): 37-40.

An astute analysis of the poem, but more of a call to see Parker as a poet, and not simply as a light verse writer.

181. Robe, Lucy Barry. <u>Co-Starring Famous Women and Alcohol</u>. Minneapolis: CompCare Publications, 1986.

Basing her analysis on Keats's and Kinney's lives of Parker, Robe accounts for Parker's excessive behavior because she was alcoholic.

1987

182. Gallagher, Brian. <u>Anything Goes: The Jazz Age Adventures of Neysa McMein and Her Extravagant Circle of Friends</u>. New York: Time books, 1987.

A first-rate life and times study of McMein and other Round Table members. Gallagher's balanced estimations make the book worthwhile reading.

183. MacDermott, Kathy. "Light Humor and the Dark Underside of Wish Fulfillment: Conservative Anti-Realism." <u>Studies in Popular Culture</u> 10.2 (1987): 37-53.

Light humor "naturalizes" the inherent contradictions of man and of the circumstances he creates; it offers no alternative but to "do what the scenario" says to do: don't fight against the inevitable.

1988

184. Feibleman, Peter. <u>Lilly: Reminiscences of Lillian Hellman</u>. New York: William Morrow, 1988.

About Hellman by an intimate acquaintance of hers, this book contains interesting anecdotes about the relationship between Parker and Hellman; for instance, they argued over who had slept with the "lowest-down men." Part of this book was reprinted in <u>Cosmopolitan</u> December 1988: 140-42.

185. Garmaise, Freda. "I'd Rather be in Philadelphia." <u>The Village Voice</u> 5 April 1988: 46.

A totally glib article about the problem of how properly to dispose of Parker's ashes.

186. Meade, Marion. <u>Dorothy Parker: What Fresh Hell Is This</u>? New York: Random House, 1988.

The best of the biographies yet written. Its notes and sources are most valuable for scholars. The biographer's insights into the nearly incomprehensibly complex character of Parker are those around her make good beginnings to refute or to agree with.

<u>The Christian Century</u> 17 February 1988: 171.
Clayton, Sylvia. <u>Punch</u> 15 April 1988: 30-31.
Kakutani, Michiko. The New York <u>Times</u> 9 January 1988: 17.

Kirkus Review 15 November 1987: 16-17.
MacKay, Shena. Times Literary Supplement 6 May 1988: 497.
Publisher's Weekly 27 November 1987: 74.
Rubin, Merle. The Christian Science Monitor 25 May 1988: 20.
Updike, John. The New Yorker 25 April 1988: 109-112.
Vosburgh, Dick. The Listener 21 April 1988: 33.
Whitman, Alden. The Chicago Tribune 24 January 1988; sec. 14: 6.
Wright, David. The Spectator 23 April 1988: 30-31.

187. "Remains of Dorothy Parker to go to NAACP Headquarters." Jet 11 April 1988: 54.

The final disposal of Parker's ashes; this article maintains that her will, leaving her estate to Martin Luther King, was controversial twenty years ago.

188. Showalter, Elaine. "Women Writers Between the Wars." Columbia Literary History of the United States. Ed. Emory Elliot. New York: Columbia University Press, 1988. 822-41.

Although Showalter does not specifically mention Parker, she does give a sensible, comprehensive view of the conditions and expectations--of, by, and for--women writers during the time she delineates.

189. Smith, Jane A. "Parker Ashes' Burial Marks the End of the Story." [Baltimore] The Sun 21 October 1988; sec. D: 1, 7.

This article details the burial of Parker's ashes.

190. Walsh, Winifred. "Show Puts Spotlight on Dorothy Parker's Life." [Baltimore] The Evening Sun 20 October 1988; sec. D: 6.

A review of Laurel Ollstein's one-woman play based on Parker's life: Laughter, Hope, and a Sock in the Eye. The play was presented after the interment of Parker's ashes.

191. Warren, Ann L. "Word Play: The Lives of Four Women Writers in Hollywood's Golden Age." Diss. University of Southern California, 1988.

In spite of "prescribed topics, plots, and messages," Parker, Zoe Akins, Vera Caspary, and Lillian Hellman were able to produce screenplays of high quality.

1989

192. Higham, Charles and Roy Moseley. Cary Grant: The Lonely Heart. New York: Harcourt, Brace, and Jovanovich, 1989.

Parker and Campbell worked on Grant's first big screen hit, The Awful Truth. The script went through at least four versions before it was finally shot; Parker and Campbell did not receive screen credit.

1990

193. Calhoun, Randall. "Autobiography in the Drama of Dorothy Parker." M/MLA, Kansas City, November, 1990.

The biographical considerations with Parker are as complicated as those concerning Jonathan Swift.

194. Gill, Brendan. "Dorothy Parker." A New York Life: Of Friends and Others. New York: Poseidon, 1990. 144-50.

A portrait of Parker acting the role of a sad and weary Mrs. Parker. Gill borrows heavily from his 1973 Introduction to the Portable Dorothy Parker.

195. Lazarus, A. L., ed. A George Jean Nathan Reader. Toronto: Associated University Presses, 1990.

Lazarus does an excellent job of collecting Nathan's informal and critical essays, but the strength of the book is its glossary full of dates and details about people in and around New York at the turn of the century and in the 1920s.

1992

196. Calhoun, Randall. "The Character of Constant Reader and Mrs. Parker in Dorothy Parker's Constant Reader Essays." Twentieth Century Literature Conference. Louisville, KY, February 1992.

The Constant Reader Essays form an integral part of Parker's canon and best represent the persona of Mrs. Parker in print.

Appendix:
Three Views
of Parker

"The Legend of
Dorothy Parker"
Richard E. Lauterbach

There is a plump little dark-haired lady now nearing fifty-one who might have been America's greatest woman writer if she had only held her tongue. As it is, her four thin volumes of verse and her three slim collections of short stories are credentials enough for a place close to the pinnacle.

Dorothy Parker, the reluctant wizard of the wonderful wisecrack, has only herself and her friends to blame for her brilliant failure as a literary giant. The things she said and the things they said were her undoing. If it had been less easy to talk so well, then perhaps all the rich promise of her quick eye for people, of her tightly tuned ear for language, might have been put on paper, bound into novels, produced as plays. But her skill in fencing with a rapier tongue swept her, too young, to a select literary heaven-- whence the bright intellectuals of the gay twenties trumpeted her glib glory.

With such a build-up, it was never possible for a fundamentally ease-loving person to cast aside her oral slings and arrows in favor of solid, earthy work. When motivated by love or hunger she penned perfectly cadenced, bitter little verses, or occasional short stories. She became in her heyday the symbol of super-sophistication. Describing herself and other female writers of the old "smarty-pants" school, Mrs. Parker observed:

> We were gallant, hardriding and careless of life. We were little black eyes
> that had gone astray . . . a sort of Ladies' Auxiliary of the Legion of the
> Damned.[1]

The reputation for the wonderous wisecrack, which changed the course of Dorothy Parker's career before it ever matured, is not entirely her fault. In Hollywood they tell a story about Sam Goldwyn having dinner with Mrs. Parker. During the meal he turned to her and asked "Do you really say all those things which the papers report that you say?" Dorothy smiled, batted her long black lashes and parried, "Do you?"

In both instances the answer is "No." Any anecdote about a Hollywood producer with a garbled vocabulary and genius for <u>non sequitur</u> is eventually retold about Goldwyn. And for twenty years most quotable <u>bon mots</u> emanating from U. S. literary circles were attributed to Dorothy Parker.

The concoction which Alexander Woollcott labelled as so odd a blend of "Little Nell and Lady MacBeth" was born Dorothy Rothschild on August 22, 1893, at West End,

N. J. Her father was Jewish, her mother was Scotch. When Dorothy was very young, her mother died and she was taken to a convent in New York, from which she remembers only that if you spit on a pencil eraser it will erase ink. She was, by her own description, a plain, disagreeable child with stringy hair and a yen to write verse.[2] Her unhappy stay at the convent culminated in her dismissal for writing an essay which the Mother Superior considered horribly unfunny.

Deciding that Dorothy wasn't going to become a teacher, her father did not put her back in school, hoping she would soon marry and therefore not require a complete education. Dorothy beguiled her way into a job writing fashion captions for Vogue at the lavish salary of ten dollars a week. On the side she swelled that income by writing and selling light verse and playing the piano for a children's dancing class.

While she was struggling along at Vogue, she married Edwin Parker, a handsome young man from Connecticut whom she had known for most of her life. He was a Wall Street broker, serious and correct. They lived together for four or five hilarious days until his division sailed for France. When he came back two years later, the Parkers began rollicking down the high, wide, and handsome speakeasy road that smashed so many marriages in the twenties.

After the Armistice Mrs. Parker shifted her talents from Vogue to Vanity Fair. This urbane monthly, under the editorship of Frank Crowinshield, was then publishing the work of such writers as Heywood Broun, Edna St. Vincent Millay, John Dos Passos, Stephen Leacock, Floyd Dell, F. Scott Fitzgerald, John V. A. Weaver, Donald Ogden Stewart, and Grantland Rice. Working in almost glorious anonymity, Mrs. Parker earned twenty-five dollars a week, wrote picture captions with an exact count of 14 and a half which had to have a punch in them, and was friendly with a young pundit named Bob Benchley.

Mrs. Parker soon became the perfect lunching companion for Vanity Fair editors. Addicted to plain suits and cute little red hats, she was shy, a good listener and minxy rather than devastating with her modest sense of humor.

In those Prohibition days, the bright young people drank their lunches and feasted on dry wit. Mrs. Parker learned fast, both in and out of the office. In a few months she was not only doing all the Vanity Fair picture captions but also writing articles under pseudonyms.[3] She became increasingly popular with the staff, especially with Benchley, who was managing editor, and Robert Sherwood, dramatic editor. Mrs. Parker made a practice of calling them "Mr. Benchley" and "Mr. Sherwood," which she still does as a gag.

Mrs. Parker wasn't exactly fired from Vanity Fair in 1921.[4] She wrote tartly and with restrained sophistication about most of the New York matters which she examined and reviewed for the magazine. But the storm began to brew almost immediately after she started to grind out sharp play reviews as a pinch hitter for P. G. Wodehouse who was on his summer vacation. She hit too hard. Editor Crowinshield fretted over her biting dissections and lightning really struck when she reviewed Billie Burke's performance in W. Somerset Maugham's Caesar's Wife, saying "Miss Burke, in the role of the young wife, looks charmingly youthful. She is at her best in her more serious moments; in her desire to convey the girlishness of the character, she plays the lighter scenes rather as if she were giving an impersonation of Eva Tanguay." (Miss Tanguay was a vaudeville performer with wild, wooly hair who sang a song called " I Don't Care.")[5] When Crowinshield received angry letters from Florenz Ziegfeld, David Belasco, and Charles Dillingham, he suggested to Benchley that Mrs. Parker be taken off reviews.

Benchley next day offered his resignation, hoping that such a decisive action would change the editor's mind. He was quite surprised when Crowinshield shook his hand and said, "Gee, Bob, I'm sorry to see you go." Whereupon Benchley and Parker quit, formed a writing team, opened an "oversized broom closet" office in the Metropolitan Opera building. They called the firm "Utica Drop Forge and Tool Co., Benchley and Parker, Presidents," but never had enough money to pay for having the name lettered on the door. They tried doing a play, but the problem of naming the characters held up that project interminably. Dorothy suggested calling them 1, 2, 3, 4, 5, but found that stage directions like "1 moves upstage while 2 shrinks against backdrop," were more like bad chess than good theatre.

Mrs. Parker, with an office, a typewriter, and an appetite, finally starved herself into writing. She did some play reviews for Ainslee's and began turning out a little fiction.[6] It took her then, as now, as long as a month to smooth the prose of one very short story. She spent most of her sober hours dreaming up new excuses for not working. A favorite was writing menus on a large mirror of fancy luncheons she'd like to eat. The first two paragraphs of a Parker book review stayed in the typewriter until the paper yellowed and crumpled. The other president of the Utica Drop Forge was no more assiduous. The first line of a Benchley essay beginning, "Now that wages are coming down," stayed in his typewriter so long that wages were going up again before he got around to finishing it. This line became a running gag for Mrs. Parker, who would prefix every remark on the social scene with "Now that wages are coming down." It invariably made Benchley sick with laughter.

In 1923 they gave up their office and later wangled space at the old humorous weekly Life, edited by Bob Sherwood, who had quit Vanity Fair a few weeks before Parker and Benchley.

During these years, Mrs. Parker's reputation as a wag began spreading, largely because she had two of New York's brightest circles acting as her personal publicists. One was the Algonquin crowd which included Franklin P. Adams, Alexander Woollcott, Heywood Broun, and others. They met at the Algonquin Hotel for lunch, and each day carried away with them the latest and brightest Parkerisms. F. P. A. spread the pointed word in his column and at his regular poker games with Broadway celebrities. Woollcott, who had made his reputation out of the conversation of others, delighted in conveying Parker's remarks back to the people they were directed against. This luncheon group, orginally self-christened "The S. J. Kaufman Post of the American Legion," grew into what was known as the "Critics' Round-Table." The table grew larger, and when curious crowds began to flock to the Algonquin to listen, the regulars went back to eating in speak-easies for privacy.

Another more Bohemian group gathered at the studio of Neysa McMein, a cover artist. Mrs. Parker frequented these alcoholic teas, and finally took an apartment under Neysa's studio, which complicated the Parkers' already confused home life. They were divorced in 1928.

Sophisticated magazines were carrying an occasional Dorothy Parker poem or sketch. In 1924 Elmer Rice suggested they collaborate on dramatizing one of her stories. The play, called Close Harmony, ran four weeks. On the fourth Wednesday Mrs. Parker wired Benchley collect: "CLOSE HARMONY DID A COOL NINETY DOLLARS."

The publication of Enough Rope in 1926 firmly established Mrs. Parker as a poet. By 1927 the book had gone into eight printings and hit a record high for U. S. poetry sales. It is still selling well today.

But most of the smart set were talking about Mrs. Parker's unrhymed witticism rather than her verses. Woollcott gave the kiss of fame to her bright sayings at a weekend house party which he attended with Mrs. Parker. They were thrown in with a motley group of guests who bathed infrequently. When Woollcott wondered where they came from and where they might be found at other times, Mrs. Parker whispered, "I think that they crawl back into the woodwork."

Inspecting the inadequate washing facilities on that same weekend, Woollcott noted an aging toothbrush hanging on the wall above the chipped basin. "What do you suppose our hostess does with that?" Woollcott asked. Mrs. Parker, after a moment's study, answered, "I think she rides it on Hallowe'en."

The upshot of a long series of verbal bull's-eyes was the formation of a group known as "Woollcott's Vigilantes," banded together in self-protection. Anyone who heard a Parker crack about one of the others would report it immediately. It made for some fine fights.

Very early in her career, the literary and theatrical crowd liked to be "in the know" by tagging Dorothy Parker's name onto every new crackling gag. Her fame and her stories traveled abroad and came back. Mrs. Parker feels that her act was never so good as her billing. She even indicates that there mightn't have been an act at all if it hadn't been for Benchley. This Benchley stoutly denies. Furthermore, he states categorically that Mrs. Parker, when sober, has never made an unfunny crack. Most of the second rate ad libs repeated with her by-lines are misquotations or not hers at all. Recently columnists, especially Winchell, have been prone to quote Dorothy Parker on topics probably dreamed up by an over-anxious press agent. This is always a source of annoyance to Mrs. Parker. Even the late Alexander Woollcott once wrote a nostalgic story about Mrs. Parker in which he claimed that she had MEN painted on the door of her office just to break the monotony. Actually, Mrs. Parker only talked of doing it.

While hardened to the inferior stories propelled by the magic of her name, Mrs. Parker still winces when something she really authored is credited to another. It was Mrs. Parker who reacted to the news of President Coolidge's death with the cool, "How do they know?" On a magazine piece on Wilson Mizner, this tidbit was thrust into his mouth.

Another thing which arouses her ire is a misquotation of "Men seldom make passes at girls who wear glasses." She resents the use of the word "never" instead of "seldom." She often wears glasses herself.

Many of Mrs. Parker's genuine gems are lost to readers because they are too frank to print. Fortunately, her present husband, Alan Campbell, occasionally overhears a good one and repeats it. One example has to do with his wife's comment on a lady politician whose character was being gleefully shredded over martinis. One of the women at the cocktail party said in her defense, "But really, she's awfully kind to her inferiors."

Mrs. Parker quipped, "Where does she find them?"

Until 1925 Mrs. Parker worked on the old Life doing articles, stories, and reviews. Shortly after the New Yorker began publication she moved her acid pen over there, and portioned out her weekly vitriol against the puny efforts of the publishing industry in reviews signed "Constant Reader." Once, at the end of a criticism of A. A. Milne's sugar-saturated whimsy, she recorded that fact that "Tonstant Weader frowed up."[7]

During the next decade Mrs. Parker did a great deal of traveling abroad, and her interests in things international developed apace. At least one of the periodic European junkets had a higher purpose. In 1937 she went to Spain "without any axe to grind" to see what and wherefore of the bitter Civil War. Writing about her experiences afterward, she said:

> "I didn't bring messages from anybody. I am not a member of any political party. The only group I have ever been affiliated with is that not especially brave little band that hid its nakedness of heart and mind under the out-of-date garment of a sense of humor. I heard someone say, and so I said it too, that ridicule is the most effective weapon . . . Well, now I know . . . ridicule may be a shield, but it is not a weapon."[8]

When she came back, firmly convinced of the Loyalist cause, she worked hard to arouse U. S. sympathy against the Fascists. All her scorn was turned into this channel, against the isolationists, the fence sitters. At a party given by Leon Henderson in Washington she sat on a piano and pleaded for funds for Spanish Children. Her words moved her so she cried. When a photographer tried to get a picture of her misery, Henderson threw him out bodily. At that party, Mrs. Parker declared soberly,

> "A humorist in this world is whistling by the loneliest graveyard and whistling the saddest song. There is nothing funny in the world any more."[9]

The trip to Spain crystallized a social consciousness which Mrs. Parker had been nicely sublimating since she was a child. Occasionally it cropped up in her short stories or over some dramatic event. She was arrested in 1927 for "sauntering and loitering" near the scene of the Sacco-Vanzetti trial in Boston, although her active participation was no greater than that of hundreds of liberal intellectuals. She had merely marched in a protest parade.

Mrs. Parker recalls the first incident in her life which caused her to think in social terms. One wintry day she stood at the window of an apartment on West 72nd Street with her aunt who pointed at the poor, tired old men shoveling the streets clean during a snowstorm. The aunt remarked to her young charge that thanks were due to God for sending the snow as it gave the unemployed an opportunity to work. The child Dorothy thought that men ought to have the <u>chance</u> to work even in good weather.[10]

After Spain Mrs. Parker's writing became more serious but there was little market for it. Editors wanted the charming, sophisticated Dorothy Parker, the old brittle stories, the nostalgic mooncalf poems. This reaction only soured her more completely on humor and light verse. Invited by the Congress of American Writers in 1939 to talk at their poetry session, she entitled her discourse, "Sophisticated Verse and the Hell With It."

She turned her old ruthlessness on the glittering adjectives used to describe her own work:

> Out in Hollywood where the streets are paved with Goldwyn the word 'sophisticate' means, very simply, 'obscene.' A sophisticated story is a dirty story. Some of that meaning has wafted eastward and got itself mixed up into the present definition. So that a 'sophisticate' means: one who dwells in a tower made of a Du Pont substitute for ivory and holds a glass of flat champagne in one hand and an album of dirty post cards in the other.[11]

With these words Dorothy Parker completely turned her back on New York, her old hangouts and cronies. She and her second husband buckled down to work in Hollywood. Looking back now on her collections of verse and short stories, Mrs. Parker takes pride only in "Soldiers of the Republic," a singularly effctive story about Spain. But she is far better known than many fine authors who have published a hundred times as much. Her publisher estimates that on a per word basis she is probably the world's highest paid writer. Her poems and stories appear repeatedly in collected volumes and anthologies, and stories are constantly adapted for radio and stage.

Her verse has been all things to all critics: "sly and philosophical" to Russel Crouse, "robust" to Laurence Stallings, "biting and terse" to Henry Hazlitt, and to Woollcott, a "potent distillation of nectar and wormwood, of ambrosia and deadly nightshade." Her prose to Robert Sherwood was the "superior of Ernest Hemingway added to Ring Lardner added to Aldous Huxley added to Rebecca West."

But at bridge parties, and stag Dinners Mrs. Parker is not remembered as the author of the O. Henry prize-winning story, "Big Blonde" or as the dialogue writer for Pride of the Yankees. She's the wisecrack artist who summed up Channing Pollock's The House Beautiful as "the play lousy," who said of Katharine Hepburn's acting, "she runs the gamut of emotions from A to B."[12] She's the mistress of the deadly verbal thrust who wired a famous actress when that thespian finally had a baby (after making conspicuous entrances during her prolonged pregnancy) "GOOD WORK. WE ALL KNEW YOU HAD IT IN YOU." Dorothy Parker's work has been heavily conditioned by four men in her life. When her early marriage with Edwin Parker floated on the rocks, she fell in love with Charles MacArthur, now married to Helen Hayes. Three years of that bred only frustration and a volume of bitter love poems. The next heart throb was John Garrett, a socialite. The third was John McClain, a reporter, about whose Victor Maturish framework Mrs. Parker made the classic crack, "His body has gone to his head." Her second husband, Alan Campbell, is number four. They were married in 1933 when he was playing juvenile leads in summer stock. While Campbell was touring in Denver, Mrs. Parker received an offer for them to go to Hollywood. They borrowed money to buy a second-hand flivver and drove to the coast. They soon drove a Packard and lived in a mansion. Up until this second marriage Mrs. Parker's life has been a series of high plateaus between heartbreaks. She usually crawled out of the pits slowly, pulling herself up by a series of bitter verses, stories and parties. Since she achieved comparative stability with Campbell, the plateaus have leveled out, the bitter verses swell up no more, the stories are so much drudgery and the parties are less frequent. With Campbell in the Army some of her "old friends" hope that the literary output will start again.

After nine years of being one of Hollywood's most highly paid scenarists, Mrs. Parker scorn for the tinselled town has not abated. She believes one of the troubles with the movies is

> that everybody in Hollywood thinks he can write, including the producers.
> I don't believe the films have anything to do with writing except in a
> crossword puzzle kind of way. Writing a script is drawing together a lot
> of ends which can be worked into a moving picture.[13]

Parker and Campbell have collaborated on tough, realistic pictures like Mary Burns, Fugitive, gay, screwball items like Hands Across the Table and The Moon's Our Home, serious Hollywood self-analysis like <u>A Star is Born</u>; ironically their biggest box-office draw was the saccharine <u>Sweethearts</u>, a 1938 musical hit with Nelson Eddy and Jeanette MacDonald. The Campbells sweated out their time in the studios like so many days in purgatory to pay for their earthy bills. The only picture that gave Mrs. Parker any satisfaction "aside from the check every week" was the scenario for Lillian Hellman's <u>The Little Foxes</u>. After the filming of this stage hit had started, she received a frantic phone call in the middle of the night from Sam Goldwyn. "I've seen the rushes," he shouted, "and that picture's communistic, it's communism pure and simple I tell you."

"But, Sam," Mrs. Parker remonstrated gently and with inspiration, "the story is set in the early 1900's. There wasn't any communism <u>then</u>."

"Thank God," Goldwyn exclaimed. He hung up, contented.

While her husband, a lieutenant in the Air Force, shuttled around for training, Mrs. Parker lived in a dowdy two-room apartment in a New York apartment hotel, which she aptly described as "the kind of a hotel where businessmen install their mothers and then run."

In the Army, Campbell, although he has a solid reputation of his own as a writer, finds most soldiers know of his wife. They refer to her as "a newspaperwoman" and occasionally confuse her with Dorothy Thompson. This confusion, incidentally, is shared by hundreds of others--to the delight of neither Dorothy.

Dorothy Parker still has her old charm. Her conversation is animated, intelligent, not unkindly. She is short, about five feet, with dark hair that bommerbangs over her forehead, large dark eyes and a tired look. She has a nervous, shy, gamin manner relieved by a quick, warm smile. Her voice has an unusual timbre, sometimes throaty, sometimes high. No one has ever heard Mrs. Parker laugh at one of her fabulous wisecracks. She just goes on with the conversation as if she had only said "How do you do?"

She still likes dachshunds and Hemingway, cries very easily, is extremely generous and intensely self-deprecating, avoids publicity, likes to be lazy.

She is the center of any room full of people. This, she says, has always upset her. "How would you like to walk into a party and have a dozen women look up and say with their eyes, 'So, you're Dorothy Parker. I dare you to say something nasty.'" The tragedy is that Mrs. Parker loves being with people, dreads the fact that her reputation precedes and follows her. On one occasion at a first night the woman next to her turned and asked, "Are you Dorothy Parker?" In self defense, Mrs. Parker said, "Yes, do you mind?"

Mrs. Parker would gladly trade her secured niche as a foremost American wit for one thick, earthly realistic masterpiece. She would gladly forget her own prediction:

> Three be the things I shall have till I die:
> Laughter and hope and a sock in the eye.[14]

She would even hurl mud at her own epitaph, EXCUSE MY DUST. Her contribution to the 20th Century Culture, unless she should reverse her field, is the elevation of the wisecrack from the speak-easy barroom to the level of Bartlett's <u>Familiar Quotations</u>.

Notes

1. <u>New Masses</u> 27 June 1939: 21.

2. "Miss Parker Never Poses," The New York <u>Times</u> 8 January 1939; sec. 9: 4.

3. Helen Wells was Parker's pseudonym for prose while she worked at <u>Vanity Fair</u>; she wrote poetry and some prose under the name Helene Rousseau.

4. The actual year was 1920.

5. "The Oriental Drama," <u>Vanity Fair</u> January 1920: 94.

6. Parker wrote her monthly reviews "In Broadway Playhouses," for <u>Ainslee's</u> from May 1920 until July 1923.

7. <u>New Yorker</u> 20 October 1928: 39.

8. "Incredible, Fantastic . . . and True," <u>New Masses</u> 23 November 1937: 15.

9. <u>Time</u> 16 January 1939: 55.

10. "Not Enough," <u>New Masses</u> 14 March 1939: 3.

11. <u>New Masses</u> 27 June 1939: 21.

12. <u>New Yorker</u> 21 March 1931: 36; The New York <u>Journal American</u> 27 December 1933.

13. Marguerite Tazlaar, "It Seems That Hollywood Gags Dorothy Parker, Not Vice Versa," The New York <u>Herald Tribune</u> 25 April 1937.

14. "Inventory," <u>Life</u> 11 November 1926: 12.

"Whatever You Think Dorothy Parker Was Like, She Wasn't"
Wyatt Cooper

"I was," she said, "just a little Jewish girl trying to be cute."

She entered the room like an apology. Tiny and startlingly delicate, she moved with steps that were short and brittle, and she appeared to be so fragile that you feared she would shatter if you touched her.

The first image that comes to my mind is this: She sits in her accustomed place in the living room of the house in California she shared with her husband Alan Campbell. In her lap is the ever present dog, a yapping brown poodle. Beside her on the sofa are her reading glasses, and in front of her is a large ashtray filled with remains of the cigarettes she smokes constantly. Cellophane from a discarded Chesterfield package catches fire and the flames go unnoticed while she complains of the dearth of talent to be found in the pile of books of every size and subject that crowd the top of the coffee table. One of those days of everlasting monotonous sunshine is drawing to a close, and Alan has made Scotches for the two of them while I sip No-Cal soda, feeling somehow guilty and unforgiven for being a teetotaler. This would be sometime in 1961. Born nearly seventy years before to a fairly prosperous cloak-and-suiter (her description) named J. Henry Rothschild ("My God, no, dear! We'd never even heard of those Rothschilds!) and his wife, a former schoolteacher of Scotch extraction (" . . . who promptly went and died on me," she explained bitterly), Dottie had never become reconciled to her mixed parentage.

On this day she received from a publisher a request that she write an autobiography. She exhibits the crumpled letter and her eyes sweep the room in hopeless supplication of those invisible but omnipresent forces that so capriciously shape our destinies; the huge, pleading eyes seem never to stop searching for some sort of sympathetic understanding that they damned well know they aren't going to find.

"I'd never be able to do it," she says, "but I wish to God I could!" The ladylike voice progresses from resignation to a final note of triumph and defiance. "I'd like to write the damned thing, just so I could call it Mongrel!"

She was right. She couldn't. And, of course, if she could, she would have to call it <u>Mongrel</u> because that term came about as near as anything to expressing how Dorothy Parker saw herself: as a mongrel that wanted to be a thoroughbred. It isn't the whole story. <u>Mongrel</u> doesn't even explain all that much, but it is a beginning. Dottie had little impulse toward public self-analysis, at least not of the dispassionate and objective sort. She had no trouble, God knows, finding harsh words with which to <u>dismiss</u> her life and work, from: "I was following in the exquisite footsteps of Miss Edna St. Vincent Millay, unhappily in my own horrible sneakers," to the more brutal, ". . . just a little Jewish girl trying to be cute." But these statements, though they had truth in them, are a way of evading a more revealing truth. Not for Dottie the psychoanalytically oriented confessional style of breast baring that has been a common vogue of our times, and I, for one, say for this relief much thanks. It's too late for me to have to start thinking of her as a walking example of the Electra Complex, or to examine her writing for signs of Penis Envy or other popular psychological ills. She was what she was and she wrote what she wrote and none of the terms one might think of tell us anything that the work doesn't. "She was part of nothing and nobody except herself; it was this independence of mind and spirit that was the true distinction," her longtime friend, Lillian Hellman, said at her funeral. Miss Hellman also said that Dottie wanted her tombstone to tell the world, "If you can read this, you've come too close."

When, in the last months of her life, and a few years after the remark quoted at the beginning of this piece, she seemed to want to get her story down ("It would give me something to live for," she said), sitting for a few dozen hours talking into a tape recorder while I, who saw her not only as a thoroughbred but as best of breed and best in show as well, prodded her with apprehensive questions, she began by saying, "Let's make it gay; if it's not fun, there's no point in telling it," and then plunged into a narrative that was all one color and that color was black. It owed more, I think, to her early (and late) enthusiasm for Dickens than to the actual facts, if one assumes that facts must behave themselves and not vary too wildly from one recording session to the next. If the accuracy of her reporting fluctuated, the mood did not. She could (and did) stand one's hair on end with a chronicle of the adversities of a waif with the unfortunate name of Dorothy, a chronic victim whose misadventures were enough to make a piker out of de Sade's Justine. "I apologize for introducing nobody but dreadful characters," Dottie would interject cheerfully as she waded on in a saga of a childhood filled with such obstacles as ignorant nuns ("Well, how do you <u>expect</u> them to treat a kid who saw fit to refer to the Immaculate Conception as 'Spontaneous Combustion'? Boy, did I think I was smart! Still do") hostile children ("They weren't exactly your starched-crinoline set, you know. Dowdiest little bunch you ever saw") at the Blessed Sacrament Convent ("It was practically around the corner and you didn't have to cross any avenues, whatever that means. Never mind you couldn't learn anything"), while at home, a house on West Seventy-second Street ("It's still standing, I believe. They sell trusses there now"), was a dearly loathed father ("On Sunday's he'd take us on an outing. Some outing. We'd go to the cemetery to visit my mother's grave. All of us, including the second wife. That was his idea of a treat. Whenever he'd hear a crunch of gravel that meant an audience approaching, out would come the biggest handkerchief you ever saw, and in a lachrymose voice that had remarkable carrying power, he'd start wailing, 'We're all here, Eliza! I'm here. Dottie's here. Mrs. Rothschild is here--'"), two unsympathetic older brothers and a sister ("I remember my brother coming along the street once with a friend. The friend pointed at me. 'That your sister?' 'No,' my brother said. That helped. There was an enormous gap there, you see; you can't bridge that, ever. Nine years between my sister and me. She was a real beauty, my sister: sweet, lovely, but silly"), a wretched stepmother ("She was crazy with religion. I'd come in from school, she'd greet me with 'Did you love Jesus today?' Now, how do answer that? She was hurt because the older ones called her 'Mrs. Rothschild.' What else? That was her name. I didn't call her anything. 'Hey you,' was about the best I could do"), and malicious servants ("In those days they used to go down to Ellis Island and bring them, still bleeding, home to do the laundry. You know, that didn't encourage them to behave well. Honest, it didn't"). Exaggerations, of course, but creative exaggerations that throw a fascinating light on what the truth must have been.

Our sessions invariably turned into visits, and, as one of the things we had in common was a shameless lust for gossip, the resultant tapes, except for the times when I had the presence of mind (and the discretion) to shut the damned thing off, reveal much more happy (and inventive) speculation about the secret lives of some of the more beautiful of the "Beautiful People" than about Dottie's days among the golden circle at the Algonquin Round Table, a circle, which, in any case, she maintained she'd never been a part of ("Mr. Benchley and I weren't there for the simple reason that we couldn't afford it. It cost money, and we weren't just poor, we were penniless"). If it was hard for her to remember her own statistics, she had no such difficulty with those of the aforementioned beautiful folk, recalling with deadly accuracy just how much so-and-so inherited from which side of the family and who was once married to whom and for how long and (what's more) <u>why</u>. She conscientiously followed the comings and goings of that group through the columns; her curiosity was insatiable and her memory infallible. She had her favorites and her prejudices, and, from the number of times she protested that she would have gone to Truman Capote's historic ball if he had asked her, adding with a bitter laugh, "Which he <u>didn't</u>!", it was clear that she was hurt by being left out.

She was called "Mrs." Parker because, as she put it, "There was once a <u>Mr.</u> Parker." Somebody said of her that she only married her first husband in order to take his name. Mr. Benchley and Mr. Sherwood addressed her in that manner in the old days and it stuck. I've heard Alan introduce her as Miss Parker, and people who met her late in her life tended to call her "Miss" but I always liked the "Mrs." There was something special and singular about it, something romantic and dignified that seemed right for her. It suggested another era to me, the nineteenth century, perhaps, or earlier, when actresses were simply a "Mrs. Gilbert" or "Mrs. Bathwell" or "Mrs. Siddons."

Biographies will be written about her, then more will be written after that, and people will say they're marvelous and maybe they will be, but I'm willing to start taking bets that they won't get anywhere near the truth of her. How can they? The truth of her was <u>that</u> complex, and complex truths resist examination. They play tricks on you. It's the problem anybody has who sets out to describe any unique personality. You talk and talk and talk and the listener gets an impression and it may even be an interesting one, but it is only remotely like the original. Try to describe W. C. Fields to somebody who has never seen him, if you want to get an idea of the difficulty. Dottie was an original. She was unique. None of the words fit. (Cooper's Law: If you didn't know Dorothy Parker, whatever you think she was like, she wasn't. Even if you did know her, whatever you thought she was like, she probably wasn't.)

If I sound as if I am about to reveal to you exactly what she was like, would someone in the front row please get up and kick me where it hurts. The decent thing to do is admit that I can't and then get on with it. What one does in the end is fall back on retelling the stories about her and repeating the things she's alleged to have said (most of which she disclaimed), and the result is something that could go to Hollywood and be played by Miss Eve Arden, but it's not the Dorothy Parker I knew. May I offer one slight attempt to describe her by saying that a tiny part of the truth of her is that she could never, never, under any circumstances, be played by Eve Arden? Or by anybody else for that matter, notwithstanding the fact that many have tried. She was the model for so many plays that Alexander Woollcott once wrote her that he'd just gone to a play and neither he nor she was a character in it! Come to think of it, I believe I remember that Miss Arden (as well as Tallulah Bankhead, et al.) did a turn one summer as a character patterned after Dottie in George Oppenheimer's Here Today, in a part originated on Broadway by Ruth Gordon, who then went on to write and appear in a play or two of her own with roles that bore more than a casual resemblance to Mrs. Parker. (Miss Gordon's Over 21, a charming account of a famous writer joining her husband at an Army base in the South, as Dottie did when Alan Campbell enlisted in the Second World War, was also made into a movie with Irene Dunn in the part that was not Dottie and Alexander Knox in the part that was not Alan). Dottie once said that she'd like to write a play about herself but was afraid that Ruth Gordon would sue her for plagiarism.

Probably the best-known description of her is that of Alexander Woollcott, ". . . so odd a blend of Little Nell and Lady Macbeth." It is very funny and very clever, but it is also misleading. She did not affect the sweetness for any ulterior purpose; rather it sprang from her desperate wish to be what the manner suggested. If it had been bogus it wouldn't have been as effective as it was. If she said, "Doesn't she have the loveliest voice?" of a poor soul who had been talking for some time in a particularly rasping one, it was in large part because she really wished it were true. To an actor with a most unfortunate nose and no chin to speak of, who told her of his hopes in Hollywood, she said, "Oh, they've been searching for a new Cary Grant," and he was able to accept the flattery because there really was something quite genuine about it, or at least in the intention behind it. (Let's face it, he was able to accept the compliment because he was a damned fool, but that doesn't alter my point.) Dottie's sad eyes were infinitely regretful that the world is filled with unpleasant voices and Pinocchio noses, and she made her little effort to improve upon God's slipshod handiwork by giving voice to things as they should be. The inside of her head must have been a battleground. Her desire to be a lady (and she was a lady and a great one), soft-spoken, gracious, delicate, charitable, and well-mannered (and may I be struck dead if she wasn't those things), was constantly at war with her incredible mind, a critical mind, brilliant, precise, and to the point. It was her misfortune (and her fortune) that she saw the absurdity of everyone, including herself; not just piecemeal, either; she saw it whole, entire, all at one time, and sometimes, when one was with her, one would look at people and see them with her X-ray vision (an experience not recommended for casual social intercourse) and would find oneself as dismayed by the phenomena as she must have been. Out of this dismay came those little purrs of sympathy and murmurs of encouragement and the outrageous compliments that misled many an innocent to run on and on, pouring out his heart to her. Her mind, I don't have to tell you, won out in the end, as it must, and asserted itself by the devastating remark, the aptness of which usually passed over the head of the victim, so spellbound was he by her kindly radiance. Moss Hart used to enjoy telling how she charmed his wife, Kitty Carlisle, at their first meeting. The two women sat together on the sofa. Dottie said, "Tell me all about yourself," and Kitty did. At length. She ran through all the high points of her career up to that point. "And there I was," she was saying, "at the Capitol Theatre at ten-thirty in the morning, walking out on a stage for the first time in my life to face the thirty-six hundred people . . ." while Dottie was clicking her tongue and exclaiming softly "How could they do that to you!"

Unhappy aspects of life genuinely pained her, but the pain never stopped her from staring disaster square in the face. Once, in Hollywood, soon after she and Alan had reconciled for the last time (they were married off and on from 1933 until his death in 1963), we were having one of our periodic forest fires, and thousands of acres and hundred of houses were being destroyed. I dropped by Alan and Dottie's, as was my neighborly custom, and found her listening to an account of the fire on the radio. I took Alan aside and asked if he though she would like to see it. He said that she was dying to, but she would have to be persuaded. I broached mentioning offhandedly that the holocaust was visible from a nearby hilltop, and that I had been thinking of driving up for quick look. "Oh, I couldn't bear it! What a terrible sight it must be!" she was saying as she pulled on a sweater and headed for the door. We got to the hilltop and couldn't see anything. We went further, and still couldn't. Should we keep going? Might as well. We traveled, finally, some ten or fifteen miles, with Dottie protesting all the way, until suddenly there it was, the entire horizon aflame. Miles of fire. Dottie's face was hidden in her hands, but she was peeking out between her fingers. "It's like Dante's Inferno, isn't it? The end of the world!" she was saying in genuine distress. "Think how frightened all the little animals are: the little squirrels, the little rabbits, all the little birds," then, without a change of voice, "Do you think we could get any closer?"

She didn't hit anybody who wasn't as big as she was, and she never picked unworthy targets. Her barbs were aimed at sham, pomposity, and pretension. Let us consider her celebrated encounter with Mrs. Clare Boothe Luce. The details are doubtless familiar: the two women arrive simultaneously at the door of a restaurant. Mrs. Luce gestured for Dottie to go first, saying, "Age before beauty." Now, Mrs. Luce, we all know, passed some pretty funny remarks in her early days, before she switched careers (she passed some pretty funny ones afterward, too, but never mind that), but "Age before beauty" will not go down in history as among her best. It will win no prizes for originality. Why, we were saying that in high school down in Quitman, Mississippi, around that time, and we didn't even know there was such a thing as wit. It seems a safe assumption that the phrase contained more hostility than humor. It just wasn't Mrs. Luce's night. Certainly it is clear from all accounts that she spoke first, threw down the gauntlet, so to speak, and as she is not a lady totally incapable of taking care of herself, one suspects that her most ardent supporters would have to concede that Mrs. Parker was justified in striking back. Under these circumstances, it is nice that our Dottie was able to rise to the occasion. And rise she did. "And pearls before swine," she said as she glided past, doubtless to the applause of the angels.

The same Mrs. Luce was the object of another of Dottie's oft-quoted remarks, and it is a particular favorite of mine. On being told that Mrs. Luce made a habit of being kind to her inferiors, Dottie asked, "Where does she find them?" With that line she managed to slay not only the unslayable Mrs. Luce, but the whole notion of condescending graciousness. Because she had quite a splendid contempt for the wisecrack and the wisecracker, she was inclined to put down the over-inflated reputation of the Algonquin wits as fiction. "It was no Mermaid Tavern, I can tell you. Just a bunch of loud-mouths showing off, saving their gags for days, waiting for a chance to spring them. 'Did you hear about my remark?' 'Did I tell you what I said?' And everybody hanging around, asking, 'What'd he say? What'd he say?' The whole thing was made up by people who'd never been there. And may I say they're still making it up? Woollcott was ridiculous. He had a good heart, for whatever that was worth, and it wasn't much. Mencken was impossible. George Kaufman was a mess. I see nothing in that talent at all. . . . Oh, I suppose I do, but you know what I mean. It's just that there was so much praise. . . . Nathan is missed. None of the others are." (Nathan, reviewing a musical, once said, "All the show girls looked like David O. Selznick." You know, we could use that today.) Her relations with most of the regulars (though not with Robert Benchley and Robert Sherwood, her colleagues at Vanity Fair, both of whom she adored) were pretty much an on-and-off thing. She and Mr. Kaufman went through periods of not speaking, in spite of the fact that a grudging affection remained on both sides. Once, at the Round Table, responding to a humorously anti-Semitic insult from one of the habitues, Mr. Kaufman jokingly threatened to leave, adding, "And I'll expect Mrs. Parker to accompany me halfway." During one other of their prolonged estrangements, Mrs. Kaufman, the brilliant Beatrice, decided to stage a reconciliation. Dottie was accordingly invited to the Kaufman establishment in Bucks County for the weekend. All went cozily on Saturday. Drinks were drunk, wits sparkled, and affection flowed. On Sunday morning, however, disaster struck. Dottie happened to be the first one down for breakfast, and, there in a special box on the front page of the drama section of The New York Times, was a reprint of an article she had written for the Chicago Tribune ("Who expects anybody in New York to see something you wrote for Chicago?") in which she referred to "that singularly nasty little play by Mr. Kaufman and Mr. Hart, The Man Who Came to Dinner." Obviously, this would never do. Mr. Kaufman was very fond of his newspaper, and liked to spend a leisurely breakfast over it. She had to work fast. She tucked it under her arm, scurried up the stairs, and locked it in her suitcase. George came down for breakfast. No newspaper. The staff was called in and questioned sternly. Mr. Kaufman was a gentle and sweet-natured man when all was going well, but could be quite wintry when faced with negligent servants, and this occasion was no exception. During the inquisition Dottie hovered around, innocently wondering aloud whatever could have happened to it! Breakfast was got through, with Beatrice being charming, Dotty chatty, and George disgruntled. For lunch, the party journeyed over to Moss Hart's nearby place to consolidate the reunion. His paper had not been stolen. He drew George aside; the mystery of the disappearing newspaper was solved; a frosty afternoon was had by all, and the negotiations were off.

She felt sorry for anybody who had no humor. Of Fitzgerald, whom, as a person, she liked best of the serious writers, she said, "He was attractive and sweet and he wanted to be nice--Ernest never wanted to be nice; he just wanted to be worshiped. He was a bore then, and he remained so--but the damndest thing about Scott, he didn't know what was funny. He could be funny in his books, but not in life. I remember once in Antibes we were coming out of a restaurant, and there was a little man selling nuts. He had them beautifully arranged on a tray, and Scott tipped the tray over. Intentionally. He couldn't understand why that wasn't funny. 'Wasn't that funny? Wasn't that funny? But I gave him a hundred francs!' He couldn't understand why that made no difference." Of Zelda: "She was living in the day of the shock technique. That wears off very quickly, don't you think? Sitting at a dinner where nothing in particular was being said, she would turn to a neighbor"--here Dottie assumed an outlandish Southern accent--"'Ah do think Al Jolson's a greater man than Jesus Christ, don't yew?' She wanted to be thought of as 'fast'--a speed." When Alan, Dottie, and I were working at Fox Studios, they had a secretary who had absolutely no sense of humor. This fascinated Dottie and she and Alan used to promise each other sleds for Christmas if they could get her to smile. Dottie swore that everything about the girl was artificial, and I believe it was true. Breasts, eyelashes, hair, fingernails, teeth, all seemed false. Dottie used to try to surprise her in the restroom, hoping to catch her with all or some of the beauty aids removed. She kept wondering if there was anything at all there. Every day at lunch, they would report to me the secretary's personal phone calls, which were the major events of their day. Once, when the secretary had two tickets to a movie premiere, she spent the morning calling various fellows, trying without success to find a date. She was, needless to say, unaware that the pair were eavesdropping, and, when Dottie guilelessly inquired who was taking her to the movie, she replied airily, "Oh, I'd rather just go with a nice girl than with some man I don't like." It was our favorite saying for a while and we used to say it to each other rather a lot, and roll about with laughter. We took long lunch hours, going off the lot and driving down toward Santa Monica to find a place to eat. Getting away always took a long time because Dottie would go to the rest room, which was filled with secretaries talking, and get into a booth to listen. Each day she would stay longer, and Alan would get impatient, as we were waiting in the car, but when she appeared she had many goodies to report, and she remembered every word; if she didn't it was no matter, for she had made up something better. She was intolerant of affectation. One of our more narcissistic neighbors, describing a minor automobile accident in which she'd received a small scratch on her face, said archly, "I did hope there wouldn't be a scar." Dottie muttered, "As opposed to all those women who like looking as if they went to school at Heidelberg."

I don't suppose anybody ever thought of her as old. She wasn't. Even as I write this word I'm struck by the inappropriateness of it. Her fragility had nothing to do with age; the deep lines across her cheeks came not from the piling up of the years, but from staring wide-eyed at the human comedy. The mind remained quick and severe and young, with the anger and daring and hope of youth. I was never aware of the difference between her age and Alan's (he was some ten years younger) or, for that matter, the difference between her age and mine.

Probably everybody has somebody with whom he is never completely himself. The reasons for this may be varied--awe of a hero, respect for a talent, or just plain fear. In all the years I knew Dottie, and however often I saw her (and for a long time it was several times a day, for we lived a few doors apart and worked at the same studio), I was never totally at ease with her . . . well hardly ever. Not for long at a time, anyway. I could not escape seeing myself as I imagined I looked to her, an Ichabod Crane, all awkwardness and absurdity, the nervous laugh always at the ready just in case, grinning and simpering with an embarrassing eagerness to please. I never stopped feeling, somehow, like an adolescent covered with runny pimples. Alan assured me from time to time that if evening approached and they had not heard from the Sharecropper (for Sharecropper I was called, in recognition of my Mississippi origin, a background Dottie accused me of making up in an attempt to be interesting; later, when I bought a house, the Campbells' maid was solemnly instructed that henceforth she must announce that the Landowner was calling, erasing my former title), Dottie would start wondering why not, and she has been known to go to the telephone and dial my number herself, and there are few who can make that claim. Nevertheless, I was never sufficiently reassured, and advisedly so. Another friend of hers, who used to see her at the Volney Hotel after she moved back to New York, swore to me that she had never said unpleasant things about me in his presence, but after all I could not forget that I'd sworn the same thing with equal fervor, and I had had to cross every one of my fingers behind my back as I did so.

When I told Lillian Hellman that she was the one friend of whom Dottie consistently spoke with respect, affection and admiration, Miss Hellman said, "People have told me that through the years, and I always found it hard to believe, but so many have said it I've finally come to accept it."

She resisted friendship with all her might. God forbid she should let anybody get the idea she was popular. Neglect was infinitely preferable. The phone would ring in her room. She would exclaim, "Ah, here's fresh help!" and answer in an apprehensive voice. Upon hearing the name of the caller, she would curtly say "Not in," then turn to me: "I don't want to speak to Mr. X now or ever, do you?" Later, in the same visit, she would complain that she never hears from the same Mr. X anymore. Once, when I went to pick her up to bring her to a dinner at our house, she paused outside the hotel entrance to drink in the wonder of the city at night. "It's the first time I've been out after dark since I got back to New York," she said, forgetting that she'd just been telling me about some monster of a play somebody had dragged her to a few evenings before. It's easier for a neglected girl to know who she is. It was not by accident that she wrote those poems in which the romantic girl's passion is rewarded by a sock in the eye.

This affinity for distress extended to money matters. When royalty checks came in, they were hastily put away in the backs of bureau drawers, to remain there, unopened, for years, while she went on worrying about how she could pay the rent.

And God help anybody who tried to come to her aid. Alexander Woollcott's description of Mrs. Patrick Campbell in her declining days, as "a sinking battleship firing on her rescuers," can be applied here with no fear of exaggeration. There was something quite fierce and splendid about it. Not long after Alan's death, we were sitting in the living room of the California house. The heat was stifling, for the windows, which went all the way to the floor, could not be opened lest the dogs get out. There arrived on the scene a very altruistic lady, a former movie star as a matter of fact, as gracious as she was charitable, who had gone to the trouble earlier of measuring the windows and then having screens cut to fit. With the cheerfully bustling air of the well intended, she lugged the screens while Dottie went on effusively about her inability ever to repay "such kindness, such sweetness, such compassion, such beneficence . . . ." While Dottie continued in this vein, the lady asked me to find a hammer and nails, where upon Dottie abruptly stopped her recitation of praise, turned to me, freezing me with a gaze of exaggerated (and unwelcome) sympathy, and said, "If there's anything I can't stand, it's a bossy woman!"

During this time, helpful people brought her food, for otherwise she did not eat. Alan once told me before she'd cook anything, she'd go into the kitchen and eat raw bacon. One saw quite a turnover in new faces, as none of the good samaritans lasted long. They all started out with much enthusiasm, but retired, after a while, looking somewhat subdued. One neighbor, who happened to be the least bit effete, brought a couple to look at the house, which Dorothy wanted to sell in preparation for the move back to New York. While the prospective homeowners gingerly picked their way among the little piles of doggie waste (it had a way of accumulating after Alan was gone), the neighbor perched tentatively on a chair facing Dottie. "It's so kind of you to do this." Dorothy was saying, "but, then, that's just the way you are, warmhearted, tender, compassionate, obliging. . . ." The fellow gushed a bit, quite pleased with himself, all out of proportion really, as he did expect to make a commission on the deal. He then allowed as how he'd better see how the clients were doing. He was barely out of his chair, certainly not out of earshot, before she said, "There he goes, tossing his little

Shirley Temple curls."

I doubt that this is a distinction that would hold up in court, but I really don't think it was the person who had rallied around to help for whom she meant the back of her hand. Not the person, but the self-congratulating pleasure that the do-gooder takes in his deed--that's what aroused her ire. Being grateful for an extended period produces a hell of a strain, and, as Virtue was obviously rewarding itself, she couldn't resist a little annihilation.

The incident of the Shirley Temple curls reminds me of a story Alan told me (it is irrelevant here, probably, but we needn't let that stop us), of the night he and Dottie got tattooed with matching tattoos, a star on the inside of their upper arms. It had seemed a good idea at the time, though she was later to complain that it had condemned her to long sleeves for the rest of her life. All Alan remembered of the night was that they were in a bar or something in Greenwich Village, and a rather delicate sort of fellow recognized Dottie and asked her, for some reason, if she liked fairy stories. "My dear," she said, "let us not talk shop."

During the Twenties and the Thirties she must have been the most quoted woman in America. At the time I knew her, she denied almost everything attributed to her. She sometimes denied things on general principle, I think, as she genuinely resented having her witticisms repeated to her, but more often than not the quotations were neither hers nor truly funny. I have seen her in a rage when a misguided person told her he adored a tacky little poem that had been widely circulated and falsely credited to her. It concerned Miss Marion Davies and William Randolph Hearst, and Dottie had nothing whatever to do with its composition. Apart from the general squalor of it she pointed out, "It rhymed 'honor' with 'madonna!'" Young (and old) girls often said to her "I've always loved your lines, 'Men never make passes at girls who wear glasses.'" If Alan were present, he would break in and correct them sharply: "'Seldom,' not 'never.' Men seldom make passes. . . " Dottie was quite capable purring the while, "Unfortunately, my dear, I never said it," a reaction that came almost automatically to her. That line, which is a poem actually, called News Item, is her best-known saying; people know it who do not know her name.

Which reminds me of an incident at the unemployment office. When Alan and Dottie finished their work at Fox (on a script of The Good Soup, rumored to be for Marilyn Monroe), I persuaded them to file for unemployment compensation, which I was already drawing. It is a perfectly honorable procedure, and a rewarding one. You got quite a lot, considering it was tax free; it seems to me that it was about $75 a week, and for the two of them it amounted to a worthwhile sum by the end of the month. All you had to do was go in once a week and sign a card saying they you were available for work. It was pleasant and even a rather chic thing to do; you not only caught sight of such stars as Marlon Brando from time to time, but you also ran into old chums you hadn't encountered for ages, whom you were happy to see as long as you didn't have to spend a lot of time with them. The parking lot always had a Rolls or two along with an abundance of sporty Cadillacs and we once decided that you saw just as many celebrities there as you would lunching at Romanoff's; furthermore, as Dottie was quick to comment, "It's a much nicer set." The first time you go, however, there is a certain amount of bother. Papers must be filled out, and you are sent from desk to desk and asked such questions as "Have you been looking for employment?", "Are you enrolled in any school?", and "What other skills or experience have you that might be of use in other fields?" They never bat an eye at the large sums you have been paid for your studio services; they've heard it all before. On the way down, I coached Alan and Dorothy carefully. The coaching was necessary because both were behaving as if they were about to perjure themselves into prison. We kept assuring each other heartily that, after all, we paid enormous taxes and were entitled to our rights like any body else. Alan and I collaborated on filling out their preliminary forms, as it was an undertaking for which neither of us had any talent, and for which Dottie was hopeless. We could not, however, accompany her for the necessary interviews. We stood watching as she was shuttled from clerk to clerk, looking like a lamb on its way to slaughter. "Ah, she'll be all right now," Alan said as she approached one desk, "that one has glasses on." Sure enough, the lady with glasses looked up, asked a question, grinned broadly, took off her spectacles, shook hands, and called several other girls over to touch the author of the familiar lies. We were too far away to hear what was being said, but could see several pairs of lips moving as they recited the poem to her, and Dottie's expression on this occasion was one of deep gratitude. Everyone was most cooperative after that and it was even arranged that the Campbell's reporting time would coincide with mine so that we could make a weekly jaunt of it.

Norma Place, where they lived in West Hollywood, was only one block long. At some point in pre-history Norma Talmadge had had a studio on the spot and it was for her that it was named. Dottie called it Peyton Place, West. The frame building that had been Miss Talmadge's dressing room still dominated the little street. It was the largest house on the block and had been cut up into several apartments, in one of which lived Estelle Winwood. Her front room was quite near the sidewalk and one could pass by at almost any time and see her, somewhat on display, like a mannequin in a shop window, perpetually pouring tea, always carefully groomed and wearing a hat. The neighboring houses had once been the non-descript homes of railroad workers, fairly uniform in lack of design, but in recent years they had been taken over by people connected "with the Industry," as they say out there, and the facades done over in a sort of Regency style (for want of a better term) that has evolved in that area, and nowhere else. Nina Foch, Carleton Carpenter, John Dall, and Alan were among the longest term residents, the pioneers, so to speak, but other moderately well-known personages came and went. I remember Dottie's delight when Tuesday Weld's mother moved in, and Dottie would ask the neighbors, "Have you met Tuesday's Weld's mother, Wednesday, yet?" Everyone knew everybody else, there was much dropping in on each other, few secrets were possible, and nothing that went on was beneath Dottie's notice. The bank, the post office, the laundromat, and the supermarket were clustered around the corner and down the hill, and if you had an errand in any of those places, you were likely to encounter Troy Donahue or the like, and find out who was working today on what film, who had gone to the beach, and who was having drinks with whom. There was also a bar called the Four Star, where one might glimpse Patsy Kelly shooting a mean game of pool, or a former wife of Louis Hayward passing the time with a couple of pals and a few assorted dogs. Dottie's arrival in the area had caused a momentary sensation, of course, and she became an instant landmark. She was pointed out politely as she took the dogs for walks, and she returned from those outings a mine of information. Once, at night, she saw Estelle Winwood (who, she said, used to be around the Algonquin in the old days, and "she was creaking, even then"), driving along in the dark, blissfully unaware that she had forgotten to turn on the headlights, but with the interior lights burning brightly. (Later, when I mentioned that Miss Winwood was acting in <u>Camelot</u>, Dottie commented, "Playing a battlement, no doubt.") Now and then we had a little extra excitement, like when a character lady's canary got out and all the fellows joined (unsuccessfully) in trying to recapture it, while the tearful owner jogged along, calling out to the fugitive bird, and Dottie tried to keep up, offering comfort as best she could. Or maybe somebody got drunk and fell off a porch and broke a toe--that kind of thing happened from time to time. Rumors were forever spreading--that Judy Garland was visiting one of the residents, or that Dorothy Dandridge had looked at a house that was for sale, or that a certain couple was breaking up; we took a lively interest in such things. Once everybody was invited for the unveiling of a portrait of one of the most popular Norma Placers. His living room was small and the portrait was big. In it, our host was life-size and stark naked, seated, facing front, with carefully drawn genitals that seemed to tumble out at you. Dottie was most genteel and admiring, murmuring things like "It's so real, you almost feel he could speak to you, don't you?"

But the biggest sensation of all was Bathsheba Glyn's rape. (That is not her real name, of course.) Miss Glyn, an authoress with a number of plays and scenarios to her credit, had a habit of lying nude in her bedroom watching television, and her window shade did not seem to reach all the way to the bottom of the window. Now, to be fair, it should be pointed out that this window was not readily visible from the street; you were not likely to see it unless you happened to be hanging around in her neighbor's driveway, but we did a lot of hanging around in each other's driveways in those days, and if you had any excuse whatever for being in that particular driveway, Miss Glyn's charms were there to be seen, and so near that, as Alan said, "If you couldn't actually reach out and touch them, they were certainly within spitting distance." Not half bad charms, either, all things considered. As a sort of running gag, Alan and I were always inviting each other to stroll down and take a look before turning in, and once or twice Dottie, who never entirely believed it, was about to go with us and see for herself, but would lose her courage before we got there. Imagine then, her fascination when news spread that poor Bathsheba had been raped at five-o'clock of a morning. Dottie expressed horror like everybody else, but only when company was present. She relished every detail, and details were not sparing. Since Bathsheba had called in a few neighbors, as well as the police, as soon as her surprised guest had departed, it didn't take long for word to get round. Apparently, she had fallen asleep watching <u>The Late Show</u>, leaving the lights on. It seems safe to assume that some casual passerby was overcome by the sight and lost control of himself, but, according to Bathsheba, the intruder told her (in a postcoital conversation over drinks) that he had seen her in the supermarket, become obsessed by a passion for her, and, knowing that he could never possess her any other way ("I don't know why people jump to such conclusions!" said Dottie), he had taken this tack. He was eighteen years old, or so he told her, and he was blonde--Bathsheba could tell by the texture of his skin, as she was not allowed to see his face, which was covered by a shirt. We spent some time trying to figure out how he maneuvered his drink with that shirt over his head, but reluctantly concluded that in desperate situations such things can be managed. She had promised to cooperate on condition he would afterward discuss his reasons for such outrageous behavior, an arrangement to which he agreed with alacrity. I am omitting some of the more explicit details as hardly suitable for a man's magazine, but would feel remiss if I did not report Dottie's reaction to the disclosure that a certain jar of vaseline had figured in the act, since the lad found some difficulty effecting the entry, ". . . because he was so large or she was so small--in either case, a fantasy," said Dottie. She refused to believe any of it, even after police found footprints and the kitchen knife with which he had threatened his victim. Dottie further claimed to have heard a rumor that Bathsheba was to be arrested for contributing to the delinquency of a minor by giving him the alcoholic beverage. It was with reluctance that we departed for the studio on those days, so fearful were we of missing new developments. Little writing got done, in any case, as we were in constant touch by telephone, working out new theories and speculations.

It is often said of married couples,"They couldn't be happy together and they couldn't be happy apart," and this certainly applied to Dottie and Alan. They were two of the most engaging people in the world, and absolutely right for each other. Probably they were too right for each other. Their relationship was an extraordinary one, incredibly close, each strongly identifying with the other, but also mutually antagonistic and somehow fearful and bitter toward the other. When I first saw them together--it must have been in 1955 or '56--they had been separated for quite a while, and the experience was so disturbing to me that the intervening years have almost succeeded in putting it out of my mind, and remembering it even now is oddly discomforting. I had known Alan only casually; I had seen him here and there and, though he was one of the most charming, witty, and sociable gentlemen alive, he also had a surprising defensiveness, an off-putting chip on the shoulder, that made me wary of him. I was surprised then, when, in the elevator after a gathering at George Kaufman's, he suddenly asked, like a man desperate not to be alone, "I have to go see Dottie. Will you go with me?" As my previous encounters with Mrs. Parker had not been pleasant ones--this was an unhappy period in her life--I must have hesitated, though it is doubtful that I hesitated long, my curiosity being what it was. She lived then (as she did later) at the Volney, and my memory is of a stark, bare, colorless, and impersonal room, with a large bone on the floor, dog toys on the gravy-colored sofa, a dog of course and an agonized Alan facing a stricken-looking Dottie, who was, as incredible as it seems now, actually fat. My impression was of a sad, bewildered young girl, angrily trapped inside an inappropriate and almost grotesque body. Of the desolate conversation, I remember only that she apologized repeatedly: for the disorder of the room, for her own appearance, for the behavior of the dog, and for the absence of anything to drink. There was a sense of unreality about it: the darkened room, the sad and lost lady, the man ill-at-ease and poised for flight, and the stranger to them both, with no reason whatever for being present. It was painful to witness the estrangement of two people who were forever to be deeply involved with each other. Loneliness and guilt were almost like physical presences in the space between them, and they spoke in short, stilted, and polite sentences with terrible silences in between, and yet there was a tenderness in the exchange, a grief for old hurts, and a shared reluctance to turn loose.

I am glad that I came to know and love them later in better times, when they had great fun together, as they must have done in earlier and younger days. In Hollywood in 1960 their spirits were gay; they delighted in each other's humor and found pleasure in each other's company. They had the kind of unspoken communication of those who know all there is to know about each other.

They were very alike, much more alike than most people realized. Not only their humor--Alan wrote the funniest letters I've ever read--but their critical judgments were almost interchangeable. Even their backgrounds had certain parallels. Alan's father was of Scotch extraction and his mother was Jewish. Coming from Richmond, Virginia, and from a social class that concerned itself with such things, he had a feeling of not belonging that matched Dottie's own. Also, they were similarly embarrassed by private emotions. Dottie was incapable of admitting to any degree of happiness; shortly after she came to Norma Place, I heard someone at a party ask where she was staying, and, with the shame faced mien of an adolescent caught in an indiscretion, she replied, "At Alan's, isn't that disgraceful?" Many years before, someone had said to her, "Dottie, what are you complaining about? You're married to a charming, handsome man who adores you. What more do you want?" Dottie shot back, "Presents!"

When they awoke on the morning of their second wedding day (in 1950; they had been divorced three years earlier), Dottie coyly pulled the sheet over her face, and said, "Mustn't see the bride before the wedding." At the reception, someone remarked that many were present who had not spoken to each other for years, and Dottie rejoined, "Including the bride and groom."

She was incurably jealous, and accused him of infidelities that, according to him, did not exist. He had a happy capacity for friendships, many of them with cultivated and interesting women. Of one, who was perhaps a little more formal and unbending than most, Dottie said in anger, "I know you're not laying her. If you were, you'd have splinters in your prow."

As time went on, they complained more and more about each other. They took turns, actually. One day she would say "I don't know why Alan behaves as he does when he's drinking. He used to be able to drink and still be fun." The next day Alan would say the same thing of her. If he said, "I didn't know the paper had come," she would say, "I didn't try to hide it," or the lines could as easily be reversed. He used to come over to my house and announce grumpily, "I'm supposed to get out of the way so Dottie can do her Esquire piece. It's already five days late and she's not going to do it. I put a hair on the typewriter, and when I get back, it'll still be there, wait and see, and she's going to claim she's finished it and sent it in." And he would be right. Her book reviews appeared less and less frequently. The magazine would call to ask when it could be expected and she would declare in all innocence, "I can't imagine why it hasn't arrived. I sent it days ago," when she hadn't written a line of it. She went on reading the books, she talked about them brilliantly, and she wanted to write, but the fears of inadequacy, from which she'd always suffered, in common with so many other first-rate writers, became more and more paralyzing.

Their feelings about each other were a blend of pride and exasperation. Alan was constantly starting home-improvement projects, adding a bathroom, or making the garage into a guest cottage to be rented out, and they were rarely completed. Dottie would announce with the air of a true martyr, "I don't know where Alan is; he just pulled two boards up out of the floor and went off to the post office!" Or if he took a chair to be covered in a pretty fabric--he had a strong nest-building instinct--Dottie would share his enthusiasm for the result, taking loving pride in his taste, but, shortly afterward, when the dogs had done their inevitable destruction to it, she was almost gleeful in pointing out the damage.

Sometimes they seemed determined to behave symbolically; when Dottie arrived with her poodle Cliche, Alan, who up to then had seemed content without a dog, went out and bought a bad-tempered Sealyham puppy, and the two animals were never at peace. From their first meeting, they engaged in a running contest to see which could wreak the greater havoc.

At the same time, Alan and Dottie could be fiercely protective of each other. When she suffered through quite a bit of repair work on her teeth, Alan was visibly distressed by her pain.

Once we were driving along in my car and Alan was describing some untalented screenwriter, saying, "He would write a line like, **You're mashing the hell out of my finger!**" Dottie was busily reacting, saying, "Imagine writing a line like that!" and I, ever eager to learn, was trying to figure out what was wrong with the line if the character's fingers were actually being mashed, not connecting it with the fact that I was also, at that moment, pressing a button, the function of which was to raise the window on Alan's side of the car. I had no way of knowing that he'd stuck his fingers down into the space where the window was rising, and it took some time and quite a lot of yelling on Alan's part to make the connection for me. Dottie laughed heartily at this predicament, reversing her former position by saying, "It seemed like a perfectly good line to me," until she saw that there was actually blood on his fingernail, and then she was all concern for him and mad as the devil at my idiocy.

Whatever their anger at each other, they presented a united front when guests were present, each elaborately ignoring any misadventure on the part of the other. One night Miss Cathleen Nesbitt and I were invited for dinner, and, when we arrived, I recognized the glassy, unfocused look in Alan's eyes as a signal that we were headed for trouble. Drinks stretched on and on, with Alan making unsteady trips to the kitchen from time to time to check the progress of a roast. Dottie was fine--his bad behavior brought out her best--she was entertaining and amusing, as was Miss Nesbitt, who is surely one of the most attractive people in the western hemisphere. She spoke charmingly of her affection for Dottie's poem, "One Perfect Rose," and told us about seeing Noel Coward's new musical, Sail Away, describing it in quite gracious terms, while Alan interrupted unpleasantly and frequently, snarling "Let's face it, what you're trying to say is, it stunk!" That was not what she was trying to say, but she never lost her aplomb, nor did Dottie, as stomachs began to rumble and dinner failed to appear. Alan's trips to the kitchen took longer and longer and he angrily refused any offers of help. It was well after ten o'clock before food was forthcoming, and we were so busy not noticing his lurching walk which was, by now, that of a sailor on deck in the worst sort of storm, that it was not until I had a fork loaded with salad on the way to my mouth that I noticed the presence in it of long strips of gaily-colored aluminum wrap. God knows what Alan had thought he was doing as he shredded it so carefully, but there it was disappearing down Miss Nesbitt's elegant throat, while Dottie complimented her husband on the excellence of his cooking. Alan despaired of ever totally pleasing her. He said that no matter what he did, she felt victimized. When World War II began, she went about muttering that any man worth his salt would be in there fighting. Then, when he enlisted, she bitterly accused him of deserting her in perilous times.

She was filled with sympathy for all of society's victims. She and Mr. Benchley were, as is well-known, fined $5 for marching against the execution of Sacco and Vanzetti. This sympathy extended to anyone accused of a crime; so long as they were found guilty, she was convinced of their innocence. It was clear to her, at the time he was in jail, that Dr. Sam Shepard had been railroaded. On the other hand, Lizzie Borden, having been acquitted, would be forever guilty in Dottie's eyes, and she took it personally when a book written a few years back asserted her innocence. "I can sympathize with almost any wrongdoing," she once told me. "People are horrified by child molesting, but it seems perfectly understandable to me. The only criminal activity with which I don't completely identify is arson."

I once heard Alan contemptuously say of a certain irresponsible couple "They simply aren't citizens!" Conversely, Alan and Dottie were citizens. They were civilized persons. When Dottie taught in a Los Angeles college for a while, she hated the students, feeling that they were too quick to settle for too little, the range of their vision was too short--she claimed that they hated her. When she heard that Christopher Isherwood said the students were mad about her and fought to get in her course, she laughed and said, "You know how much sense Christopher makes!" Her feeling about the students didn't extend to the Negroes. She believed in their future, and she left her estate to Martin Luther King Jr., whom she had never met, because she respected what he had done. She adored the memory of President Roosevelt ("He was God; you didn't exactly feel you were slumming with him"), and she thought Mrs. Roosevelt was a heroine ("What a woman! So decent, so fair minded, and, it's hard to believe, but when you met her, she was the most beautiful woman you ever saw"). Of the Thirties, she said, "They were progressive days. We thought we were going to make the world better--I forget why we thought it, but we did." And, of course, like most literate persons, she was passionate about Adlai Stevenson. She never ceased to have great hopes for the young, her dislike of those students not withstanding, and she never stopped feeling passionately involved in the issues of the day.

In June of 1963, I was in Tuscaloosa, Alabama, where Governor George Wallace was making his brief stand in the door of the university to bar enrollment of two Negro students--for a couple of hours until the National Guard could be mobilized to overwhelm him. The National Guard consisted of university students who did weekend military training and, with the eyes of the entire world focused on the historic event, one was startled to move among the assembled militia and hear them asking each other questions like, "Are you taking English Lit again this term?" I had nothing whatever to do with any of it, needless to say. I was simply a fascinated observer, only allowed to be there because I was a self-invited guest of the president of the university, a relative of mine. I wrote Alan and Dottie long daily accounts of the human side of the events leading up to the encounter in the doorway (and those events were very human, indeed, and surprisingly humorous as well) and it was there that I received word of Alan's sudden death. Shaken and emotional, I called Dottie, not really expecting her to be in any condition to come to the phone. She did, however, and there ensued a most disconcerting conversation. While I was still making blubbery and incoherent noises of sympathy, she cut me off by saying, as calmly as if continuing a conversation interrupted only five minutes earlier, "The whole world thanks you for what you're dong." I couldn't think what she was referring to, unless it was the act of calling her. "I could hardly not--" I began, but she went on, "And let's face it dear, it's not for yourself you're doing it; it's for all mankind--" By now I was hopelessly at sea. "I think we can say Alan died with your letters clutched in his hand." Then I had a vague idea of what she was trying to do. She was removing herself from her grief by talking of something else, something untrue, and she was outrageously giving me the credit for accomplishing the integration of the university. (She sometimes paid one a compliment so unreasonable that it was presumptuous even to deny it. One's only recourse was silence and pretending not to have heard it.) I asked her who was with her, and she replied that no one was, although I could hear voices and had recognized that of their close friend, Bill Templeton, when he had answered the phone. I ran through a list of their friends and she said flatly that she had heard from none of them, which was, of course, not true. She was in a state of suspended animation, moving automatically, and she seemed to want to talk. She gave me an account of her discovery of his body, speaking as one might to a newspaper reporter, getting the facts straight. She said, that he'd been awakened at a certain time, and that when she touched him "rigor mortis had already set in." This last she said with some coldness as if that condition were somehow his fault. A final affront.

In the four years she lived after that, she was to describe the same thing to me many times, omitting only the references to rigor mortis. It was a moment she returned to again and again. Just as she was to mention over and over that Alan's mother, who still lives in Virginia, had insisted on having the funeral in Richmond. The doctor had advised Dottie not to go ("I didn't know what 'in shock' meant, I was it") and I am sure that it was just as well, her relations with her mother-in-law being what they were.

Of course the idea of Dottie having a mother-in-law of any sort was unsettling at best, and Dottie lodged many a complaint against the senior Mrs. Campbell. "The way she gushed over me when we got married, calling me 'my little daughter' (I wasn't her little daughter; I wasn't her little anything!) while she went around telling everybody I had 'snatched that boy out of the cradle,' just because I happened to be a year and a half older than Alan. You would have thought she was the only mother that ever lived." She had not been happy with Mr. Parker's family either. "His grandfather had been chaplain of the Senate, and he used to call us together for family prayers. 'Oh Lord, grant to the unbeliever in our midst, the light to see the error of her ways. . . .' The unbeliever, in case you don't recognize her, was me! 'Stranger within our gates' was another term he tossed around." Of Edwin Pond Parker II, her husband, whom she met at a summer hotel at Bradford, Connecticut, she said, "He was beautiful, but not very smart. He was supposed to be in Wall Street, but that didn't mean anything. We were married [in 1917] for about five minutes, then he went off to war. He didn't want to kill anybody, so he drove an ambulance. Unfortunately, they had dope in the ambulance. Morphine. You know, that's not good for you. Not healthy. Well, it was one sanatorium after another, so finally I ran off to the Riviera with a Trotskyite." She divorced Mr. Parker in 1928, "In Connecticut, where you can get it for roller skating." When I mentioned this recently to Beatrice Ames, who was once Mrs. Donald Ogden Stewart, she roared with laughter. "Little Charlie Parker a drug addict? Impossible! He was the most harmless little man you ever saw. That Dottie! She's awful! Isn't it marvelous?"

"I should be dead," Dottie said several times that last year, "everybody I ever cared about is." Death was much on her mind. She had been talking of moving, and one day one of the reasons came out. "Do you know what they do when you die in this hotel? They used to take them down on the big elevator in the back, but it's not running and they take them down that front elevator, and you know how small it is. They have to stand you up."

Her rooms, again, were bare and impersonal, though more cheerful than the one I remembered from years before. Except for a Christmas card with a picture of my son on it on the bureau in her bedroom, there were no photographs, no attempts at decoration, and no clues to the identity of its resident, apart from the inevitable pile of books on the coffee table. Even those she did not keep. Publishers continued to send books to her, and as soon as she'd read them, they were pressed on the next visitor. There were only two visible mementos of her life. One was an old edition of her poems or stories, only recently sent to her by a stranger, who had, through the years, cut pictures of her out of the papers and glued them in. When I said that the photographs were beautiful, she said, "My dear, those are pictures. They could fix those up." When I said that it was a fascinating thing to have, she said gruffly, "Want it?" and I put the book down. The other souvenir, and the only thing so far as I could see that she had salvaged from the California house, was a set of Napoleon's generals, thirteen porcelain figures, that we had come across in a junky sort of antique store in Santa Monica during one of our lunch hours. They were installed in the Campbell living room and Alan even put a special light over them. Here at the hotel Dottie had gotten somebody to put a shelf in the middle of the a wall, and Napoleon, backed by his stalwart generals, brooded down on her as she went about her daily occupations. When I took Carter Cooper, an extremely self-possessed and brilliant child who was then just past his second birthday, up to see her, he strolled in, shook hands, and indicating the figures with a tilt of his beautiful head, said, "You like Napoleon?" She was convinced that I'd coached him to say it before we entered the room, until they sat down and had a conversation about Mr. Napoleon putting the crown on Mrs. Napoleon's head, about Baby Napoleon as King of Rome, and Napoleon setting fire to Russia. It happens that our child (who came into this world with a college education) preferred The Life of Napoleon in Pictures to Winnie the Pooh, a literary judgment with which Dottie found herself in complete agreement. She was fascinated by children, and seemed to like them, but a certain a degree of mistrust was apparent in her manner, as if waiting for the little tykes to betray themselves and confirm her darkest suspicions.

One of her passions was Mrs. John F. Kennedy; she was full of admiration for the quiet grace with which that lady conducted her life under incredible pressure and, when I told her of meeting Mrs. Kennedy, she wanted to hear everything about her; what she wore, how she spoke, what we talked about, and could she possibly be as enchanting as Dottie fancied her to be? We promised Dottie that if she would come with us--she had recently been in the hospital and almost never went out--to a recital at the U.N. by Libby Holman, we would invite Mrs. Kennedy. Unfortunately Mrs. Kennedy was unable to join us, though she expressed regret at not being able to meet Mrs. Parker, and delight at hearing that she was alive and around. I, accordingly, conveyed this disappointment to Dottie, who agreed to come anyway. The evening went well; she was enthusiastic and energetic, making a luncheon date with Mr. Main Bocher, chatting as happily as a school girl with Miss Eugenia Sheppard, whose column she followed conscientiously, and, at the concert, enjoying a reunion with Miss Holman. After such an excursion, her spirits were high for days, and she delighted in describing it to her friends, though something in her made it necessary that she balance her diversion with some show of vexation, and her pleasure in this particular evening did not keep her from complaining that we had got her out under false pretenses by promising her Mrs. Kennedy. Another evening, when she was to come to our house for dinner, the city was hit by the worst snowstorm of the season. Cars could not move and the sidewalks were piled so deep with snow and ice that only the most hardy could navigate. She insisted that she could make it, however, and when Harvey Breit went to pick her up, she happily invited him up to her room to zip her dress. "After thirty years of marriage," she explained, "you miss such things." They set out on foot determinedly but she had to give up before they'd gone a block. Her disappointment was so keen that my wife suggested we give a party for her and ask people she'd like to see--some she knew, some she'd like to meet, some she'd enjoy looking at, and some she'd enjoy talking to.

Mr. and Mrs. Gardner Cowles, Mr. and Mrs. William S. Paley, Mr. and Mrs. Bennett Cerf, Mr. and Mrs. Samuel P. Peabody, Mr. and Mrs. Martin Gabel, Mr. and Mrs. John Barry Ryan II, Mr. and Mrs. Louis Auchincloss, Mrs. Arthur Bunker, Miss Gloria Steinem, Miss Jean Parr, Duke Fulco di Verdura, Mr. Herb Sargent, Mr. Richard Adler, and Mrs. Oliver Smith accepted, and Dottie followed all developments with joyful anticipation, but about a week before she suddenly said, "You know I can't go there with Mrs. Paley and all those people. What in God's name would I wear?" It is true she had no clothes. Alan used to take her to buy her dresses, and I don't imagine she had ventured into a store since. But we were prepared for this. My wife was, of course, fascinated by Dottie, and somewhat worshipful, an attitude that was mutual; after their first meeting, Dottie had a dream in which she, Dottie, was the size of a pygmy, and Gloria was tall, towering toward the sky. The dream-Dottie circled around and around, looking up at the tall beauty. She could even describe the dress my wife wore in the dream--it had gold leaves on it, small ones at the top, growing larger toward the bottom. Gloria never heard her breathe an unkind word about anybody. Dottie was always at her most genteel in my wife's presence, with malice toward none and charity for all. Gloria had always wanted to see Dottie in some kind of Chinese robe, delicately embroidered and elegant, and, when, a few months before this, Gloria started wearing caftans as maternity dresses, she often expressed the desire to have one made for Dottie. Having no measurements to go by, it was made in size three, of yellow brocade with gold trim encrusted with little pearls. I took it over to Dottie, and she sat looking at it and touching it in the manner of an orphan with a Christmas present she can't quite believe is meant for her. She went into the bedroom to try it on, and emerged after a long time to say that she didn't know how to get into it. I put it on the floor, and, as one would in dressing a child, I lifted her feet to place them inside the dress, pulled it up, and fastened it around her. The stand-up collar, the soft color, and rich materials emphasized the essential femininity of her face. She stood looking at herself in the mirror and she was transformed. It was as if for a long time she had been unaware of her beauty, and suddenly she could see what she had forgotten. The dress was too long by at least six inches. I offered to have someone come in to shorten it. "No," she said immediately, I want it long. Then I have to lift it, like this . . . . " She pulled herself tall, and with one hand raised her skirt like an Edwardian lady about to step into her carriage. "I want to have that haughty look," she said, which she had. She minced about the room, head held high, body erect and proud, steps ladylike and sure, while her eyes followed her progress in the mirror.

Gloria Steinem and Herb Sargent brought her to the party, and she entered the room trembling but looking magnificent, like the last dowager empress of China, a creature frail and exquisite but a power not to be tampered with, a lady of grace and modesty but well aware of her own value. She was not unlike a great actress who may have been away for a while, but who knows her audience is still waiting for this appearance, and she's going to make it a triumphant one.

I saw Mrs. Paley catch her husband's arm. "Bill," she said quietly, but with some awe in her voice, "do you know who that is?" And Mr. Paley went over to sit beside Dottie and talk of previous meetings. Others came to her, and she was unfailingly gracious and charming and impressive. The evening had a certain amount of glitter; everybody looked just right, and Dottie's eyes took in every detail of the women's clothes, jewelry, and hairdos; each item was tucked away in her mind to be produced at will later on.

I had a moment with her and whispered that her slippers and bag were perfect. She put on her sorely-tried-but-ever-patient face and said with mock dignity, pronouncing each syllable with elaborate care, "Mr. Cooper, promise me that you will never, never go to Saks to buy gold slippers and gold handbag with Sara Murphy and that Nurse!" Sara Murphy is the legendary Mrs. Gerald Murphy, who, along with her late husband, were objects of idolatry to Scott Fitzgerald and were the models for the glamorous couple in Tender Is The Night. "And promise me further," Dottie went on, "if you do go to Saks to buy gold slippers and gold handbag with Sara Murphy and that nurse, you <u>won't</u> go to Schrafft's for a tea afterward!" She was seated on my right, of course, and as we took our places at table, she spoke glowingly of the room with the red tablecloths, the gleaming silver, the glowing candles, the flowers arranged with such artful casualness (my wife does these things with tolerable style), but when someone remarked that the wine glasses were beautiful, adding, "I always think that wine tastes so much better in lovely glasses, don't you?", Dottie, quick as a flash, said, "Oh, yes, paper cups aren't right," and I was seized by a fit of nervous coughing.

She got on well with Mr. Auchincloss on her other side; she admired his work; he admired hers; it was their first meeting, so that was fine. When it was time for her to turn back to me, we exchanged a few formal remarks and then realized that, after all the years of talking, of letting our hair down and shooting straight, man-to-man as it were, we had, under the presence of elegant circumstances, nothing whatever to say to each other, and we began to laugh.

Three months later she was dead. I know that night meant something to her. There was something splendid and touching and defiant in her brave vanity, and I like to remember her in that golden dress, which she was not to have on again until she was buried in it. Many years ago she wrote a poem.

Needle, needle, dip and dart,
  Thrusting up and down,
Where's the man could ease a heart,
  Like a satin gown?

See the stitches curve and crawl
  Round the cunning seams--
Patterns thin and sweet and small
  Like a lady's dreams.

Wantons go in bright brocades;
  Brides in organdie;
Gingham's for the plighted maid;
  Satin's for the free!

Wool's to line a miser's chest;
  Crepe's to calm the old;
Velvet hides an empty breast;
  Satin's for the bold.

Lawn is for a bishop's yoke;
  Linen's for a nun;
Satin is for wiser folk--
  Would the dress were done!

Satin glows in candlelight--
 Satin's for the proud!
They will say who watch at night,
 "What a fine shroud."

"Bittersweet"
Joseph Bryan, III

This is going to be about Dorothy Parker, but I'll need a minute to get around to her. Even then, please don't expect an analysis of her personality, or speculation about her ultimate place in American literature. All I intend to do is set down, informally, a part of what I remember about her, including some of her remarks that I've never seen in print, and that I think deserve saving.

Well, then, I was a youth in Richmond, Virginia, I had a friend named Alan Campbell. His house was near ours, and we were together often, until he went off to the Virginia Military Institute, and I went elsewhere. Ten years passed before I saw him again. I had become the second-string theater critic for Time, and one evening in the 1928-29 season, I was sent to review a steamy drama called Congai, which involved an Indo-Chinese half-caste (Helen Menken) and her handsome son Ouven. The son looked familiar, despite a thick layer of Max Factor's "Light Egyptian." The program explained it: "Ouven . . . Allen [sic] Campbell." I remember almost nothing about the play except, irrelevantly, that Ouven wore a maroon blazer; but I remember going backstage for a pleasant reunion. Thereafter Alan and I ran into each other from time to time, and it was one of our chance encounters--I'm coming to the point at last--that he introduced me to Dorothy (whom he had just married, I discovered later, or perhaps was just about to marry).

The occasion was a dance in New York, in October 1933. I date it by the fact that, a week earlier, The New Yorker had published a profile I had written about Rosa Lewis of the Cavendish Hotel in London. The first person I recognized at the party was Alan. He said "Come along at once! Dottie Parker is here and she's dying to meet you."

Dying to meet me? Dorothy Parker? I followed Alan to where she was sitting. I don't know what he said, but she waved me away. "Joe Bryan? Oh, no! Oh, no! Whoever you are, you're certainly not Joe Bryan! If this is a joke, buster, it's not funny!"

I babbled "Yes, I am!" or maybe "Honest, it's me!" but she went right on: "Oh, no! Not little Dorothy. Not with the Curse of the Parkers hanging over her head! Dorothy's never going to meet the man who wrote that marvelous Rosa Lewis piece! That's reserved for rich, attractive girls. They get to meet Joe Bryan, but not poor, plain little Mrs. Parker!"

I stood there like a great gowk, still mumbling that inane "Honest--" until finally she said, "You <u>swear</u> your are?" Then, to the room at large, "Go away, all you dreadful people, and leave this <u>special</u> man with me! Go away, <u>all</u> of you!--and as for <u>you</u>," she said, wheeling on me, "<u>you sit down</u>!" I sat. She stared at me, and a moment passed before she said, "You're going to think this very strange. I've just met you, and here I'm about to ask you an impertinent question. It's not 'Will you collaborate on play with me?' but 'How soon can you start?'"

Imagine it!--the famous Dorothy Parker, the brilliant poet and short story writer, the wittiest woman in New York, asking an unknown cub to collaborate with her!--Not <u>asking</u> me; <u>ordering</u> me! In the years ahead, I often heard her describe herself, when embarrassed, as "dimpling and blushing, digging my toe in the sand, twisting my handkerchief in my two great things of hands." That's what I did then. We agreed to meet at her apartment at eleven the next morning, and I went home wrapped in a pink mist.

Her apartment was at the extreme end of East 49th Street, downtown side. She'd said "eleven," but I couldn't possibly get there before ten thirty, so I had to walk up and down, killing time. On the stroke of eleven, I told the doorman, "Mr. Bryan to see Mrs. Parker, Please."

He rang her. She was along time answering, but finally he said, "Mr. Bryan, madam . . . Mr. <u>Bryan</u> . . ." He turned to me: "Will you spell it, Sir?" I spelled it, and he repeated, "B, R, Y, A, N, madam . . . Yes, Madam." He turned to me again: "Mrs. Parker asks what you wish to see her about." I don't know how I made myself heard over the noise of my heart cracking, but I must have succeeded, because presently I found myself in the elevator, even though I was already achingly aware that she'd had no recollection of our glittering plans from the evening before. It proved to be worse than that: she had no recollection even of our having <u>met</u>.

I saw Dottie many times afterwards; indeed, she lived with my wife and me for a while; but never once was that first evening ever mentioned. For all she retained of it, it had never happened.

A number of playwrights and novelists who knew Dottie well used her as a model for a character--usually a wisecracking woman, with either good looks or their remnants; she drinks too much; if she isn't suffering through an unhappy romance at the moment, one is just behind her; and often the threat of suicide hangs in the air. (Yes, Dottie had looks in her younger days. Mrs. Pat Campbell told her, "You're a pretty, pretty cobra!") One of her first and most lifelike incarnations was as "Lily Malone," in Philip Barry's <u>Hotel Universe</u>. Barry describes Lily as "able to impart to her small, impudent face a certain prettiness," which was bang true of Dottie; and he gave Lily lines that are purest Parker. For instance:

> ALICE: What a fool I am, really!
> LILY: (Sweetly.) Please, dear, let <u>me</u> say that.

That same year, 1932, "Mary Hilliard" in George Oppenheimer's <u>Here Today</u> was drawn from Dottie. Ruth Gordon created the role; she must have enjoyed it, because she later wrote <u>Over 21</u>, in which "Paula Wharton" was Dottie again. Dottie once said she wanted to write her autobiography, but was afraid that George and Miss Gordon would sue her for plagiarism. Her bitter title for it would have been <u>Mongrel</u>, presumably because she was cross-bred, her father being Jewish and her mother Scottish (Alan Campbell's father was Scottish and his mother Jewish). George Kaufman and Moss Hart, in turn, put her on stage as "Julia Glenn" in Merrily We Roll Along (1934). The stage directions describe Julia as "a woman close to forty [Dottie was forty that year]. She is not unpretty, but on her face are the marks of years of quiet and steady drinking--eight, ten hours a day. . . . She wears something from about three years ago, and which wasn't quite right then." A man offers to get her a drink and asks, "What are you having?" and Julia says, "Know what I'm having? Not much fun." Dottie as ever was!

She was also "Daisy Lester," a nightclub singer, in Charles Brackett's Entirely Surrounded (1934)--a roman a clef dedicated to her. Daisy is a speaking likeness of Dottie--Daisy, with her "great melancholy eyes . . . a tiny, dark figure in a blue dress with peasant Embroidery on the sleeves." Listen to this line of Daisy's and you'll hear Dottie's own voice:

You couldn't have turned a dog away in that storm. Not even Mrs. Herrick, and I may say that Mrs. Herrick looked like an old belle who'd spent the best years of her youth turning dogs away.

If you saw Audrey Hepburn in War and Peace, fatten up her image and age it and--however absurd it may sound--you'll have an approximation of Dottie as she looked then, in the mid-1930's: the same height (about five three), the same wistful black eyes, the same black bangs and topknot. But whereas Miss Hepburn was slim and trim and chic, Dottie was always tousled, and a little--well, dingy. Moreover, she was addicted to dirndls ("with peasant embroidery on the sleeves"), a costume that made her seem both dumpy and dowdy. Not that this ever bothered her. Her idea of dressing up for the evening was to add a tulle scarf to whatever she'd been wearing all day. If it is true that women dress to impress other women, this explains Dottie's indifference to fashion. She didn't care a damn what women thought of her or her appearance. What men thought, yes, but not women. She didn't like women. As far as I know, only two of her close friends were women: Bee Ames (who had been married to Donald Ogden Stewart) and Lillian Hellman. Dottie's friendships were liable to sudden, violent reversals. If she ever turned on Miss Hellman, I never heard about it; but she repaid Bee's long years of loyalty and generosity by making a woman very much like her the butt of a cruel short story. I myself can strip my sleeve and show the marks of Dottie's claws. Come to think of it, she had a couple of marks of her own: a small blue star tattooed on her right shoulder, and scars across her wrists. I don't know anything about the tattoo, but it was no secret that the scars came from a halfhearted attempt at suicide with a razor in the 1920s. A later attempt--no more resolute--with sleeping pills moved Benchley to warn her, "If you don't stop this sort of thing, Dottie, you'll make yourself sick!"

Pretension always invited her derision. Her "Diary of a New York Lady" crucified a woman we all knew--silly and affected, but harmless--who had somehow offended her. Later, Dottie said of her and her set, "Their pooled emotions wouldn't fill a teaspoon." The wife of a friend of mine, unfortunately given to sprinkling French phrases throughout her chatter, once said, "Tant pis!" in Dottie's hearing. Ever afterwards, Dottie made solicitous inquiries about her: "How's old tant pis these days? Still full of it?" Yet she herself crossed her 7s, continental-style, and she gave at least three of her poems titles in French, one with a word misspelled.

Any collection of her slashes would show that though several of the most famous had men for their targets--"He's a pony's ass," for instance, and "He's a rhinestone in the rough"--most were aimed at women. There comes to mind the lady who "spent her time in London sliding down a barrister." Another lady--she had finally married the gentleman who had been sheltering her for some years--received this telegram from Dottie next day: WHAT'S NEW?   A sentimental occasion like a wedding always brought something absurd from her--or like Christmas, as witnesses the telegram she sent my wife and me from Hollywood: IN ORDER TO WISH YOU A MERRY CHRISTMAS I AM INTERRUPTING WORK ON MY SCREEN EPIC, LASSIE GET DOWN.

Theater people seemed to provoke her special displeasure. I don't need to quote what she said about Katharine Hepburn's acting in The Lake; it's Dottie's best-known quip. When someone mentioned Meg Mundy, then starring in The Respectful Prostitute, Dottie affected never to have heard of her: "Meg Mundy?   What's that, a Welsh holiday?"   She said of a certain English actor, a notorious homosexual, "He simply buggers description" (apropos, she also said that "Verlaine was always chasing Rimbauds").   Clare Boothe Luce, stepping aside to let Dottie precede through a door, rashly remarked "Age before beauty!"   She said it with a laugh, but Dottie was not appeased; she snapped "--and pearls before swine."   She also said, "'Clare--Booth--Luce': sounds like the motto of a girls' school."

To be sure, almost any quip would be mothered on Dottie, if it was witty enough and savage enough--unless, of course, it had a Washington angle, in which case it became Alice Longworth's.   The two ladies intersected at one point.   Mrs. Longworth said that Calvin Coolidge "looked as if he had been weaned on a pickle"; Mrs. Parker, on being informed that he was dead, asked "How can they tell?"

My wife and I lived in or near New York from 1932 to 1938, and we ran into Dottie occasionally at a friend's or at some restaurant.   One evening we were having nightcaps with Frank Sullivan at 21 when Dottie entered alone and, seeing Frank, whom she loved, came to our table.   Frank welcomed her with "Hello, you Jew-hater."

Dottie flung herself on his lap and clawed at his fly, demanding, "Which side does it open on?"

Presently St. Clair McKelway brought over a man whom he introduced as a psychiatrist.   This was at a time when almost everybody was complaining about the shortage of apartments--almost everybody but Mac, who announced that only a few hours' search that morning had turned up a perfect one: inexpensive, comfortable, excellent location.   Dottie touched the psychiatrists's arm: "A patient for you, Doctor!"

Her apartment was at the New Weston hotel.   I remember the housewarming. Sullivan's present was a neat little package of eggshells, coffee grounds, orange peel, and soggy crusts.   "There's nothing like garbage," he explained, "to make a house a home."

Dottie asked Benchley what she should do with it, since she hadn't yet bought a garbage can.   Bob said, "Put it in your bed and pull the sheet over it."

"Never!" Dottie said nobly.   "That's the coward's way out!"

I went to the apartment one winter afternoon.   A wispy young writer had just left, and Dottie gave an incredulous account of his visit.   His blue sneakers had surprised her-- it had been snowing all day--but she had been dumbfounded by his voice, which was "so high it was audible only to a dog's ear."   Her first Christmas at the New Weston, someone asked if she had hung up her stocking.   "No," she said, "but I hung up the hotel."

I think it was Cory [Ford] who told me that one.   In those days, before World War II, such remarks of Dottie's as I heard were quoted to me by mutual friends who saw her oftener and knew her far better than I--people like Ford and Sullivan, Kaufman,

Woollcott, Don and Bee Stewart, and Bob Benchley. Particularly Bob. There was a special friendship between him and Dottie. His full, formal name was Robert Charles Benchley, but for some private reason she always called him Fred. The poems in her Sunset Gun include "For R. C. B.," and her Death and Taxes is dedicated "To Mr. Benchley." She was with him when he reached one of the most important milestones in his life: his first alcoholic drink--the first, as the years passed, of a formidable series they would have together.

George Kaufman was not as close to her as were the others; but it was he who told me about a dinner at Lillian Hellman's on a summer evening when Louis Adamic, author of The Native's Return and other books, turned up in a white cotton suit, rather rumpled, and Dottie remarked in a loud aside, "Looks like he's come to sell us some leaf tobacco!" Another summer evening, she went for drinks at the apartment on West 47th Street that Woollcott shared with Harold Ross. Charlie MacArthur was there, in a suit like Adamic's, plus an open shirt and a wide-brimmed raffia hat; he was even smoking a thin cheroot and holding a tall frosted glass. Dottie addressed him respectfully: "As the American consul here, sir-". My wife and I saw Dottie most frequently just after the war, when we were all living in Bucks County, she and Alan at Fox Farm, near Pipersville, and we a few miles away at Fiddler's Green, near Doylestown. Sid and Laura Perelman were close by, too, and George and Bea Kaufman, and Moss Hart and his recent bride, Kitty Carlisle. After a dinner, we often played The Game--the one in which one team draws up a list of ten words or names or phrases and gives it to the captain of the other, who has to act them out in pantomime for his teammates to identify as quickly as they can. The Kaufmans and Harts (no slouches as actors themselves) often had one or two professionals from their shows down for the weekend, so competition was hot. Alan was excellent at pantomime, and Dottie was excellent at lists. I have kept a couple of hers, in her round, finishing-school handwriting. Here is one:

I'd die for dear old Rutgers. Peter Pan. You don't know your ass from your elbow. Fly Away, Kentucky Babe! Have you a little fairy in your home? Pride and Prejudice. Block that Kick! Parallel lines meet in infinity. Misery loves company. You too, Brutus?

Once when Dottie was doing the pantomime, she signaled that the word contained four syllables (this was permitted), and then began to nibble, delicately and daintily, at an imaginary morsel: in-grace-she-ate.

She was on her good behavior that evening. But as the months passed and her marriage fell apart, she became bitter and cruel, especially towards Alan's mother--"the only person on earth," said Dottie, "who pronounces the word 'egg' in three syllables: 'ay-yuh-guh.'" She told me once that she had seen Mrs. Campbell wearing a hat "that would have looked young on Joan"--our daughter, then aged twelve.

One day at our house she switched her sights from poor, harmless Mrs. Campbell to Moss Hart, the gentlest and kindest of men. She pretended to believe that "Moss" was not his real name and began coaxing him to admit it. Moss said mildly that it actually was his name; his parents had given it to him, and he'd never had another. Dottie laughed this aside: "Oh, come on, Mossy! This is old Dottie--you can tell her! What is it really?--Moses? Morris? You can trust me! Besides, it's nothing to be ashamed of. Plenty of nice people change their names! Tell Dottie now: is it Moscowitz?"[1]

She kept it up until anyone more combustible than Moss--which was almost anyone else at all--would have smacked her chops, but he took it quietly until she ran down. And then, if you please, she turned on Kitty! I didn't hear their dialogue. Kitty remembered it to me long afterwards:

"When Dottie realized she wasn't going to get a rise out of Moss, she came over and sat by me, sweet as sugar cane, and begged me to tell her about my debut on the stage. I should have known she was half-loaded, but I didn't, and I--little Miss Innocence--plunged ahead. It was in <u>Rio Rita</u>, I said, the title role, and the theater was the famous Old Capitol, in New York. I was all wound up, describing the thrill of walking in the footsteps of the great stars who had played there, when she put her hand on my arm and breathed, 'They made you do <u>that</u>? Oh, you poor <u>child</u>! That <u>huge</u> place, and all those people out front <u>staring</u> at you, waiting to <u>devour</u> you! Just to <u>think</u> of it makes my heart <u>ache</u>!'

"I said it wasn't that way at all! They were a marvelous audience, and I enjoyed every minute of it. Dottie said, 'You don't have to pretend with <u>me</u>, dear. How <u>brave</u> you are! What a <u>brave</u> girl! Oh I <u>admire</u> you so!' I can't swear there weren't tears in her eyes. I kept protesting that there'd been nothing for me to be brave about--that I'd absolutely loved it--but Dottie kept oozing sympathy and calling me 'You dear, brave <u>Baby</u>!'--and then, suddenly, I woke up. She was putting me on, trying to see how much of her molasses I'd swallow. I felt like a <u>fool</u>!"

Kitty wasn't the first whom Dottie had made feel like that--it was the same technique she had used on me the evening we met--nor, by far, was Kitty the last. She was probably saved from worse savaging by Dottie's dropping her cigarette lighter, which bounced under the sofa. I had to kneel to reach it, and when I knelt, my knee joints popped and crackled. Dottie rubbed her hands together and spread them toward me. "Ah," she beamed, "there's nothing like an open fire--!"

The Campbells sold their farm and were divorced in 1947, to everyone's distress, especially our children's. They liked Dottie, but they loved Alan. He played their games with genuine enthusiasm. He had a fund of riddles and jokes and nonsense jungles. He was "cozy" and never unkind. Dottie too would entertain them, but her principal audience was always herself, as when she told them, "the little-known fable of Aesop and the Wolf":

"Well, Aesop was walking through this forest one day, when he came upon a great big wolf caught in a trap. The wolf begged him, 'Please, nice Mr. Aesop, help me out of this cruel trap!' So, Aesop did, and when the wolf was free, he bit Aesop on the ankle and said, 'Now go write a fable about <u>that</u>!'"

Another of her stories (but <u>not</u> for children) was about the bumpkin who went to visit his rich cousin in the big city. The host showed him around the huge, sumptuous apartment: the Louis Seize salon, the library, the dining room, the master suite, the sauna, the conservatory. "And now," he said proudly, opening another door, "here's where I keep my collection of phallic symbols."

The bumpkin goggled and giggled and gave his host a nudge: "You know what they <u>look</u> like, don't you?"

Still another favorite was about the haughty lady at a fashionable church wedding. She felt a timid tap on her shoulder and turned to see a meek little woman in the pew behind, mouthing something incomprehensible and gesturing toward the back of her skirt. The haughty lady said sharply, "What are you trying to tell me, madam? Is it--by some preposterous chance--that I have an eggbeater caught in my fringe?"

The meek little woman whispered, "Yes."

I remember a true story of hers--at least, she said it was true. She went to a dinner at Somerset Maugham's Villa Mauresque, at Cap Ferrat, where she met Humbert Wolfe, the English poet, for whose work she had profound respect (as do I). No one else there seemed to know who he was, and as course followed course, without a word being addressed to the quiet, slightly drunken little man in the rusty dinner jacket, Dottie saw he was getting more and more restive. Finally, she said, he rapped on his glass and announced loudly, but thickly, "I have just lost a very precious emerald! I must ask that the doors be locked, and that everyone present submit to a search!"

Dottie also loved overheard remarks, and she was hurt if anyone expressed a suspicion that she had overheard the best of them when she was talking to herself. Of course, she was always armed with "substantiating" details: "It's true, I tell you! Scout's honor! I was sitting on the right side of the bus (Dottie in a bus? Her story collapses right there), about four seats from the front, and this woman in the seat ahead told the other woman--may I fry in hell through all eternity if I've changed a syllable!--she told her 'Mad, I don't say. Odd, I do--sitting nude at the piano!'"

"I couldn't have made that up, could I?"

Yes, she could have--Dottie, and nobody else.

Granted that she was wonderful company, life with her was life on thin ice. You never knew when she would turn on you and denounce you as a fascist, an anti-Semite, a warmonger, a geoplanarian, a neo-Malthusian, or something equally ridiculous. Almost any epithet would serve. It didn't need even a smidgen of justification. The barb of her wit made it stick where it hit, and the victim was tagged forever after. He had been given instant immortality--of the wrong sort--like the man from Porlock, and courtier who farted in the presence of Queen Elizabeth I, and the Hollywood producer of whom Dottie said, "He hasn't got sense enough to bore assholes in wooden hobbyhorses."

She was never a girl to back away from a word just because it wasn't in Elsie Dinsmore's vocabulary. Sid Perelman told me that during one of his hitches in Hollywood, the studio assigned him an office adjoining Alan and Dottie's. Alan's desk was near the common wall, and Dottie's was at the far side; thus, Sid couldn't help hearing most of Alan's remarks, whereas Dottie's were only a mumble.

One afternoon he heard Alan say brightly, "I've finished that scene now, Dottie! I'll read it to you, and you can tell me how you like it." He read. "Well, what do you think?" Her answer was a muttered monosyllable. Then Alan's voice again, shrill and clear and anguished: "Dottie, I've asked you ten thousand times not to use that word!"

I'm not sure what Alan did immediately after the divorce. I remember going to see him in New York when he shared an apartment with Tom Heggen (who wrote Mister Roberts), but that was for only a short while; Heggen died in the spring of 1949. Dottie came to stay with us that summer--rather, with my wife; I was working in Washington and was home only on weekends. Our household consisted of us and our three children, Mamie the cook, and four dogs. Mamie had been a dresser for the Dolly sisters. She was small and black and was a quiet drunkard. When the fit was on her, she simply kept to her room, even though it might be an evening when we were having guests to dinner or, more likely, the next morning. Dottie called her "a tower of Jell-o." On one of Mamie's "mornings," it fell to me to get breakfast. I asked Dottie what she'd like. "Just something light and easy to fix," she said. "How about a dear little whiskey sour?. . . Make it a double, while you're up." "While you're up" was one of her pet additives. She'd tear a strip off some poor wretch, then add reflectively, "And his wife's a shit too, while you're up." Another of her pets was "for my sins," as in, "I had to go to this dreadful party, and there, for my sins, I saw--" All parties were becoming "dreadful." I think she continued to go to them only because they gave her something to do, and because they offered her fresh targets. She took her dog to one of them, where it promptly vomited on the rug. Dottie explained to the hostess, "It's the company."

The Doylestown of Dottie's summer with us had a ceremony called "viewing." When someone died, friends and even acquaintances were expected to call at the bereaved house and view the corpse. The first we heard of this aboriginal custom was when our daughter Joan reported in gleeful excitement that the grandmother of a schoolmate had "passed"; viewing would begin the following afternoon, and "Please, Mummy, will you take us, please?" My wife was horror-struck, but she finally surrendered under a flurry of lefts ("Everyone in school will ask why we weren't there!") and rights ("Aw, gee, Mummy! You never let us have any fun!"). Next afternoon was scalding hot, my wife told me; she and Dottie dropped the children off at the crepe-hung door, and waited in the car, both of them melting in the furious heat. When the children came back, my wife asked, "Are you glad you went? How did the old lady look?"

Joan glanced at her mother's damp, rumpled dress and sniffed, "She looked better than you do!"

Dottie rushed to the rescue: "Maybe, but don't forget she's been on ice all day!"

My friend Stockton Rush and his son John, aged six, stayed with us one weekend while Dottie was there. Saturday night was a rough one. Sunday morning, when Stockton tottered down to breakfast, he asked me shakily, "Be all right if I cut my throat?"

Dottie came in just then. She told him, "Move over on the blade and make room for me!"

All that day she watched young John Rush playing with our children. She was fascinated by the way that he--like "Pigpen," in the "Peanuts" comic strip--accumulated layer upon layer of grime without seeming to try. "I could take John into 21," Dottie said, "and leave him at the center table while I went to the ladies' room for no more than a moment, and when I came back, he'd be covered with tar!"

When her stay with us ended, I brought her bags downstairs for our drive to New York. One was a large, heavy Vuitton. She watched me struggling to fit it into our small car and remarked, "I know! They feel like they're full of wet sand before you've packed even a handkerchief."

I saw her again, just after Dame Edith Sitwell gave a reading in New York and, recognizing Dottie in the audience, bowed to her and paid a generous compliment to "your grett Ameddican pwettess, Miss Doddothy Wadden." (These are not misprints; I have transcribed the line exactly as Dottie, still enraged, quoted it to me.)

"'Wadden'! for Christ's sake!" she snarled. "Why that goddam limey--!" and went from strength to strength.

Someone teased her, "It's no use getting sore! You've got to expect public recognition like that. After all, you're an international celebrity."

"Yeah," Dottie said. "That's me; the toast of two continents--Greenland and Australia."

She herself once gave a reading or a talk; I didn't hear it, but I remember her account, often repeated, of the woman who came up to her afterwards and gushed, "Oh, Miss Parker, I can't tell you how many sleepless night your books have saved me!"

More and more she was surrendering to self-pity, self-mockery, self-diminishment, and to openly and bitterly reviewing her old loves. She couldn't keep her tongue off them, as if they were so many aching teeth. The names of only a few have stayed with me: John Garrett, Charlie MacArthur, John McClain, Alan Campbell, Ross Evans. I can't contribute even a minor footnote to her romances with Garrett and MacArthur; I never knew either of them, so I didn't pay much attention to her breast-beatings and recriminations. But although Dottie and McClain had blown up before I met her--just before--and she had already married Alan, McClain and I were close friends, and I could hardly help being exposed to, and absorbing, some of the lingering radiation from the fallout.

John was the male equivalent of a Rubens nude: a big, blond, handsome hunk of "roast beef and cold cream." His friend David Niven called him a Teddy bear. A single glance at him was all that Dottie needed: she hadn't dropped her handkerchief at his feet so much as flung it into his lap, John had picked it up. His good looks were only one of his assets: he was jolly; he chuckled; he had a nice wit and nice manners and a gentle drawl. Marion, Ohio, was his hometown. He had arrived in New York by way of Brown, where he played football, and Kenyon; and when I met him (about the same time that Dottie did), he was reporting ship news for the Sun, in a column called "On the Sun Deck." He and I were almost exactly the same age; we had many mutual friends; both of us liked to think that we were writers; both of us were from "the sticks": and both of us enjoyed an occasional glass of the old and bold. In short, we saw a good deal of each other, and I could hardly help watching his side of the affair with Dottie develop.

It went smoothly and merrily at first. Ardor matched ardor. In addition to the physical satisfaction, John was flattered (and somewhat dizzied) at being take up by this famous, brilliant woman and introduced to her famous, brilliant friends; and Dottie, for her part, was proud to parade him, an attractive ten-years-younger man, as proof that she was still seductive. But eventually the day came when John's ardor began to flag, whereas Dottie's did not. If anything, it increased. She became voracious and insistent. She telephoned him every few hours, even at his office, with your-place-or-mine suggestions, until John, in desperation, found himself beginning to plead imaginary assignments and fake engagements.

He didn't have to fake many or for long. He was that precious rarity, the personable Extra Man, with clean fingernails and a smooth tongue; and hostesses were quick to grab him not only for their dinner parties but--as the word got around that he was a beau sabreur--for other, more private, entertainments. Dottie's diagnosis was "His body has gone to his head."

So, dining and weekending, drawling and chuckling and flirting, up John went, leaving Dottie behind to curse and wail, to call him a climber and an ingrate. At fashionable estates from Old Westbury to Bernardsville, guest books began to carry this entry, in John's clear, beautiful handwriting:

> From east to west,
> The nation's guest
> --John McClain

Dottie said of an extremely rich Long Island hostess at whose house he had become almost a weekend fixture, "He'll be back as soon as has licked all the gilt off her ass." But he on honey dew had fed, and he didn't come back. It was over.

Alan Campbell caught her on the rebound, or perhaps she caught him. Anyway, they were married in October 1933. He was utterly different from John, less lover-husband than a housekeeper-companion, always at hand to straighten her hat, escort her to a party and back, and mix her Bromo the next morning. The marriage lasted until 1947. I don't know where or how she met her next, Ross Evans. She first brought him to Fiddler's Green in 1949: a pleasant, shambling, hobbledehoy with huge, lump-toed Army boots that instantly inspired our children to call him "Li'l Abner," in tribute to Al Capp's lamented naif, Abner Yokum. Dottie soon thought better of Li'l Abner and, to our delight, remarried Alan a year later. They stayed married this time.

Bee Stewart told me a story about Dottie that has been printed before, but since this is the authentic version and is a credit to the three people concerned, I'm going to repeat it:

In one of Dottie's flat-broke periods, early in the 1930s, Bee telegraphed her friend John Gilbert, who was then at the peak of his fame and prosperity, I WANT TWO THOUSAND DOLLARS FOR SOMEONE WHO SHALL BE NAMELESS. Gilbert sent the money at once, asking no questions. Well, the talkies came in, and soon it was Gilbert's turn to be broke. He asked Bee if she though he could collect any of his many loans. Bee notified Dottie, who promptly returned the two thousand in full--whereupon Gilbert sent her an enormous basket of roses with a card saying, "Thank you, Miss Finland!" (Younger readers may need reminding that after the Great War, Finland was the only nation that paid its war debts to the U.S.A.).

Alan died in Hollywood in June of 1963, and his body was sent home to Richmond, where I had returned to live. His family asked me to be a pallbearer, with several others of his boyhood friends. I assumed that Dottie would come to the funeral, so I telephoned Hollywood and left an invitation for her to stay with us. No answer. The next I heard, she was in New York, in a suite at the Volney Hotel. At first, I used to ring her when I came to town and ask if I might stop in for a drink, but she was always "just going out"; and if I called well in advance, it was always, "If only, you'd phoned five minutes earlier!" I was reassured to learn before long that she was avoiding almost everybody, so I stopped bothering her.

The last time I saw Bee Stewart, a few weeks before her death in 1980, she told me about Dottie's in 1967. She came to Bee's apartment one evening and sat around drinking vodka until Bee decided it would be best to get her home and to bed. She loaded Dottie into a taxi and paid the driver to make the delivery. Half an hour later, her phone rang and she heard a mumble: "My bes' frien'! Mos' loyal frien'! On'y frien'! Goo' nigh'!" Next morning, June 7, a maid at the Volney found her dead. Dorothy's Yellow Brick Road had ended in potholes and mire and squalor, and no kindly Aunt Em and Uncle Henry were waiting there to hug her and comfort her.

She left no family, nor any estate except her literary rights (which went to the NAACP), nor any personal possessions except a few books and some clothing. Over the years, she had bought little and kept less. Almost everything given her, she handed on to someone else--including six original drawings by James Thurber, which she gave to me. Bee said that she was buried in a cloth-of-gold caftan given her by Gloria Vanderbilt. She had composed her own epitaphs long ago:

EXCUSE MY DUST

and

THIS IS ON ME.

Note

1. Moss's autobiography, <u>Act One</u>, relates how he became the office boy at "Augustus Pitou, Theatrical Enterprises." Like Dottie, Mr. Pitou refused to accept his name, and always called him "Mouse."

Classified Primary Index

General Index

Campbell, Alan, 14, 15, 22, 26, 135,
142-44, 151, 160
Capote, Truman, 22, 113
Capron, Marion, 1, 5, 62
Carlisle, Kitty, 134
Case, Frank, 8, 13, 91, 92
Ceplair, Larry, 19, 110
Cerf, Bennet, 94, 107
Chase, Edna Woolman, 4, 5, 96
Churchill, Allen, 103
"A Christmas Guide to the Best
   Fiction," 26
Clive, James, 48
Close Harmony, 13
Clurman, Harold, 104
Coast of Illyria, 25
Coleman, John, 48
Cooper, Morton, 99
Cooper, Wyatt, 2, 3, 101
Connelly, Marc, 9, 13, 28, 101
"The Conning Tower," 8
"Constant Reader," 13
Corley, Edwin, 12
Corwin, Norman, 110
Coward, Noel, 34
Cosmopolitan, 25
Crowinshield, Frank, 93
"Crowinshield in the Cubs' Den," 4
Curtiss, Mina, 47
"The Custard Heart," 17, 24
Crowinshield, Frank, 2, 34
Crouse, Russel, 43,

d'Usseau, Arnaud, 25
Daniels, Earl, 92
Dayton, Dorothy, 89
Death and Taxes, 13
Denis, Brian, 109
DeVoto, Bernard, 90
Dialist, 88
"Diary of Our Own Samuel Pepys,"
Dietz, Howard, 104
Dillingham, Charles, 6
Donovan, Bill, 10
Dos Passos, John, 99
Douglas, Ann, 106
Douglas, George H., 113, 116
Drennan, Robert, 9, 101

Dresner, Zita Atkin, 112
Drutman, Irving, 62

Eastman, Max, 89
Eatenson, Ervin, 50
Edman, Irwin, 46
Edwards, Anne, 115
Emerson, Dorothy, 89
Engle, William, 50
Enough Rope, 13
Ephron, Nora, 104
Escar, Evan, 108
Esquire, 26
Evans, Ross, 25, 159-60

Fadiman, Clifton, 47
Farnham, Marjnia, 95
Farrar, John, 24
Faulkner, William, 18, 34
Feibleman, Peter, 28-29, 117
Ferber, Edna, 10
Fields, W. C., 133
Fitzgerald, F. Scott, 18, 23, 26, 28
Fitzgerald, Zelda, 136
Ford, Cory, 12, 100, 154
Forester, E. M., 116
The 49'ers, 9
Frank, Gerold, 26
Franklin, Robert C., 62
Frewin, Leslie, 116

Gaines, James R., 107
Gallagher, Brian, 8, 117
"The Game," 25,
Gannett, Lewis, 46
Garmaise, Freda, 117
Garrett, John, 159
Gibbs, Wolcott, 49, 92
Gilbert, Julie, 108
Gill, Brendan, 10, 28, 104, 105, 1
Gilmer, Walker, 102
Gilpin Charles, 15
Gish, Lillian, 102
Goldwyn, Samuel, 129
Gordon, Ruth, 12, 106, 110, 134
Gorman, Herbert, 42
Graham, Gladys, 44
Graham, Sheilah, 21, 26, 102

Lynes, George Platt, 33
Lyons, Leonard, 97

MacArthur, Charles, 18, 159
McCarty, Norma, 47
McClain, John, 159
MacDermott, Kathy, 117
MacLeish, Archibald, 20, 21, 113
McClain, John, 30
McKennedy, Ruth, 47
MacShane, Frank, 110
Mankiwicz, Herman, 34
McMein, Neysa, 10, 86
Mailer, Norman, 107
Mair, John, 47
March, Frederick, 20
Marks, Jeannette, 87
Marston, Annie Eliza, 1
Martindale, James, 61
Marx, Groucho, 19
Marx, Harpo, 98
Masson, Thomas L., 87
Matthews, T. S., 44, 46
Maugham, William Somerset, 6, 94, 124
Maurois, Andre, 95
Mayer, Louis B., 18,
Meade, Marion, 1, 11, 117
Melzer, Sondra, 115
Meredith, Scott, 105
Millay, Edna St. Vincent, 10, 132
Millet, Fred B., 94
Mitsch, Ruthmarie H., 116
Morehouse, Ward, 62
Mosedale, John, 111
Mostel, Kate, 108
Murphy, Gerald, 11,
Murry, Bill 9

Nardi, Marcia, 50
Nash, Ogden, 46
Nast, Conde, 4
NAACP, 31
New Masses, 14, 17, 19
New Yorker, 8, 11-12, 13, 24, 126
"News Item," 13, 139
Nobbe, George, 46
North, Sterling, 44, 48

No Siree!, 9

Odets, Clifford, 20
O'Hara, John, 18, 96
Oliviere, Laurence, 20
Ollstein, Laurel, 31
O'Neill, Eugene, 8, 10
"One Perfect Rose," 13
Oppenheimer, George, 12, 15, 28, 29, 100, 134, 152
"The Oriental Drama," 6,
Orvis, Mary Burchard, 95
"Our Office," 4

Parker, Edwin Pond, 2-3, 133
Pearl, Jane Helen, 112
Pemberton, Murdock, 8
Peck, Everett, 32
Peck, Gregory, 20
"People," 92
Perelman, S. J., 21, 111, 155
Pett, Saul, 14, 28, 62
Photoplay Author's League, 18
Plomer, William, 47
Pollock, Channing, 8
Poore, Charles, 47
Prescott, Orville, 90
Puk, Francine, 114

"Queen of the Round Table," 100

Redman, Ben Ray, 46
"Resume," 13
Rice, Elmer, 13, 98, 125
Richart, Bette, 98
Riddel, John, 44
Robe, Lucy, 116
Robeson, Paul, 34
Robinson, Edward G., 20
Roberts, Ray, 50
Robinson, Henry M., 44
Rogers, Richard, 19
Roscoe, Burton, 45
Rose, Carl, 32
Rosenburg, Harold, 45
Rosenfield, John, 48
Rosmond, Babette, 104
Ross, Harold, 9

About the Author

RANDALL CALHOUN is Assistant Professor of English at Ball State University, Muncie, Indiana. He is working on a complete edition of Dorothy Parker's stories, poetry, and essays.

*9 7 8 1 6 2 6 5 4 1 8 6 3 *

Recent Titles in
Bio-Bibliographies in American Literature

Lloyd Alexander: A Bio-Bibliography
James S. Jacobs and Michael O. Tunnell

Donald Windham: A Bio-Bibliography
Bruce Kellner

Walter M. Miller, Jr.: A Bio-Bibliography
William H. Roberson and Robert L. Battenfeld

www.ingramcontent.com/pod-product-compliance
Lightning Source LLC
Chambersburg PA
CBHW020401100426
42812CB00001B/143